To Dean and Rebecca,

With deepest affection
and gratitude
beyond words,

Charlie
4/5/2011

You were part of the
writing of this book
more than you know.

BONE DEAD, AND RISING

BONE DEAD, AND RISING

Vincent van Gogh and the Self before God

CHARLES DAVIDSON

CASCADE *Books* · Eugene, Oregon

BONE DEAD, AND RISING
Vincent van Gogh and the Self before God

Cascade Books
An Imprint of Wipf and Stock Publishers
199 W. 8th Ave., Suite 3
Eugene, OR 97401

www.wipfandstock.com

ISBN 13: 978-1-60608-616-2

Cataloging-in-Publication data:

Davidson, Charles

  Bone dead, and rising : Vincent van Gogh and the self before God / Charles Davidson.

   xxiv + 250 p. ; 23 cm. — Includes bibliographical references and index(es).

   ISBN 13: 978-1-60608-616-2

   1. Gogh, Vincent van, 1853–1890—Religion. 2. Gogh, Vincent van, 1853–1890—Psychology. I. Title.

ND653 G7 D25 2011

Manufactured in the U.S.A.

With constant thanksgiving for Ethlyne, Mark, Kate, Nancy and Bill

In loving memory of Charles and Katherine, and Dan

"The soul is a mirror before it becomes a home."
From Alphonse de Lamartine's *Cromwell*

—Quoted by Vincent van Gogh
Letter 100 ~ June 5, 1877 ~ Amsterdam

"In spite of everything, I will rise again: I will take up my pencil,
which I have forsaken in my great discouragement,
and I will go on with my drawing."

—Vincent van Gogh to his brother, Theo
Letter 136 ~ September 24, 1880 ~ Cuesmes

"This original self, with the print of God's thumb still upon it, is the
most essential part of who we are and is buried deep in all of us as a
source of wisdom and strength and healing which we can draw upon
or, with our terrible freedom, not draw upon as we choose. I think that
among other things all real art comes from that deepest self—painting,
writing, music, dance, all of it that in some way nourishes the spirit."

—Frederick Buechner, *Telling Secrets*, 44–45

"The gaps are the thing. The gaps are the spirit's one home, the alti-
tudes and latitudes so dazzlingly spare and clean that the spirit can
discover itself for the first time like a once-blind man unbound. The
gaps are the clifts in the rock where you cower to see the back parts of
God; they are the fissures between mountains and cells the wind lances
through, the icy narrowing fiords splitting the cliffs of mystery."

—Annie Dillard, *Pilgrim at Tinker Creek*, 269

Contents

Illustrations

Foreword

MOST ANYONE WHO PICKS up this volume will have had a personal experience with the paintings. My earliest recollection of learning about Vincent van Gogh was as an adolescent seeing "The Starry Night" (1889) for the first time. I was particularly drawn to its "blueness." It has remained my favorite van Gogh painting through all the years of adult life, enhanced only a bit more by Don McLean's 1971 hit song, "Vincent (Starry, Starry Night)." Why and how, I wonder, does a painting stick with us over time? The vivid colors? The distorted images? The dramatic story of a man who cut off his own earlobe? Blue? Though these are the more accessible explanations, the predilection for one of his paintings may constitute what I call "a van Gogh imprinting," that is, a formative experience so early and so impressive that it retains permanence within the self. Charles Davidson suggests an even deeper meaning for the emotional power of Van Gogh's paintings: "He is existentially no different from the rest of us. Like the rest of us, he is in pain."

In *Bone Dead, and Rising: Vincent van Gogh and the Self before God* we encounter an empathic wrestling with the themes of Van Gogh's life: the women he loved and/or tried to love; the often stabilizing, though conflict-rent relationship with his younger brother, Theo; the bitter disappointment in his clergyman father and the emotional inadequacy of his mother; the fluidity of experiences with joy and sorrow, life and death; the role of his Christian spirituality even as he became disengaged from institutional religion; the vocational search for an identity; the intense devotion to art and to his companion "Dame Nature"; and the desperate, desperate struggle with loneliness and depression.

The task undertaken here is enormous and one that has occupied Davidson for fifteen years. Considering the wealth of material already written about van Gogh and his own oeuvre of over 800 letters, the facility with which Davidson handles this massive amount of data is impressive. While the work is offered as a psychobiography in the genre of a psychology of religion case study, the reader will find an unexpectedly sensitive and artistic rendering of the life, spirituality, and work of van Gogh. The analysis is incisive and utilizes, among others, the psychodynamic theories of Freud, Kohut, and Winnicott, as well as the theological and philosophical insights of Kierkegaard and Tillich. Yet, I hasten to add these perspectives are masterfully, and hence, painlessly, interwoven throughout the book with the more technical detail relegated to footnotes.

Many scholars have addressed the question of Vincent's mental illness. The speculations include epilepsy and hypergraphia, lead poisoning from paint, multiple sunstrokes, major depression, and bipolar disorder. Whichever diagnosis one may choose, it would not be overly dramatic to describe van Gogh as a tortured soul, both religiously and psychologically. *Bone Dead, and Rising* captures the anguish with which Vincent lived, and it grasps, in a new way, the intimate relationship between the religious and the psychological in this particular psyche.

What follows is an artistic production, a verbal painting inspired by the life and work of its subject. As such, *Bone Dead* is better left to the reader's experience than summarized here. However, I will caution the reader to anticipate being drawn into the same introspection about the human condition that so occupied Vincent. In the midst of the beautiful paintings, encountered here, again, for many of us, there will also be no escaping a feeling of tragedy, no escaping emotional contact with the pain of a man who knew not his own self-worth, nor the magnitude of his talent, who lived the whole of his life with little artistic recognition. Given our contemporary vantage point, it seems impossible, and yet, as Paul suggested in his first letter to the Corinthians, "we see through a glass darkly."

Don McLean perceived the "suffering for sanity" and lamented, finally, "I could have told you, Vincent: This world was never meant for one as beautiful as you."[1]

Lallene J. Rector
Garrett-Evangelical Theological Seminary

---

1. Readers may access Don McLean's song "Vincent (Starry, Starry Night)" illustrated with Vincent's paintings at http://www.youtube.com/watch?v=dipFMJckZOM.

Prologue

To enter the experiential world of Vincent van Gogh is to encounter not only the complexities of his rich inner life but also those mysteries and paradoxes that defined him as a person and an artist, including ways in which his deep pain and suffering led him to a profound vision of God, discernible in his art.

This narrative interpretation of Vincent's life and work explores various theological, psychological, familial, and cultural aspects of a young man intent upon becoming a cleric like his father, who as a maturing adult discovered his true self and vocation through intense personal struggle as an artist embarked upon a passionate spiritual quest. To mitigate any mistaken overlays of interpretation, this account relies on words coming directly from Vincent's own pen—expansively and eloquently self-observant as he was—combined with illustrations from many of his highly expressive paintings.

Invariably, within every life lived authentically as a spiritual journey, more than one person of significant influence is at work behind the scenes in the formation of one's personality. In each case, one's thoughts and actions are sometimes consistent and then again contradictory, sometimes self-serving and then again self-transcendent. Here the reader will also meet some of those people who had a hand, either positively or negatively, in shaping the life and work of Vincent van Gogh.

READERS' INTERESTS

More than one kind of reader may take an interest in the story that unfolds within these pages. A great many may simply be somehow curious about van Gogh. Still others may be devotees of his art, for whom his life and art continue to be a compelling attraction. These may include pastors, priests, and laity challenged with understanding the internal perplexities and struggles of persons on whose behalf they are called to render spiritual care. Still others may be mental health clinicians, such as pastoral counselors, psychotherapists, psychologists, psychoanalysts, physicians, nurses, and allied health professionals, entrusted with the welfare of persons whom they have the privilege of serving in healing relationships. Likewise, teachers of these and other disciplines, who are attuned to the significant connections between psychology and spirituality, may find Vincent to be a person they would eagerly invite to join their conversations in the clinic and the classroom. By no means least, among potential readers are those visual artists who deem their vocations to be a spiritual calling, or who wonder about whether it is.

In the present narrative, readers are introduced not only to Vincent van Gogh but also to the thoughts of others who are able to shed light upon Vincent's personality, his life, and his work. Among these is the Danish existentialist philosopher-theologian Søren Kierkegaard, who died two years after Vincent's birth, and who was, like Vincent, both a student and critic of church and cultures. So was Paul Tillich, a giant among twentieth-century theologians conversant with the fields of psychology and art. Both Kierkegaard and Tillich had important things to say about the anxiety and despair that have been endemic to nineteenth- and post-nineteenth-century Western civilization. The present interpretation also features the contemporary American philosopher and psychologist Ken Wilber, whose transpersonal psychology and "integral theory" offer assistance toward gaining an enlarged view of Vincent's spiritual life and, by implication, our own. For those who seek a clearer understanding of Vincent's inner psychological world, the perspective of Self Psychology, as conceived and developed by the psychoanalyst Heinz Kohut and others, is employed as a psychological framework for this intimate portrait of Vincent, which may also be thought of as a study in both the theology and psychology of religious experience.

I want readers be aware of the limitations, as well as the positive ramifications, of any approach to psychological interpretation. As the Jesuit psychoanalyst William Meissner, the biographer of both Ignatius of Loyola and Vincent van Gogh, has written: "the psychoanalytic lens . . . is necessarily very selective in what it brings into focus. . . . It provides little more than a partial portrait, limited in scope and implication, that should offer a unique perspective on this dynamic and complex figure. If we can achieve some clearer picture of his humanity, it should do no violence to his spirituality and his sanctity."[2] Meissner reiterates that such an interpreter's purpose is "not merely to establish and validate the facts of [the] subject's life, but to see beyond, into the heart and mind of the [person]," although such an undertaking always involves a "concealment factor . . . since motives are by their nature largely concealed even from the subject."[3] For this reason, among others, I have sought to present the person of Vincent van Gogh with admiration, respect, and humility, and with as much objectivity as possible, while acknowledging that subjective biases inevitably influence interpretive writing of this nature.

In the interest of full disclosure, I should mention that as a person of Scottish, English, and French descent, my cultural and religious backgrounds are primarily southern, urban, east coast North American, Protestant Reformed, and Presbyterian, while Vincent's were northern European lowland, Protestant Dutch Reformed, and continental French, a century earlier. As for the focal perspectives of this book, the theological dimensions of Vincent's life and religious experience remain primary for me, while the psychological ones are secondary. This is reflected in the fact that my vocational commitments have been as a pastor, psychotherapist, and teacher of theology, philosophy, and pastoral care and counseling, accompanied by a life-long love for poetry and jazz as forms of creative expression, all of which in one way or another have influenced my writing through the years.

Several portions of this book fall into the category of "poetic license." In an attempt to construct an approximation of his "felt reality," when his own words were not available as factual evidence, I have sought to portray what I had imagined to be true of Vincent, given what I had known of him from many years of absorption in his letters and art. Here, of course, greater risks of straying from the truth arise, even if taken in the service of a more complete understanding. One such occasion, for example, is that in which I have interpreted what it might well have been like for Vincent to approach his final moments while contemplating death by suicide.

The subjective substratum for the use of such poetic imagination is what in the lexicon of Self Psychology is called "vicarious introspection,"

2. Meissner, *Ignatius of Loyola*, xxvi–xxvii.
3. Ibid., xxi–xxii.

whereby one person seeks by means of "empathic attunement" to enter into another's subjective experience in order better to understand it. To define this idiomatically, to be "empathically attuned" is to accomplish what we mean when we say we are seeking to "walk in another's shoes," as nearly impossible as this may seem. Yet, this is precisely what I have sought to do in page after page of this narrative. I have rarely done so alone. Rather, it has often been in the unconscious if not conscious company of other "witnesses" who, in one way or another, through the use of their minds, emotions, and imaginations, have sought to make sense of Vincent's life, just as they have their own, by exploring those subjective realities that comprise the basic phenomenological fund of our commonly shared humanity.

PROCEDURAL CONSIDERATIONS

For those who may be interested in the kind of qualitative research[4] that I undertook while living in close proximity to Vincent through detailed analysis of his more than 800 letters and 900 paintings, plus many of his 1,000 drawings, suffice it to say that the task was complex and at times daunting, yet deeply exhilarating and inspiring. Not least, of certain peak occasions, when I actually stood in sustained meditation before a number of his paintings and portraits on display in various places, encountering close-up and first-hand the ecstasies and agonies that had leapt boldly from the brushes he once held in his hand as he produced his magnificent works of art—it would be untruthful to say that such moments were anything less than deeply religious experiences.

4. This particular form of qualitative interpretation is sometimes referred to formally as "grounded theory," wherein "the relationships of themes constitute the theory, which is grounded in (is inductively developed from) the data" (Heppner et al., *Research Design*, 264). As a phenomenological treatise it looks beneath the surface of facts to the substrata of subjective meanings that constitute "the motives and beliefs behind people's actions" (Taylor et al., *Introduction to Qualitative Research*, 4). It is similar in many respects to Erik Erikson's psychobiography, *Young Man Luther*, of which Donald B. Meyer wrote: "Erikson finds that [in a particular period] . . . Luther underwent the decisive crisis of his life. This was his crisis of 'identity.' It began with his decision to be a monk; by every means he knew Luther tried to become what, so far as he knew, he wanted to be; and he failed. The triumphant conclusion to his crisis was a consequence of a breakthrough to a higher stage of self-integration, a fuller recognition of the grounds of selfhood" (Meyer, "A Review of *Young Man Luther*," 174).

For the sake of mining the many "treasures" contained within the 1,700 printed pages of Vincent's letters—which are like veritable doors and windows opened upon his inner life—I devised a detailed system of codification, whereby symbols and colors were assigned to specific categories of subject matter throughout *The Complete Letters*.[5] These enabled close examination of numerous topics, including Vincent's personal relationships, the dynamics of his families of origin, statements about himself, his work, and other people, as well as thoughts and images he held of the church, of God, and of Jesus Christ. Much of the thematic coding and grouping of subject matter pertained to particular concepts and principles of Christian theology and psychoanalytic Self Psychology. Specific dates, events, and turning points in Vincent's life were noted, a chronological synopsis of which appears at the end of this book.

Perhaps it is true, as Norman Denzin concluded in his essay "The Art and Politics of Interpretation," that "no one else but this writer could have brought this . . . corner of the world alive in this way for the reader."[6] To whatever extent this might be true, I hope and trust that my efforts will accrue to your enjoyment, enlightenment, and positive growth as a reader. A portrayal of Vincent's work is in no need of introduction to the world of art or art criticism, broadly or narrowly defined. Yet, it is surprising how many potential beneficiaries of his artistic and literary legacy have never seen one of his paintings nor read one of his letters. Many are unaware of the fascinating story of his life, with the exception of the scintillating, often spurious folklore surrounding the scandalous fate of his famous "ear"—itself too often an object of instant "interpretation," divorced from the whole of his story.

Throughout my years of reflection about Vincent van Gogh, and as recently as midstream in this writing, moments of sudden awakening occurred, bringing a new level of clarity. This is one of the many reasons as to why an encounter with Vincent is supremely engaging, somewhat like certain conversations taking place between pastor and parishioner, or counselor and counselee, in which true epiphanies suddenly arise. Moments of elation occurred for me more than once as I was working through the epochal events and tedious minutia of Vincent's life.

5. For bibliographic information about *The Complete Letters*, see "Sources and Citations" at the conclusion of the Acknowledgments.

6. Denzin, "Art and Politics," 323. The operative social scientific model for this interpretation of van Gogh's life is the postmodernist one set forth by Denzin (ibid., 313–44).

Practically every human emotion emerged during protracted immersions in the pathos of his story, which is one that transcends the era in which Vincent lived, and speaks powerfully to our own.

As I have stated, any number of "characters" are involved in the saga of a person's life over the course of time. In Vincent's case, some of them lived out their scripts from within him, while others took their stance from without, each with respective and, at times, conflicting roles to play in regard to his developing self-integration. As with Vincent during his most self-transcendent moments, we might also dare to believe that the most important and decisive influence for one's life is the very "God" to whom the psychoanalyst Heinz Kohut pointed us in Eugene O'Neill's drama "The Great God Brown," wherein just before his death William Brown declared: "Man is born broken. He lives by mending. The grace of God is glue."[7]

So, dear reader, as you listen attentively to what Vincent had to say about his life, may you find yourself attending all the more deeply to your own life, in continual discovery of its sacred meanings and purposes. The act of interpretation never ceases until life as we know it ceases. Thereafter, what is not yet fully known and understood will reside, at the very least, as I believe, within the mind, the will, and the loving activity of God, the Final Interpreter of all of life.

7. Kohut, *Self Psychology*, 169.

Acknowledgments

I WISH TO EXPRESS MY heartfelt gratitude to those who have accompanied me throughout this hallowed journey. As critical readers, whose thoughtful reflections and suggestions have contributed in important ways to the final form and content of this book, the following persons are especially to be thanked: Dr. Ross Mackenzie of Richmond, Virginia, long-time friend and mentor—retired as the director of the department of religion at the Chautauqua Institute of New York—who, also, more than thirty-five years ago was my graduate professor in church history and historical theology at Union Theological Seminary in Richmond—painstakingly and lovingly poured over every word of the manuscript, making pertinent comments and raising appropriate questions; Dr. Terrence Tice, friend and confidant for the past twenty-five years—a pre-eminent Schleiermacher scholar now living in Denver, Colorado, who for many years was professor of philosophy and education at the University of Michigan—offered extensive encouragement, meticulously and lovingly critiqued each chapter, and provided rich discussion and germane suggestions; Dr. John Campbell, personal friend and colleague—a pastoral psychotherapist in Brevard, North Carolina, and an exceptionally insightful supervisor of my work in pastoral counseling some years ago—introduced me then to the work of Heinz Kohut, for which I remain inexpressibly grateful; Dr. Cliff Edwards—currently professor of philosophy and religion at Virginia Commonwealth University in Richmond, and a long-time van Gogh aficionado and scholar who made significant contributions to my own thinking about Vincent's life, art, and religious experience—is quoted within the narrative with great appreciation for his having held firmly to an unapologetically theological view of Vincent's life and art; and, Dr. Lallene Rector—currently dean of the faculty and professor of pastoral theology and psychology of religion at Garrett-Evangelical Theological Seminary, Evanston, Illinois—as a teacher and practitioner of Self Psychology and as my doctoral advisor, enthusiastically supported the subject I had chosen for my research and writing, adding her own perspectives and insights about Vincent's personality. My former professors and supervisors, Drs. Wesley Brun, Richard Erikson, David Hogue, Stephen Long, Patricia McCluskey, Ms. Laura Sell, and the Rev. Nathan Brooks also made significant contributions to my learning, not only for this singular undertaking, but also and especially by way of theoretical and clinical preparation for my practice and teaching of pastoral care and counseling.

No one has known me longer or been more supportive and encouraging of me personally and of my writing than my dearest friend, Dr. Dean K. Thompson, recently retired president of Louisville Presbyterian Theological Seminary. Since we first met as students at Union Theological Seminary (now Union Presbyterian Seminary) in Richmond, Virginia, our conversations have covered almost every conceivable subject for some forty-five years, including many a special and familial occasion when we gathered to celebrate or to mourn pivotal and precious events in our lives. It was he, in addition to my wife, who lovingly and carefully pored over the galley proofs of these pages, as but one of the many gifts and graces for which I owe him the deepest personal gratitude in abiding friendship.

Others, too numerous to name, in their own special ways gave of themselves toward my growth as a pastor, pastoral counselor, and teacher, including those professional colleagues and students with whom I had the privilege of being associated within the context of cross-cultural and interracial higher education during the time I taught pastoral theology, care, and counseling at Virginia University of Lynchburg, in Lynchburg, Virginia. I am indebted especially to Dr. Ralph Reavis, President of the University, and Dr. Marshall Mays, Dean of the School of Religion.

Most of all, I give thanks for the abiding love, support, and encouragement of my beloved wife, Ethlyne, whose patience, forbearance, and insight, combined with her many hours of gentle nurture, listening, and conversation, made the writing of this book possible (and kept her husband sane throughout the endeavor!). I also express deep thanksgiving for my cherished children, Mark and Kate, without whom my journey through life, as well as my vicarious pilgrimage through the life of Vincent van Gogh, would have been significantly impoverished.

I recall especially the lovely rendition of Vincent's sunflowers that my daughter Kate painted when she was an elementary school student. To this day her painting remains a very special memory for her father. Vincent would have been quite honored to know that his painting had sparked the inquisitive imagination of a young child.

Thirty-four years ago, my then four-year-old son, Mark, and I, were on our way to church one Sunday morning during a violent thunderstorm, when he turned to me and asked: "Daddy, does God make thunder and lightening?" What can a responsible parent say to such a pure and earnest question? I said: "Why, yes, Mark, God does make thunder and lightening," whereupon Mark commanded, "God, make some thunder and lightening!" Suddenly, a great thunderbolt of lightening crashed all around us, and Mark shouted with glee: "Good, God, good!" I have recalled that profoundly serious and humorous moment more than once as I have thought of Vincent standing beneath the full forces of nature, painting to his heart's content, and with the same trusting belief and expectation that, at any given moment on just about any given day, God would uproariously reveal God's self—and would do so in such a manner that, in consequence, a certain painter might give distinct expression to the epiphany, right there upon the surface of his canvas in the middle of God's good and glorious creation. And I have since come to believe that this was so.

I wish, furthermore, to express my appreciation to my editor, Dr. Chris Spinks, and his colleagues, Mr. Matthew Stock, Ms. Diane Farley, and Ms. Kristen Bareman, as well as the other editorial staff at Wipf and Stock and its Cascade imprint. Their professional competence, comportment, consideration, and encouragement have been everything a writer could possibly want in an editor and publisher. It has been a great pleasure and privilege to work with them.

Lastly, I offer gratitude for Vincent and his brother Theo van Gogh, without whose mutual sharing the world would be bereft of one of the greatest gifts of sacred art that any artist has ever produced, through such extraordinary outpourings of heart and mind, in order that countless throngs of pilgrims could be blessed to "come and see." What is seen, above all, are intimations of that "Mystery within the mystery" from time to time yielding a fleeting glimpse of the holy and inscrutable One from whom all things visible and invisible come, and all blessings flow.

SOURCES AND CITATIONS

My source for Vincent van Gogh's personal letters of correspondence consisted of the three-volume set of *The Complete Letters* (ISBN 0-8212-0735-0) edited and published, originally in Dutch, by Vincent's sister-in-law, Theo van Gogh's wife, Johanna van Gogh-Bonger, who also translated the first two volumes into English. Mr. C. de Dood of Amsterdam translated the third volume. Mrs. Robert Amussen did a revision of the entire collection for American publication, which eventually resulted in the 1958 and 1978 editions published under the Bulfinch imprint by Little, Brown, and Company, now owned by the Hachette Book Group.[8]

Also now available are the two most recent English translations: (1) *Vincent van Gogh: The Letters* ("The Museum Letters Project") edited by Leo Jansen, Hans Luijten, and Nienka Bakker, published in 2009 in both Dutch and English under the auspices of the Vincent van Gogh Museum of Amsterdam and the Huygens Institute of the Royal Netherlands Academy of Arts and Sciences in Amsterdam, available in six hardcover, slipcase volumes (ISBN 0-5002-3865-0) and on the web at http://www.vangoghletters.org/vg/; and (2) the translation by Robert Harrison of Montreal, Canada, funded in part by the U.S. Department of Education, available online at http://www.webexhibits.org/vangogh/about/credits.html.

To view van Gogh's artistic works, consisting of his paintings, drawings, and sketches, as cited in this book, the reader may go to the website http://www.vangoghgallery.com/ and enter the titles of the works into the search field. The reader may also wish to access the complete collection of Vincent's paintings by securing a copy of the two-volume, slipcase edition of *Vincent van Gogh: The Complete Paintings*, edited by Ingo F. Walther and Rainer Metzger, translated into English by Michael Hulse and published in 1993 in Cologne by Benedikt Taschen, and printed in Germany (ISBN 3-8228-0291-3). The identical collection is also available in a smaller, hardcover version of the two volumes combined into one volume, published in 2002 in Cologne, London, Madrid, New York,

8. Today, van Gogh's letters are archived at the Van Gogh Museum in Amsterdam. We understand the copyright on these letters has long since expired, and so Vincent's letters are now in the public domain. Due diligence was made to secure permission for the use of the English translation used in this book. Our efforts included correspondence with the Van Gogh estate, the Van Gogh Museum, Thames & Hudson Publishers, and the Hachette Group.

Paris, and Tokyo by Taschen, and printed in Slovenia (ISBN 3-8228-1588-8). My footnote references to van Gogh's paintings are specific to this Walther and Metzger collection, whose pagination and content are identical in both the slipcase and the smaller hardcover editions.[9]

Footnote citations referring to the aforementioned *The Complete Letters* (Bulfinch, 1978 edition) are designated by the abbreviation "CL" (for "Complete Letters"), along with the respective number attached to a specific letter (example: "CL 100" for the hundredth letter). When a citation refers to an editorial annotation appearing in any one of the three volumes, the designation is by the volume number (1, 2, or 3) followed by a decimal point and the Arabic numeral for the page number (example: "CL 1.1" for volume one, page one). When citing correspondence written to persons other than Theo, the designation "CL" is followed by the letter of the alphabet representing the first letter in the surname of its recipient, plus the number of the specific letter of correspondence (example: "CL R2" for Vincent's second letter to Mr. Rappard). Correspondence that Vincent received from Theo is designated by the letter "T" followed by a number." Citations of Johanna van Gogh-Bonger's personal memoir of Vincent, appearing in the front of volume one, are designated as "Memoir" followed by the Roman numeral of the specific page number (example: "Memoir, x").

It is important to note that the numbering system used in the newly published *Vincent van Gogh: The Letters* (the "Museum Letters Project") is different from the original numbering system in *The Complete Letters*, employed for citations in this book. During the last several months of my pre-publication revisions, I consulted the Museum Letters Project website for corroboration of certain chronological and factual data that I had previously ascertained elsewhere. I wish to express my personal gratitude to the Van Gogh Museum letters project co-editor, Hans Luijten, for his kind and thoughtful personal assistance in several matters.

9. With respect to copyright on the paintings, a 1999 decision by a U.S. copyright court confirms that Vincent van Gogh's paintings are in the public domain (see *The Bridgeman Art Library, Ltd. v. Corel Corp.*). The basis for this decision was the court's view that a photograph of a painting in the public domain is insufficiently distinct from the original to be protected by copyright. That applies to all images used in this book.

THE MAIN THESIS

Our thesis, as presented here, is this: The achievement of a transfiguring spiritual vision is predicated, more often than not, upon regression into the depths of personal pain and suffering for the sake of the regeneration of life and love—or, as Vincent would say: the revelation of God is to be seen in following Jesus, willfully, into the Heart of Sorrow.

I hope that my efforts to express my own understanding of the life and work of Vincent van Gogh may contribute in some small fashion to the continuing quest for those deepest truths still to be discovered about him and his art—for the benefit of all who will have been deeply touched by his story, which in so many ways is our story.

CHARLES DAVIDSON
Black Mountain, North Carolina
January 28, 2011

PART ONE

The "Birth" of an Artist

ONE

A Lark in the Sky

"STRANGER ON THE EARTH"

O N THE BEAUTIFUL AUTUMN Sunday morning of the 29th of
October, 1876, a young Dutchman by the name of Vincent van
Gogh, twenty-three years of age, feeling at once solemn and anxious,
was hiking afoot in the western outskirts of London along the Thames
River "in which the great chestnut trees with their load of yellow leaves
and the clear blue sky were mirrored."[1] Embarked upon a mission, he
was clipping off the distance of three miles, headed south from the town
of Isleworth toward the Wesleyan Methodist Church in the community
of Richmond.

It was to be the first time he had ever stood in a pulpit to preach the
sermon—though we can envision him as a boy, his imagination sailing
before him like a ship at full tilt, as he climbed upward to stand for a few
moments behind the pulpit where his father had stood from Sunday to
Sunday to proclaim God's word to the people.

Looking out upon the Methodists gathered for worship, Vincent
began to speak: "Psalm 119:19. I am a stranger on the earth, hide not Thy

1. Vincent van Gogh, *The Complete Letters*, letter no. 79, hereafter cited, as in this
instance, "CL 79." Vincent's correspondence is numbered chronologically. For elaboration, see "Sources and Citations" in the Prologue. In addition to a brief chronology
provided at the end of this book, the reader may consult the Vincent van Gogh Museum
letters project for a more detailed chronology, found online at http://vangoghletters
.org/vg/chronology.html.

3

commandment from me. It is an old belief and it is a good belief, that our life is a pilgrim's progress—that we are strangers on the earth, but that though this be so, yet we are not alone for our Father is with us. We are pilgrims, our life is a long walk . . . from earth to Heaven . . .

"Sorrow is better than joy—and even in mirth the heart is sad—and it is better to go to the house of mourning than to the house of feasts, for by the sadness of the countenance the heart is made better. Our nature is sorrowful, but for those who have learnt and are learning to look at Jesus Christ there is always reason to rejoice. It is a good word that of St. Paul: as being sorrowful yet always rejoicing. For those who believe in Jesus Christ, there is no death or sorrow that is not mixed with hope—no despair—there is only a constantly being born again, a constantly going from darkness into light . . .

"We ourselves change in many respects, we are not what we once were, we shall not remain what we are now."[2]

Growing up in Holland, he had been a shy and introverted lad, coveting solitude, in contrast to his frequent fits of hot temper that made him hard to manage—and which, not surprisingly, led to his being pulled by his parents from the village school at Zundert at age nine to be tutored at home by a governess.

At age eleven, still presenting a considerable challenge to his family and teachers, he had been placed for two years in a private boarding school for boys in Zevenbergen, followed by several more lonely high school years spent away in Tilburg. Then, upon turning sixteen, with no money available for his further education, Uncle "Cent" arranged for him to try his hand at becoming an apprentice at the Goupil art firm, located at The Hague—since it was more or less "in the cards" that Vincent be groomed to follow in the hallowed footsteps of his favorite uncles.

Over the course of the ensuing seven years, before his April 1876 return to England, and before he began teaching and preaching as a pastoral assistant, he had been transferred back and forth between the firm's London and Paris branches, where he was often seen not so much to be going about his duties as an apprentice, as to be sitting in a corner

2. Ibid., vol. 1., p. 87, hereafter cited as "CL 1.87" with the use of a decimal point between the volume number and page number. For elaboration, see "Sources and Citations" in the Acknowledgments.

immersed in the study of Scripture or the art of various painters. With little or no aptitude and even less interest for learning how to operate the business, he mostly kept to himself rather than converse with the employees and customers.

Throughout these formative years, on many a day he was poking his head into an art exhibition, such as those at the Louvre, the Luxembourg, the British Museum, or the Royal Academy, there carefully observing the various displays and studying paintings of the great masters. All the while, he was collecting items for his scrapbooks and purchasing whatever he could afford at Goupil by way of prints and photographs to decorate the walls of his room. He was reading volumes of poetry, including Keats and Longfellow, alongside numerous other works of fiction, history, or biography, and as always the Bible. Occasionally on his travels he would stop to speak with someone he would meet, quite often a fellow artist, though he was chiefly given to solitude. During the period he was assigned to work at the Goupil gallery of London, with his mind frequently drifting from the immediate task at hand, he unsuccessfully fell in love with a lovely young Brixton woman by the name of Eugenie Loyer, to whose mother he was paying rent.

Overall, Vincent found his liking for the business of art to be wanting, but his passion for the art itself was all-consuming. His employers, who were equally as unenamored of him as he was of them, viewed him with an eye of critical skepticism and dubbed him an "eccentric."

At last, in January 1876, Goupil had given him notice of his forthcoming dismissal, effective as of the first of April. This would leave him without job and income. On the tenth of January he had dashed off a note to his brother, Theo, saying: "When the apple is ripe, a soft breeze makes it fall from the tree; such was the case here; in a sense I have done things that have been very wrong, and therefore I have but little to say" (CL 50). He did not indicate what had "ripened" the apple or what sort of "soft breeze" had caused it to fall from the tree.

By now his attention had been drawn to the 1866 political novel *Felix Holt, the Radical*, written by George Eliot, which, as he said to Theo, was "a book that impressed me very much" (CL 51). The story related to the changing British social order ranging from the 1830s to the time the novel was published, addressing the tensions that existed between the conservative landed aristocracy of England and a restless industrial working class, the latter being championed by the reformist sympathies of the protagonist, Felix Holt. Themes of importance to Eliot, such as differences of attitude toward Victorian women, were central to the plot.

Vincent's wide scope of reading to that time often had reflected his interest in historical matters as well as current events of the day, whether taking place in England or on the European continent. Eliot's novel had resonated with the tone of Vincent's own growing spirit of social radicalism, so much so that he passed the borrowed book on to Theo to read, asking Theo to send it to their parents before returning it to the owner.

Toward the end of January, Vincent posted a letter to Theo, declaring: "There is a phrase which haunts me these days—it is today's text, 'His children shall seek to please the poor'" (CL 52). He was referring to his reading of the tenth verse of the twentieth chapter of the book of Job: "His children shall seek to please the poor, and his hands shall restore their goods."[3]

Subsequently, in February, Vincent read Eliot's *Scenes from Clerical Life*, and made a point to mention the "tale" within it called "Janet's Repentance," which he said "struck me very much." He summarized it as "the story of a clergyman who lived chiefly among the inhabitants of the squalid streets of a town" and "died at the age of thirty-four. During his long illness he was nursed by a woman who had been a drunkard, but by his teaching, and leaning as it were on him, [she] had conquered her weakness and found rest for her soul. At his burial they read the chapter which says, 'I am the resurrection, and the life: he that believeth in me, though he were dead, yet shall he live'" (CL 55).

Back in England by the month of April, and no longer in the employ of Goupil, Vincent had decided to teach languages and math for a few months at a small school run by Mr. William Stokes in the eastern coastal town of Ramsgate. The school soon relocated to Isleworth, but Vincent quickly moved on to teach until December at another Isleworth school operated by the Reverend Mr. Thomas Slade-Jones, a Methodist minister. It was Mr. Jones whom Vincent assisted at the Turnham Green Congregational Church, located not far away from the sanctuary where Vincent preached the gospel on that auspicious autumn Sunday morning in late October. When Christmas arrived, Vincent left for Etten, Holland, to be with his family. Just as he had alluded in his sermon, it seemed that

3. From the Authorized King James Version (KJV).

he had been possessed for some time by a recurring sense of darkness and doom. He decided therefore not to return to England but instead was introduced by an uncle to the proprietor of the bookshop Blussé and Van Braam in Dordrecht, where he went to work as a clerk for a trial period of one week in the middle of January 1877. He remained there through the end of April of that same year.

Thirty-seven years later, in June 1914, in a column published in a Rotterdam newspaper—which was based upon a conversation between the writer, Mr. M. J. Bruuse, and the son of the bookseller, Mr. D. Braat, who had personally known Vincent—Mr. Bruuse offered some impressions.

> In theory Vincent had the show goods, and now and then the delivery goods, under his care . . . but whenever anyone looked at what he was doing, it was found that instead of working, he was translating the Bible into French, German, and English, in four columns, with the Dutch text in addition. . . . At other times when you happened to look, you caught him making little sketches, such silly pen-and-ink drawings, a little tree with a lot of branches and side branches and twigs—nobody ever saw anything else. (CL 1.108)

Mr. Bruuse further stated that Vincent "had not the slightest knowledge of the book trade, and he did not make any attempt to learn. . . . On the contrary, he was excessively interested in religion." As Mr. Braat had said to Mr. Bruuse: "On Sunday he always went to church, preferably an orthodox one. . . . And during the week, well, we started work here at eight o'clock in the morning; at one o'clock he went home to lunch until three; and then he came back in the evening for a few hours. For the rest, he had no intercourse with anybody; he led an absolutely solitary life. He took many walks . . . but always alone. In the shop he hardly spoke a word. In short, he was something of a recluse" (CL 1.109).

Mr. Braat's sister thereupon added: "I never thought there was anything particular about him. Honestly, I always thought of him as a real dullard. . . . And so, when he became obsessed with the idea of being a preacher, Pa told him, 'My lad, if you believe your road in life lies that way, you should take it, by all means.'" Mr. Braat then concluded of Vincent: "It looked as if he were suffering from a sense of injury—there was something lonesome about him. When you saw him, you pitied him" (CL 1.110).

It should have come as little surprise to anyone that by the time Vincent said farewell to the bookshop in Dordrecht, his life was heading in a decisively different direction from that of a salesman in art or books, though a preoccupation with both would become all-consuming.

By the month of May 1877, only several weeks beyond his twenty-fourth birthday, with singular determination, though not solely of his own accord, he landed in the city of Amsterdam. It was his explicit purpose to take up the study of theology there. His aspiration was to become a minister of the Christian gospel within the Groningen wing of the Dutch Reformed Church in which his father, Theodorus, was serving as a pastor.

Proponents of the Groninger theology, centered at Groningen University, "had rejected . . . popular rationalistic theology and emphasized the importance of the heart in Christian belief."[4] As the "moderating school" of Dutch Reformed Christianity, it "shared tenets of faith embraced by both the most orthodox and the most liberal thinkers of the time. On the one hand, it insisted on the verbal inspiration of Scripture and its ultimate authority; and, on the other hand, it denied the deity of Jesus."[5]

Amsterdam was the leading center of nineteenth-century northern Dutch urban society, commerce, culture, art, and religion. It was also home to young Vincent's paternal uncle, Cornelius Marinus van Gogh, one of five brothers who included three art dealers, a vice-admiral in the navy, and Vincent's father. Cornelius, informally addressed as "C.M." and also frequently called "Cor," was principal of the Amsterdam art firm C. M. van Gogh and an eventual partner within the House of Goupil in London, Paris, and at The Hague. Cornelius's brother, likewise named Vincent van Gogh, known to his nephews as "Uncle Cent," had established the firm. Also dwelling in Amsterdam was Jan van Gogh, the vice admiral and commandant of the Amsterdam naval yard, in whose home Vincent resided while living in the city through the middle of 1878.

On the maternal side was still another uncle, the Rev. Johannes Stricker, the husband of Vincent's mother's sister, Willemina Carbentus, also living in Amsterdam. As a Dutch Reformed minister and biblical

4. Bruins and Swierenga, *Family Quarrels,* 16.
5. Erickson, *At Eternity's Gate,* 4.

scholar who personally espoused the Groninger theology, he became the first to publish a modern Dutch "life of Jesus."[6]

Based upon Vincent's expressed desire to follow in his father's profession, the family carefully orchestrated a plan whereby Vincent would begin the study of theology through regular tutorials with his Uncle Stricker and would also learn Latin and Greek under the tutelage of the classicist Dr. Mendes da Costa. The arrangement was designed to prepare Vincent for the day when he would take the qualifying examinations for entrance into the university.

Professor da Costa later reminisced about his former pupil: "In my mind's eye I can still see him . . . his head thrust forward a little to the right, and on his face, because of the way his mouth drooped at the corners, a pervading expression of indescribable sadness and despair. And when he had come upstairs, there would sound again that singular, profoundly melancholy, deep voice: 'Don't be mad at me, Mendes; I have brought you some little flowers again because you are so good to me'" (CL 122a).

Despite Vincent's longing for acceptance, and regardless of the unflattering conclusions that others often drew about him, his aspiration to become a clergyman was authentic and sincere. In a handwritten letter in which he confided in his beloved brother Theo, who was four years his junior, Vincent said: "As for me, I must become a good clergyman who has something to say that is right and may be of use in the world; perhaps it is better that I have a relatively long time in preparation and am strongly confirmed in a stanch conviction before I am called to speak to others about it" (CL 121). Giving account of his genuine enthusiasm, along with his growing trepidation about the ultimate outcome of his studies, he spoke candidly to Theo concerning the conflict that was brewing within.

> Time passes—and quickly, too—we are almost at the end of the week. At present I am collecting Latin and Greek exercises and all kinds of writing about history, etc.; I am writing about the Reformation now, and it is getting quite lengthy. Some time ago I met a young man who had just passed his entrance examination for Leyden University. It is not easy—he told me what they had asked him. But I must keep courage; with God's help I will pass

6. For elaboration of Stricker's work, *Jezus van Nazareth volgens de Historie Geschetst* (Amsterdam: Gebroeders Kraay, 1868), see K. P. Erickson's discussion, ibid., 30–35.

this, and the other examinations, too. Mendes has given me hope
that at the end of three months we shall have accomplished what
he had planned we should [do] if everything went well. But Greek
lessons in the heart of Amsterdam, in the heart of the Jewish
quarter, on a very close and sultry summer afternoon, with the
feeling that many difficult examinations await you, arranged by
very learned and shrewd professors—I can tell you they make
one feel more oppressed than the Brabant cornfields, which are
beautiful on such a day. But as Uncle Jan says, we must always
"push on." (CL 103)

"Push on," indeed, the rear admiral had commanded. But the "push"
for Vincent to become a linguistic scholar—parsing the nuances of Greek
and Latin grammar, as capable as he was of doing so, and attending to
the rarified arguments of conventional theological discourse—mattered
little in comparison to the "pull" of an inner tug, a call to expend his
life as a missionary living among persons far less literate and socially
elevated than his learned and erudite uncles.

A "son of the manse"[7] most assuredly, and a voracious reader,
Vincent felt inextricably drawn to something deeper within himself
than could be unearthed by mining the petrified recesses of traditional
theological texts. In due time his earnest and true vocational commitments would become apparent, but in the meantime he would endure
what can only be described as a series of severe trials by fire. In order to
prove himself worthy of approbation, he gradually realized that he was
catering more to the conformist expectations of family and church than
he was answering the most profound vocational yearnings welling up
within his soul.

A brilliant linguist, fluent in French and English, in addition to his
native Dutch, and acquainted with the basics of German, he certainly
could have passed his Greek and Latin exams, but he was not at all prone
to waste precious energy in pursuit of requirements deemed by official
church councils to be essential for ordination to the ministry. It soon
became apparent that he wished instead to be engaged in the rough and
tumble, hands-on work of ministry, living among the common people,
especially the lowly, the poor, and the destitute.

Johanna van Gogh-Bonger, Vincent's sister-in-law and the wife
of Theo, noted in an editorial comment, which she inserted within her

7. Davidson, "Vincent van Gogh, Son of the Manse: A Portrait in Self Psychology,"
237.

collection of Vincent's correspondence published after his death, that at long last, or, more accurately, at short last, "in the summer of '78 he gave up studying in Amsterdam, with his parents' permission, and returned to the parsonage in Etten" (CL 1.115).

Shortly before his cessation of studies, Vincent had asserted to Theo: "Most people who have attained something have passed through a long and difficult time of preparation—the rock upon which their house was built" (CL 116). But the question remained: What exactly was the nature of the rock, and the house to be built upon it? And just how roughly or smoothly hewn were the contours of its architecture?

Four months before Vincent made the decision to abandon the path that would have led him to the doors of the university, he had received an especially meaningful visit from his father. It was on the extremely lonely Sunday night of February 10, 1878. He had just returned from seeing his "Father off at the station" and watching "the train go out of sight, even the smoke of it," when he sat down and composed an epistle to Theo, in which he unveiled his heart. "I came home to my room," he said, "and saw Father's chair standing near the little table on which the books and copybooks of the day before were still lying; and though I know that we shall see each other again pretty soon, I cried like a child" (CL 118). One can only surmise what thoughts accompanied his tears, but they poured from his depths, and, as he said, he was lonely. At the end of the letter he expressed gratitude for his "clever" Uncle Stricker from whom he was receiving lessons twice a week.

His next message to Theo followed eight days thereafter. He mentioned that on the previous Sunday he had visited the French church in Amsterdam, and there had heard a sermon by a minister visiting from Lyons speaking of "stories from the lives of the working people in the factories." The sermon lacked sophistication, but the words "came from the heart." "Only such," said Vincent, "are powerful enough to touch other hearts" (CL 119).

In the same letter he noted in passing that over the course of two days—perhaps it was a diversion from his studies, perhaps not—he had sketched out a map of the travels of the apostle Paul and had given them to a new acquaintance by the name of the Reverend Mr. Gagnebin. "I want to do such things now and then, for it certainly is very doubtful that I shall ever succeed, I mean, shall ever pass all the examinations. Five years at the least is a very long time. . . . Even if I fail, I want to leave my mark here and there behind me" (CL 119).

On the third of March 1778, he conveyed to his brother that their Uncle Cornelius ("C.M.") had told him that the artist Charles-François Daubigny had died. The lamentable news caused Vincent to reflect instantly upon his own life, concluding that "it must be good to die, conscious of having performed some real good and knowing that one will live through this work, at least in the memory of some, and will leave a good example to those who come after" (CL 120).

He had begun the letter by indicating to Theo how much he would have liked to be with him that day, given the beautiful weather and the feel of spring approaching, and then he said: "I suppose the lark can already be heard in the country, but in the city that is impossible, unless one hears the sound of the lark in the voice of some old clergyman whose words come from a heart that is tuned like that of the bird" (CL 120).

By early April, harboring even graver doubts about the course of his studies, Vincent had made an indirect reference to himself in another missive, saying that "there was once a man who went to church and asked, 'Can it be that my zeal has deceived me, that I have taken the wrong road and have not planned it well? Oh! If I might be freed from this uncertainty and firmly convinced that I shall conquer and succeed in the end!'" Twice in the letter he had repeated himself: *Nous sommes aujourd'hui ce que nous étions hier* [We are today what we were yesterday]," and added, "namely 'honest [people]' . . . who must be tried in the fire of life to become strengthened and steadied within, and be, by the Grace of God, what they are by nature."

But a few paragraphs before, he had declared: "Whoever chooses poverty for himself and loves it, possesses a great treasure and will always hear the voice of his conscience clearly; he who hears and obeys that voice, which is the best gift of God, finds at last a friend in it, and is never alone" (CL 121). Such words were clairvoyant. And when similar ones were voiced in letters written to his parents, they did not go unnoticed by his mother. Theo's wife, Johanna, once reported: "In her naïve religious faith his mother wrote, 'Vincent's letters, which contain so many interesting things, prove that with all his peculiarities, he yet shows a warm interest in the poor; that surely will not remain unobserved by God.'"[8]

8. Johanna van Gogh-Bonger, "Memoir," *The Complete Letters*, xxix, cited in text hereinafter as "Memoir" followed by its Roman numeral page number. Subsequent to the deaths of Vincent and Theo, Johanna van Gogh-Bonger, Theo's widow, reflected

While in the midst of working out math problems and translating Greek sentences, Vincent reported having suddenly quipped out loud to his tutor: "Mendes, do you seriously believe that such horrors are indispensable to a man who wants to do what I want to do: give peace to poor creatures and reconcile them to their existence here on earth?" Just what could Mendes say to that? Moreover, Vincent continued: "John Bunyan's *Pilgrim's Progress* is of much more use to me, and Thomas à Kempis and a translation of the Bible; and I don't want anything more" (CL 1.169). One could hear the thunder, admixed with anguish, in his voice.

Looking back upon Vincent's life posthumously, Mendes recalled that after every renewed attempt to conquer the excruciating difficulty of preparing for those examinations, Vincent would engage in "self-chastisement" by taking "a cudgel to bed with him" where he "belabored his back with it." He seemed altogether "consumed by a desire to help the unfortunate." "In no way," said Mendes, "could I guess in those days—no more than anyone else, himself included—that in the depths of his soul lay dormant the future visionary of color" (CL 1.171).

"CAGED BIRD"

In hindsight, Vincent bluntly referred to the year in Amsterdam as "the worst time I have ever lived through" (CL 131). After a brief retreat to his parents' home in Etten, he resolutely set forth upon his intended journey to become a missionary. Accompanied by his father and the former school principal, the Reverend Mr. Thomas Slade-Jones, Vincent suddenly found himself standing in fear and trembling before a solemn convocation of the clergy—the gatekeepers of the Committee of Evangelization of the Dutch Reformed Church at Brussels, whose critical judgments would soon humble Vincent beyond the fears of his wildest nightmares.

Vincent entreated them to grant their approval to commission him as an evangelist in the coal mining fields of Belgium. This would entail a different order of preparation than the one recently undertaken

upon many intimate details of Vincent's life, including insights and anecdotes gathered from her husband, family members, and others. She compiled altogether 642 of Vincent's letters written to Theo, in addition to letters Vincent had written to and received from others with whom he shared correspondence. Her memoir of Vincent constitutes a preface to his letters, as well as occasional commentary here and there.

in Amsterdam. To Vincent's delight, if not his surprise, the committee accepted his application.

That hurdle having been crossed, there was another court of opinion with which he must quickly reckon. It would not be his first appearance before it, for he had already faced its judges on more than one occasion. His mother, who harbored as much doubt about her son as she did hope and expectation for him, declared: "I am always so afraid that wherever Vincent may be or whatever he may do, he will spoil everything by his eccentricity, his queer ideas and views on life." Thereupon, according to the testimony of their daughter-in-law, Johanna: "His father added, 'It grieves us so to see that he literally knows no joy of life, but always walks with bent head, whilst we did all in our power to bring him to an honorable position! It seems as if he deliberately chooses the most difficult path'" (Memoir, xxviii).

The court of parental jurisdiction had once again convened. And yet, his father's disapproving judgment aside, there was a less critical, more understanding and sagacious component to Theodorus, of which others sometimes, perhaps often, caught a glimpse—more so than Vincent may have known or been willing to admit. Taking account of what he perceived to be a measure of growth on the part of his son, Theodorus wrote: "His stay abroad and that last year at Amsterdam have not been quite fruitless after all, and when he takes the trouble to exert himself, he shows that he has learned and observed much in the school of life" (Memoir, xxvii). Theodorus considered that a three months' trial phase spent in training at the Flemish School of Evangelization could bode well for Vincent. For the long haul, however, should Vincent decide to complete the training, three years of study would be required.[9]

As hopeful and promising as this prospect was for Vincent, there was yet one other court of weighty opinion before whose "councils" he must present himself if he expected to graduate. Its youthful adjudicators would surely hold forth a more kindly disposition toward Vincent than just about anyone else had, either in Brussels or back home in Etten. This court consisted of the jury of his peers at the School of Evangelization.

Their kindly disposition was not to be so kindly, however. As it turned out, by subjecting Vincent to unsolicited cruelties catering to their craving for twisted amusement—"boys will be boys," especially

9. See CL 123 for a description of Vincent's impressions of the course of studies.

when they can make fun of someone else—they spoiled just about any positive self-expectation that Vincent had in mind.

This was not a new phenomenon within the precincts of judgment to which Vincent had been subjected one way or another all his life. As long as he could recall, familiar and unfamiliar persons alike had meted out judgments contravening his self-esteem. Personal dismissal and behind-the-back snickering and sneering—the tomfoolery of those who mocked and bullied him—had adhered to him like lead paint fastened to a weather-beaten stone wall. As with many an idiosyncratic stranger, his eccentricities presented an opportunity for others to heap scorn and contempt upon him. He was invariably the odd man out.

Thus, when he arrived in Brussels for his studies as "the most advanced in Mr. Bokma's class," feeling, as Vincent put it, "like a fish out of water," he was roundly "ridiculed for his peculiarities in dress and manners." According to Johanna's report, "he also lacked the ability to extemporize, and was therefore obliged to read his lectures from manuscript. But the greatest objection against him was, 'He is not submissive'; and when the three months had elapsed, he did not get his nomination" (Memoir, xxviii).

The underlying question remained: why was he so determined not to be submissive? In his present state of mind, with his body "weak and thin," "nervous and excited," as well as deprived of sleep, his father was summoned to take him home. Perhaps that was the primary if not only clue to his stubborn recalcitrance. For there was always someone—usually it was Father—who was summoned to take him home. The prodigal invariably received a reminder that he was a prodigal.

Tell a prodigal often enough that he is a prodigal, and he will believe he is a prodigal and will act like a prodigal. Believe in a God who is forever and always supposed to be punitive, and such a God will remain forever and always punitive in the mind of the one who so believes. Tell a believer that as a child of God he is nothing but a rascal in God's sight, and he will eventually believe he is nothing but a rascal in God's sight. To wit: "I am always so afraid that wherever Vincent may be or whatever he may do, he will spoil everything by his eccentricity, his queer ideas and views on life." "It grieves us so to see that he literally knows no joy of life, but always walks with bent head, whilst we did all in our power to bring him to any honorable position! It seems as if he deliberately chooses the most difficult path."

Always, always, always—walks with head bent—knows no joy of
life—must be brought to an *honorable* position! But for the sake of *whose*
honor?

When was Vincent himself ever so much as *honored*? Certainly not
by his peers or his masters at the School of Evangelization. Nevertheless,
despite the Committee of Evangelization's failure to nominate him,
Vincent was not about to be deterred from his mission. He would not
surrender to their form of jurisprudence. Unhesitating, he immediately
struck out on his own, heading for the Belgian coal-mining district of
the Borinage where he quickly set about his work. He did so among the
miners and their families at his own expense as a self-appointed evangelist. Such was his hard and fast resolve. And, contrary to Vincent's
expectation, his father consented. There in the presence of strangers like
himself he sought to make friends. He read his Bible and visited the sick
until January of 1879, when he was able to obtain a temporary appointment as an evangelist for a provisionary period of six months.

His efforts to succeed more than doubled. He nursed "the sick and
wounded; he gave away all he possessed, clothes, money, even his bed;
he no longer lived in a boardinghouse, but in a small miner's hut where
even the barest necessities were wanting. In this way he tried to follow
Jesus' teaching literally" (CL 1.172). So, the overriding consideration
was not about the authority to whom he *would* submit, but about the
One to whom he had *already* submitted.

Nonetheless, when the probationary phase had ended, the committee summarily and categorically denied his continuance as an evangelist.
Instead of sanctioning his work, it reproved him for his overzealous ways
and his utter neglect of himself. He was formally dismissed in July. As
Johanna recalled: "The ensuing days were the most bitter of his life; he
wandered about full of cares, without faith, without work, without any
prospects, without any friends" (CL 1.172). For certain, and without the
shadow of a doubt, he had *become* the prodigal.

Yet, in the midst of his "travail in the wilderness," something quite extraordinary had happened. Pushed to the limit of self-assurance, with
nothing material to his name, nothing on his back, nothing on his feet,
and nothing in his purse, he appeared to have dissolved both inwardly
and outwardly into little more than nothing. Yet, his self-reflection,

which easily could have degenerated to the point of cataclysmic self-destruction, turned instead into a profoundly sobering and transforming self-realization.

"What shall we do now?" he asked. "Jesus was also very calm in the storm; perhaps it must grow worse before it grows better," he mused (Memoir, xxix). Amid the devastating impact of the singeing rejection he had received from the church authorities, and in spite of an overwhelming temptation to persist in thorough self-recrimination, he managed to attain no less than a high level of self-composure. He wrote to Theo with sympathetic sensitivity—not, however, about himself, but about the character and plight of the coal miners. In spirit, Vincent had become one of the coal miners. One day, in keeping with his renewed sense of mission, for six hours he deliberately descended into one of the mines, the notorious Marcasse, considered extremely dangerous with "a bad reputation because many perish in it, either going down or coming up, or through poisoned air, firedamp explosion, water seepage, [and] cave-ins" (CL 129).

During this season of his radical identification with the harsh and impoverished circumstances of the miners, one of the mines exploded—Pit Number One of the Charbonnage Belge. Many miners were burned, some severely. Believing himself called of Christ, Vincent went rapidly to their side, tending to the wounded. The words of Jean-Baptiste Denis, the baker with whom Vincent initially boarded while living and working there in the Borinage, told the story.

> Having arrived at the state where he had no shirt and no socks on his feet, we have seen him make shirts out of sacking . . . My kind-hearted mother said to him: Monsieur Vincent, why do you deprive yourself of all your clothes like this—you who are descended from such a noble family of Dutch pastors? He answered: I am a friend of the poor like Jesus was. She answered: You're no longer in a normal condition. . . . Our friend Vincent did not give himself a moment's rest day and night cutting up the last remnants of his linen to make bandages with wax and olive oil on them, and then ran to the wounded to dress their burns.
>
> The humanity of our friend continued to grow day by day, and yet the persecutions he suffered grew, too. And still the reproaches and insults and stoning by the members of the Consistory, though he always remained in the deepest abasement! . . . Yet he was always at his studies; in a single night he read a volume of 100 pages;

during the week he taught a school he had founded for the children teaching them to fear God, and at the same time he was busy
making drawings of photography and the mines. (CL 143a)

After the explosion, having remained close to the miners through
the misery, pain, and outpouring of their grief, Vincent pondered the
import of the calm that had possessed his Lord in the midst of just such
a besetting storm at sea, which portended for Jesus even worse storms
to come. Vincent had confronted a magnitude of existential human
anguish that was even more devastating than his own. He had entered
into the miners' affliction as one who willingly, and defiantly, had taken
upon himself not only their suffering but also the suffering of Jesus. In
doing so, also like Jesus, he railed against the very establishment that
had determined him to be unfit for the ministrations of the gospel: "Not
permissible, aye, just as Frank the Evangelist thought it reprehensible of
me to assert that the sermons of the Reverend Mr. John Andry are only
a little more evangelical than those of a Roman Catholic priest. I would
rather die a natural death than be prepared for it by the Academy, and
I have sometimes had a lesson from a German mower that was of more
use to me than one in Greek" (CL 132).

Life among the coal miners had brought Vincent to a turning
point, the latest in a series of turning points, which this time had
come about in a mood and manner of irreversibility. To make matters
worse, Vincent experienced an increased distance from Theo, who to
Vincent's chagrin sided with the family back home. Theo thought his
older brother had more or less lost his mind. In a translucent moment,
to mollify Theo by setting the record straight, Vincent turned the tip
of his pen into an instrument of blunt discourse: "Now if you should
conclude from what I say that I wanted to call you a quack because of
your advice, you would have quite misunderstood me, as I do not think
this of you at all. On the other hand, you would also be mistaken if you
thought that I would do well to follow your advice literally to become
an engraver of bill headings and visiting cards, or a bookkeeper or a
carpenter's apprentice—or else to devote myself to being a baker—or
many similar things (curiously different and hard to combine) that
other people advise me" (CL 132).

In fear, and perhaps in haste, Theo had falsely accused Vincent of
"idleness." The accusation sounded remarkably familiar—downright pa-
ternalistic—in fact, too much like their father. In retort, Vincent erupted

like a mountain volcano spewing forth molten lava, sliding downhill into a river of ice. "If I had to believe that I were troublesome to you or to the people at home, or were in your way, of no good to anyone, and if I should be obliged to feel like an intruder or an outcast, so that I were better off dead, and if I should have to try to keep out of your way more and more—if I thought this were really the case, a feeling of anguish would overwhelm me, and I should have to struggle against despair. This is a thought I can hardly bear, and still harder to bear is the thought that so much discord, misery and trouble between us, and in our home, is caused by me. If it were indeed so, then I might wish that I had not much longer to live" (CL 132).

The emotional distance had grown exponentially between Vincent and Theo, so much so that total silence would reign from early August of 1879 until the following summer. In the meantime, Vincent had already moved the short distance from Wasmes to Cuesmes near the city of Mons in Belgium, where he lived for a while with an evangelist whom he identified as M. Frank (CL 131). In the middle of August he paid a brief visit to his parents in Etten. Then, upon his return to Cuesmes, in the ensuing months and throughout the winter he immersed himself in his drawing and made positive use of his "melancholy" spirit by studying, as he said, "somewhat seriously the books within my reach like the Bible, and the *French Revolution* by Michelet, and . . . Shakespeare and a few by Victor Hugo and Dickens, and Beecher Stowe, and lately *Eschylus*, and then several others, less classical, several great 'little masters'" (CL 133).

In July 1880, from the Borinage, when "with reluctance" at last he broke the ice with Theo, he wrote a lengthy letter, saying: "to a certain degree you have become a stranger to me, and I have become the same to you, more than you may think." Confessing to having learned during his most recent visit to Etten that Theo had generously sent him fifty francs, he added: "Well, I have accepted them. Certainly with reluctance, certainly with a rather melancholy feeling but I am up against a stone wall and in a sort of mess. How can I do otherwise? So I am writing you to thank you" (CL 133).

Feeling still aggrieved and hurt, he nevertheless withdrew from behind his emotional armor long enough to expostulate as to what had happened. "Involuntarily, I have become more or less a kind of impossible and suspect personage in the family, at least somebody whom they do not trust, so how could I in any way be of any use to anybody? Therefore, above all, I think the best and most reasonable thing for me to do is to go away and keep at a convenient distance, so that I cease to exist for you all." In the next sentence he explained: "As molting time—when they change their feathers—is for birds, so adversity or misfortune is the difficult time for us human beings. One can stay in it—in that time of molting—one can also emerge renewed; but anyhow it must not be done in public and it is not at all amusing, therefore the only thing to do is to hide oneself. Well, so be it" (CL 133). Thereupon, he expressed his wish for an *entente cordiale* between himself and Theo, as well as with their father.

Through the self-protective maneuvers of the wounded and testy parts of his personality, Vincent had learned early in life to oscillate abruptly at times between belligerent volatility and crushing self-deprecation. This served him about as well as a double-edged sword: with the foreside striking out bitterly toward others and the backside cutting punitively into himself. Now, however, while being in a relatively conciliatory mood, he turned the lamplight of insight upon himself: "I am a man of passions, capable of and subject to doing more or less foolish things, which I happen to repent, more or less, afterward. Now and then I speak and act too hastily, when it would have been better to wait patiently. Well, this being the case, what's to be done? Must I consider myself a dangerous man, incapable of anything? I don't think so. But the problem is to try every means to put those selfsame passions to good use" (CL 133).

While living among the coal miners, sketching the visages of their beleaguered lives, Vincent had come to realize, with Theo's encouragement, that his aesthetic passions would need to be channeled far beyond his appreciation for the artistic works of others. For so many years he had been consumed by observing art. Now he must become consumed by creating art—and, not least, in the interest of earning some money.

One day, after taking a walking tour of Pas-de-Calais in the northern tip of France, in search of a job—with ten francs in his pocket, and in the spirit of a lark jumping the bush—he hopped the train to travel to Courrières. He had dreamed of meeting the well-known artist and poet Jules Breton. But he quickly ran out money and had to make the rest of the way by foot. "I was on the road for a week, I had a long, weary walk of it," he said. Then he added: "I saw, Courrières, and the outside of M. Jules Breton's studio. The outside . . . was rather disappointing: it was quite newly built of brick, with a Methodist regularity, an inhospitable, chilly and irritating aspect. If I could only have seen the interior, I would certainly not have given a thought to the exterior, I am sure of that. But what shall I say of the interior? I was not able to catch a glimpse, for I lacked the courage to enter and introduce myself" (CL 136).

The opportunity to receive personal confirmation from a fellow artist, and a celebrated one at that, had landed squarely at his fingertips like a capering bird, but he simply could not take hold of it. So he returned "the long journey" to the Borinage, penniless, and "slept either in the open air or in a hayloft. Sometimes he exchanged a drawing for a piece of bread" (Memoir, xxx). Nevertheless, despite so many things having worked against him, both from within and from without, and for reasons he may not have entirely understood himself, he did not lose faith in the possibility that eventually he would accede to the realization of his greatest potential.

"Wait, perhaps someday you will see that I too am an artist," he enjoined Theo. "I do not now know what I can do, but I hope I shall be able to make some drawings with something human in them. But first I must draw the Bargues[10] and do other more or less difficult things. The path is narrow, the door is narrow, and there are few who find it" (CL 136). Even so, in the midst of his poverty and troubled emotional state, regretful of the past, distraught over the present, and despondent about the future, wailing like a lone wolf crying in the wilderness, albeit unconsciously, he had crossed his "Rubicon." Or, at the least, he was more than midway through its churning waters. Incumbent upon him was the necessity of continually waging war against every hindrance to the fulfillment of his calling, which at the core of his God-given self was rooted deeper than an oak tree's branches could grow tall. He was never meant to be a bookkeeper or a baker. The numbers simply would not have added up, and the bread would have charred in the oven. For he was singularly destined to become a painter.

By the time of his reconciliation with Theo in the summer of 1880, he expressed the anguish he had harbored for so long in response to a

10. Famous drawing book consisting of lithographs of the human anatomy produced by painters Charles Bargue and Jean-Leon Gerôme in Paris during the mid-1800s.

world that almost universally had accused him of the same crime his brother had laid at his feet—of being no more than an "idle" person.

> This is quite a different kind of idle man; if you like you may take me for such a one! A caged bird in spring knows quite well that he might serve some end; he is well aware that there is something for him to do, but he cannot do it. What is it? He does not quite remember. Then some vague ideas occur to him, and he says to himself, "The others build their nest and lay their eggs and bring up little ones"; and he knocks his head against the bars of the cage. But the cage remains, and the bird is maddened by anguish. "Look at that lazy animal," says another bird in passing, "he seems to be living at ease." Yes, the prisoner lives, he does not die; there are no outward signs of what passes within him—his health is good, he is more or less gay when the sun shines. But then the season of migration comes, and attacks of melancholia—"But he has everything he wants," say the children that tend him in his cage. He looks through the bars at the overcast sky where a thunderstorm is gathering, and inwardly he rebels against his fate. "I am caged, I am caged, and you tell me I do not want anything, fools! You think I have everything I need! Oh! I beseech you liberty, that I may be a bird like other birds!" A certain idle man resembles this idle bird. (CL 133)

Vincent had the inherent ability, like a chameleon, to become at one moment invisible to the entire world as though he did not even exist—at least not in order to conform to expectation. And then in the very next instant—when accused of idleness, or something worse—he had the capacity to spring forth in full costume like a circus clown, making fun of himself in order to give his detractors a chance to catch a glimpse of their own feeble folly. Yet, beneath the act there sagged a very sad countenance, which said: "Circumstances often prevent [people] from doing things, prisoners in I do not know what horrible, horrible, most horrible cage. There is also—I know it—the deliverance, the tardy deliverance. A justly or unjustly ruined reputation, poverty, unavoidable circumstances, adversity—that is what makes [people] prisoners" (CL 133). Indeed, "one cannot always tell what it is that keeps us shut in, confines us, seems to bury us; nevertheless, one feels certain barriers, certain gates, certain walls. Is all this imagination, fantasy? I don't think so. And one asks, 'My god! Is it for long, is it forever, is it for all eternity?'" (CL 136).

"Prisoners Exercising (after Doré)"

But then, like the clown in the circus—having fallen down and bounced back up and dusted himself off—he said: "In spite of everything I shall rise again: I will take up my pencil, which I have forsaken in my great discouragement, and I will go on with my drawing. From that moment everything has seemed transformed for me; and now I have started and my pencil has become somewhat docile, becoming more so every day. The too long and too great poverty had discouraged me so much that I could not do anything. . . . Though every day difficulties crop up and new ones will present themselves, I cannot tell you how happy I am to have taken up drawing again. . . . The thing for me is to learn to draw well, to be master of my pencil or my crayon or my brush; this gained, I shall make good things anywhere, and the Borinage is just as picturesque as old Venice, Arabia, Brittany, Normandy, Picardy or Brie" (CL 136).

The picturesque coalfields of the Borinage notwithstanding, during October of 1880 Vincent chose to take flight to Brussels and the Brussels Academy, where he "hoped to become acquainted with other artists." There Theo, working from Paris, was able to introduce him to one who would become Vincent's good friend, the young Dutch painter Anthon van Rappard, who for a while stood by Vincent like a second brother, though not without brotherly squabbles. In a letter of reminiscence written after Vincent's death, van Rappard recollected: "Whoever had witnessed this wrestling, struggling and sorrowful existence could not but feel sympathy for the man who demanded so much of himself that it ruined body and mind. He belonged to the breed that produces the great artists" (Memoir, xxx–xxxi).

According to Johanna, while Vincent was there in Brussels, he "studied anatomy by himself, drew diligently from living models, and . . . took lessons in perspective from a poor painter." At winter's end, longing once again to be in the countryside and to reduce his expenses, he sought refuge with his family back in Etten, where he remained for eight long months (Memoir, xxxi–xxxii).

The interlude, from April through December 1881, proved to be a fateful convocation of the generations, a living drama over which the familial gods and goddesses of the hearth—had any been visible— would have been seen hovering in anxious watchfulness, shedding their tears of lamentation. In certain respects the pivotal events surrounding Christmastide of 1881 were inevitable, and quite consistent with the effect of what had happened to Vincent in the Borinage. For while he had been there among the coal miners, he had encountered what the theologian Paul Hessert called "the break"—which is that liminal space of interrupted expectation where "another Reality may be met,"[11] and where "the saint is not heroic and the Christian life is not heroism. The saint is one who is coming to terms with the reality of Christ crucified, not idealistic heroism."[12]

Vincent's dream of making his living as a commissioned missionary, the offshoot of his father's vocation as a pastor, had been thoroughly shattered during his tenure in the coalfields. It was inevitable, therefore, that a fundamental realignment of forces would have to take place, lest the lark veer from its destined path of flight—"the lark that cannot keep

11. P. Hessert, *Christ and the End of Meaning*, 73.
12. Ibid., 159.

from singing in the morning even though the soul sometimes sinks within us and is perturbed" (CL 98). In order for that to happen, the door to the future would have to fling wide open with a resounding fury.

"NO, NEVER NEVER"

"Where sympathy is renewed, life is restored"—Vincent had written during his recent travail, living among the miners' families (CL 133). So, when he arrived at the parsonage in Etten, he was glad to be at home once again where he could set about his work with renewed vigor in a comfortable environment with a roof over his head, food on his plate, and enough cash in his pocket to pay for living models to pose at his easel, thanks to the largesse of those who continued to support him, namely, his parents, and, especially, his brother Theo. He soon wrote to his brother, who had come to Etten for a visit: "It was very pleasant to have you here again, and to have long talks together about everything. I always regret that we cannot be together much more. Not that I think talking in itself so valuable, but I mean that I wish we knew each other much better and more intimately than we do now" (CL 148).

Vincent was also grateful for the forthcoming opportunity to make a brief trip to The Hague to spend some time with his mother's kin, Anton Mauve, a first cousin by marriage, who was an accomplished painter. Mauve was yet another one of those gifted mentors who steered Vincent toward the discovery of his truest self. If it is accurate to say that God secretly provides momentary glimpses of future graces embedded in present encounters, then Mauve was certainly among the "angels unawares"[13] for Vincent, as Vincent would shortly find out.

In the meantime, by the summer of 1881 there was an altogether different reason for Vincent to believe that "where sympathy is renewed, life is restored." Her name was Kee Vos, of Amsterdam. She was the recently widowed niece of Vincent's mother, thus Vincent's first cousin, and in his eyes a delicate, kind, and nurturing woman with a young child of her own. Vincent adored her, walked and talked with her, devoted his attention to her son, and quite unexpectedly, and instantly, proposed marriage to her.

13. "Do not neglect to show hospitality to strangers, for thereby some have entertained angels unawares" (Hebrews 13:2, RSV).

Her response? "No, never never!"

Vincent was mortally wounded. He felt like the wingéd lark had tumbled into a heap of fiery timbers, reduced to ashes. Yet, the pining lark—or was it the infatuated phoenix?—refused to play dead. Vincent explained to Theo:

> In the first place I must ask you if it astonishes you at all that there is a love serious and passionate enough not to be chilled even by many 'no, never nevers'? I suppose far from astonishing you, this will seem very natural and reasonable. For love is something so positive, so strong, so real that it is as impossible for one who loves to take back that feeling as it is to take his own life. If you reply to this by saying, "But there are people who put an end to their own life," I simply answer, "I really do not think I am a man with such inclinations." Life has become very dear to me, and I am very glad that I love. My life and my love are one. "But you are faced with a 'no, never never,'" is your reply. My answer to that is, "Old boy, for the present I look upon that 'no, never never' as a block of ice which I press to my heart to thaw. To determine which will win, the coldness of that block of ice or the warmth of my heart, that is the delicate question about which I can give no information as yet, and I wish that other people would not talk about it if they can say nothing better than, "The ice will not thaw," "Foolishness" and more such nice insinuations. (CL 154)

Waxing ever more eloquent, he continued:

> If I had an iceberg from Greenland or Nova Zembla[14] before me, I do not know how many meters high, thick and wide, then it would be a difficult case, to clasp that colossus and press it to my heart to thaw it. But as I have never yet seen an ice colossus of such dimensions loom up across my course, I repeat, seeing that she with her "no, never never" and all is not many meters high and thick and wide, and if I have measured correctly, might easily be clasped, I cannot see the 'foolishness' of my behavior. As for me, I press the block of ice "no, never never" to my heart; I have no other choice, and if I try to make it thaw and disappear—who can object to that??? What physical science has taught them that ice cannot be thawed is a puzzle to me. It is very sad that there are so many people who object to it, but I do not intend to get melancholy over it and lose my courage. Far from it. Let those be

14. An archipelago in the Arctic Ocean north of Russia, consisting of two islands, the northern one containing glaciers.

melancholy who will. I have had enough of it, and will only be glad as a lark in the spring!" (CL 154)

"No, never never" was the haunting refrain that would reverberate in Vincent's ears until the day he became deaf from hearing it, if ever that day should come. As he said of his grief over the loss of Kee Vos, whom he had never in the least bit gained, it "remains a wound which I carry with me; it lies deep and cannot be healed. After years it will be the same as it was the first day" (Memoir, xxxiv).

Sadly for Vincent, Kee did not permit herself the pleasure of his company. This was despite Vincent's persistent overtures. Yet, he remained hopeful and determined that he would finally overcome her stone-cold silence. Plagued with an obsession for a woman to pour out affection for him, he rationalized the impossible as the possible. And in that respect Kee Vos became his "illusion." He implored her: "'Kee, I love you as myself. . . .' Then she said, 'No, never never.' What is the opposite of 'no, never never'? Aimer encore! [To love again!] I cannot say who will win. God knows, I only know this one thing, 'I had better stick to my faith'" (CL 154).

Sometimes Vincent stuck to his judgments, as well as to his faith, to his own detriment. Soon thereafter, he wrote to Theo:

> Whoever feels so sure of himself that he rashly imagines, She is mine, before he has fought that soul's battle of love—I repeat, before he wavers between life and death, on a high sea in storm and thunder—he does not know what a real woman's heart is, and that will be brought home to him by a real woman in a very special way. When I was younger, I once half-fancied myself in love, and with the other half I really was; the result was many years of humiliation. May all this humiliation not have been in vain. I speak as 'one who has been down' from bitter experience and hard lessons. . . . And that "no, never never" is not as sweet as spring air, but bitter, bitter as nipping winter frost. "This is no flattery," as Shakespeare would say. (CL 156)

As for Vincent, when had there ever been flattery? Without so much as an ounce of flattery, Vincent had stuck to his faith during the leanest and hardest of times, which of late were most of them. As Jean-Baptiste Denis, the baker, and his wife, Esther, with whom Vincent had lived among the miners, had said of him: the fledgling evangelist voluntarily sacrificed his comfortable room in their home "in favor of that hovel outside," and lived on bread and water while feeding cheese and milk to the mice.[15] This man on a mission was no less than the very Vincent whom the inhabitants of the Borinage had crowned as "The Christ of the Coalmine."[16] So, given his most recent experience of personal deprivation—the categorical rebuke by Kee Vos—would he then suddenly go soft on his faith in the face of unrequited love—he who had so thoroughly submitted himself, in sacrifice, to Christ and the coal miners? Or, would he, like Christ, persist in the manner of deprivation that his high calling as an artist seemed to be requiring of him? If being "'*one who has been down*' from bitter experience and hard lessons" had proven anything, it had proven that "all this humiliation" had not "been in vain"—if not for the "art of making love," then surely for the "love of making art."

Certainly, Vincent would dare not let himself go "soft" on the faith like the flimsy "fabric" he had observed in the "cloth" of some who had busied themselves by touting the "true faith" while at the same time hiding the light of the gospel under a bushel in a "Falstaffian" church. "There is an old academic school," he said, "often detestable, tyrannical, the accumulation of horrors, men who wear a cuirass, a steel armor, of prejudices and conventions; when these people are in charge of affairs, they dispose of positions, and by a system of red tape they try to keep their protégés in their places and to exclude the other man. Their God is like the God of Shakespeare's drunken Falstaff, *le dedans d'une église* [the inside of a church]; indeed, by a curious chance some of these evangelical (???) gentlemen find themselves with the same point of view on spiritual things as that drunken character" (CL 133).

Who now, in fact, had gone soft? Would a true saint—if one could be found—not stand tall in the faith like a giant red oak, and not only for the love of truth but for the truth of love? What should Vincent do, given the fact that his faith, his trust, his confidence—his very livelihood— were all once again on the chopping block of public opinion? Out of sheer desire to assuage his loneliness, or simply because he was a man in essence like all other men, capable of concupiscence, should he continue his quest for a woman who might love him? Or would that be an altogether faithless and fruitless endeavor?

"Theo, all fathers of girls possess a thing which is called the key to the front door. A very terrible weapon which can open and shut the aforesaid

15. K. Wilkie, *In Search of Van Gogh*, 75–76.
16. Ibid., 77.

front door, like Peter and Paul open the gates of heaven. Well, does this instrument also fit the heart of the respective daughters 'in question'? Is it opened or shut with the key to the front door? I think not, but God and love alone can open or shut a woman's heart. Will hers ever open, brother, will she ever let me in? —God knows, I cannot tell" (CL 156).

If Kee couldn't open her own heart, then maybe there was someone else who could open it for her. That person, if the proposed plan of attack should be divinely inspired, would be no less than the Reverend "Uncle" Johannes Stricker, Vincent's former tutor in theology, and also, by a streak of hazardous luck, Kee Vos' father. With or without rightly discerning the will of heaven, Vincent exposed his daring scheme to Theo.

> Uncle and Aunt Stricker's silver wedding is approaching; Father and Mother intend to go there. I am glad you have written them before that time, for I would rather not have them come out with their 'conscientious objections' to "the untimeliness and indelicacy" of my love. . . . Do you think this mild weather will be enough to thaw the "no, never never" one of these days? Will they expel me on or shortly after the silver wedding party? God forbid. Do you think that Trojan horse in the form of a registered letter has been taken inside the walls of Troy? And if so, will the Greeks that were hidden in that horse—that is to say, the things that were written in the letter—storm the fortress? (CL 161)

In November, Vincent composed and mailed the registered letter to his uncle Stricker. He then awaited word from the troops in "Troy." So eager was he to hear from them, that in early December he made his intended journey to The Hague to see his mentor, Mauve. "I said to Mauve, Do you approve of my coming here for a month or so, and occasionally troubling you for some help and advice? After that I shall have overcome the first petites misèrer [little misery] of painting" (CL 162). In short order, Vincent gave into his ulterior motive by stepping off the distance to neighboring Amsterdam, where he sought to encounter Kee Vos. But, true to form, he had run out of money. He wrote to his father, asking for emergency assistance. His father replied, saying he "thought it so very excessive that I had [already] spent 90 guilders." Vincent then pled to Theo: "I have no money to stay, I have no money to go back. I shall wait here for a few days at all events. And I will do as you wish." Finally, as a way of inducing Theo to take pity, he appended a few words that were the equivalent of an equivocation of an oracle: "Mauve says that the sun is rising for me, but is still behind the clouds" (CL 163).

The Reverend Johannes Stricker, however, had a totally different take on the matter. "Uncle Stricker was rather angry," Vincent bewailed, "though he gave vent to it in more polite words than 'God damn you'" (CL 162). The Trojan horse, as some horses are prone to do, had backfired. The "Greeks" had not been sufficient unto the day to storm the fortress in "Troy," so well fortified was it against Vincent's ploy. The chances of his being handed the key to the gate of heaven were far better than receiving the key to unlock Kee Vos' heart. Simply put, there was no key to Kee, not even—especially not even—her father. Uncle Stricker's reply to Vincent was like the wake-up call of a trumpet blast at dawn: "Kee left the house as soon as she heard that you were here."

Despite Vincent's determination to be as "glad as a lark in the spring," his wings had been swiftly clipped and his feathers thoroughly sheered. He tumbled into the flames of despair like a bird shot out of the air.

> I felt quite lonely and forlorn during those three days in Amsterdam; I felt absolutely miserable, and . . . all those discussions—it was so dismal. Till at last I began to feel quite depressed, and I said to myself, You don't want to get melancholy again, do you? . . . Then I thought, I should like to be with a woman—I cannot live without love, without a woman. I would not value life at all, if there were not something infinite, something deep, something real. But then I say to myself, You said "she, and no other," and now you would go to another woman; it is unreasonable, it is contrary to all logic. And my answer to that was, Who is the master, the logic or I? Is the logic here for me or am I here for the logic, and is there no reason or sense in my unreasonableness and lack of sense? And whether I act rightly or wrongly I cannot do otherwise—that damned wall is too cold for me; I need a woman, I cannot, I may not, I will not live without love. I am a man, and a man with passions; I must go to a woman, otherwise I shall freeze or turn to stone—or, in short, shall be stunned. (CL 164)

Stunned he was. As he wrote to Theo upon his return to Etten in late December, his temptation was to seek solace the only way he knew how, quite like he had done in the past.

> Under the circumstances I fought a great battle within myself, and in the battle some things remained victorious, things which I knew of physic and hygienics and had learned by bitter experience. One cannot live too long without a woman with impunity.

And I do not think that what some people call God and others, supreme being, and others, nature, is unreasonable and without pity; and in short, I came to the conclusion, I must see whether I can find a woman.

And, dear me, I hadn't far to look. I found a woman, not young, not beautiful, nothing remarkable, if you like, but perhaps you are somewhat curious. She was rather tall and strongly built; she did not have a lady's hands like Kee, but the hands of one who works much; but she was not coarse or common, and had something very womanly about her. She reminded me of some curious figure by Chardin or Frère, or perhaps Jan Steen. Well, what the French call une ouvrière [a workwoman]. She had many cares, one could see that, and life had been hard for her; oh, she was not distinguished, nothing extraordinary, nothing unusual. 'Toute femme àtout âge, si elle aime et si elle est bonne, peut donner àl'homme non l'infini du moment, mais le moment de l'infini.' [Every woman at every age can, if she loves and is a good woman, give a man, not the infinity of a moment, but a moment of infinity.] . . . It was not the first time I was unable to resist that feeling of affection, aye, affection and love for those women who are so damned and condemned and despised by the clergymen from the pulpit. I do not damn or condemn them, neither do I despise them. I am almost thirty years old—would you think that I have never felt the need of love? (CL 164)

What else could have brought him more timely good fortune than the fortuitous meeting of yet another potentially endearing woman, in contrast to the one whose understandable, self-protective obstinacy had greeted him like a colossal block of ice? One thing was certain. The consolation he sought would not be found in a church.

The clergymen call us sinners, conceived and born in sin, bah! What dreadful nonsense that is. Is it a *sin* to love, to need love, not to be able to live without love? I think a life without love a sinful and immoral condition. If I repent anything, it is the time when mystical and theological notions induced me to lead too secluded a life. Gradually I have thought better of it. When you wake up in the morning and find yourself not alone, but see there in the morning twilight a fellow creature beside you, it makes the world look so much more friendly. Much more friendly than religious diaries and whitewashed church walls, with which the clergymen are in love. She lived in a modest, simple little room . . . she had a child—yes, she had had some experience of life, and

> her youth was gone, gone?—'il n'y a point de vieille femme' [there
> *is* no old woman]. Oh, and she was strong and healthy—and yet
> not coarse or common. Are those who care so very much for
> distinction always able to discern what really is distinguished?
> Dear me, people seek it often in the clouds or under the ground
> when sometimes it is quite close at hand. (CL 164)

Theo had heard as much before—bitter diatribes flaming forth from
his brother's tongue, hurled principally against "whitewashed" edifices,
the bastions of ecclesiastical orthodoxy, and thus at those, more like
than unlike their father, who had proffered lofty moral judgments that
had become anathema to Vincent's altered worldview. Vincent quickly
reminded Theo:

> Besides, as I told you before, I hate not being entirely free, and
> though I do not literally have to account to Father for every
> cent, he always knows exactly how much I spend and on what. I
> have no secrets, but I don't like to show my hand to everybody,
> though even my secrets are not secrets to those with whom I
> am in sympathy. But Father is not a man for whom I can feel
> what I feel for you or for Mauve . . . Father cannot understand
> or sympathize with me, and I cannot be reconciled to Father's
> system—it oppresses me, it would choke me. I too read the Bible
> occasionally just as I read Michelet or Balzac or Eliot; but I see
> quite different things in the Bible than Father does, and I cannot
> find at all what Father draws from it in his academic way. . . .
> And the less Father is mixed up in my affairs, the better I can get
> on with him; I must be free and independent in many things. It
> is only natural. (CL 164)

Vincent's and his father's patience and empathy for one another
had simply run their course. Having been home at the parsonage in
Etten for barely three days, after having returned from The Hague in
order to celebrate Christmas—upon the command of his father, Vincent
promptly gathered up his duds. Taking off, and arriving once again at
The Hague, he wrote Theo a brisk confession: "On Christmas Day I had
a violent scene with Father, and it went so far that Father told me I had
better leave the house. Well, he said it so decidedly that I actually left the
same day" (CL 166).

Their falling-out was a culminating crescendo, a grand finale to a
prolonged and tortuous saga. It was bound to have happened and to
have been more than a minor fissure, for the simple reason that this was

Vincent's "break" with an old and dying "reality"—such that, at last, with the door flung wide open, the lark in all its splendor might rise—and soar—into the heights of a clear blue sky.

"Wheatfield with a Lark"

TWO

A Risky Affair

"THE BREAK"

VINCENT'S BREACH WITH HIS father generated a mammoth emotional quake. Already possessing a fragile, anxiety-ridden, and depressive self, subject to repeated wounding of his self-esteem, his equilibrium had not yet recovered from the damage done to his inflated hopes and expectations regarding Kee Vos, which he described to be "a terrible blow as a death sentence" that "crushed me to the ground" (CL 154).

On top of that, his father's powerful rejection was such that Vincent's instant reaction took the form of impassioned fury. "I do not remember ever having been in such a rage in my life," he wrote to Theo from the The Hague four days after his ejection from the house in Etten.

He continued: "I frankly said I thought their whole system of religion horrible, and just because I had gone too deeply into those questions during a miserable period in my life, I did not want to think of them any more, and must keep clear of them as of something fatal."

"The real reason" for the altercation with his father, he explained, was that "I did not go to church." Moreover, "If going to church was compulsory and if I was *forced* to go, I certainly should never go again out of courtesy, as I had done rather regularly all the time I was in Etten. But, oh, in truth there was much more at the back of it all, including the whole story of what happened this summer between Kee and me" (CL 166).

Much later, from the distance of more than three years since being asked to leave home that fateful Christmas Day of 1881, and approximately seven months before his father's untimely death in 1885, Vincent would confess to Theo: "I think that Father also feels it is fatality rather than downright intention when there is sometimes such a decided difference of opinion between us. But I wish that I didn't *hit* other people,[1] that Father had not been standing *right* in front of me at times" (CL 380).

It is not clear whether Vincent was referring to an incident contemporaneous with his letter of September 30, 1884, and whether at that same time he might have struck his father physically while residing with the family in Nuenen after returning home from The Hague (CL 380). Perhaps he was recalling the 1881 Christmas episode in Etten. In either case, the effects of it were still hanging over him. He was remorseful for having lost complete control of his temper. His sister-in-law, Johanna, who was in a reasonably good position to know—presumably having heard from Theo and other members of the family just what had taken place—observed about the 1881 incident that Vincent "had become irritable and nervous, his relations with his parents became strained, and in December, after a violent altercation with his father, he left suddenly for The Hague" (Memoir, xxxii).

His father's wrath aside, Vincent's own recurrent rage indicated a deep-seated character trait and potentially fatal flaw that had produced a heap of trouble for him in the past and would continue to do so. To his credit, he retraced his ill behavior with second thoughts: "Was I *too* angry, *too* violent? Maybe—but even so, it is settled now, once and for all" (CL 166). Or, so he wished.

Realizing immediately the precarious predicament in which he found himself after his precipitous departure from home, Vincent promptly turned again to Anton Mauve, his cousin by marriage. "I went back to Mauve and said, 'Listen, Mauve, I cannot stay in Etten any longer, and I must go and live somewhere else, preferably here.'" "Well, Mauve said, 'Then stay.'" So Vincent "rented a studio" that consisted of "a room and an alcove . . . ten minutes from Mauve" (CL 166).

No matter how monumentally damaging and painful the estrangement from his father and mother had been, it did not amount to an irrevocable severance of their relationship. He had not yet been home

---

1. Translated as "But I wish to *hit no one*" (the Museum Letters Project's *Vincent van Gogh: The Letters*, no. 463).

for the last time. Nevertheless, little room was left in the brittle space between them for Vincent to beg for consideration. Vincent reported to Theo: "Father said if I wanted money, he would lend it to me if necessary, but this is impossible now, I must be quite independent of Father. How? I do not know yet, but Mauve will help me if necessary, and I hope and believe you will too, and of course I will work and try as hard as I can to earn something" (CL 166).

Whatever the current distance between himself and his parents represented for Vincent's present and future growth, it would take more than a day, a week, or a few months for him or for them to be healed of the residual effects of their emotional clash. Amid his continuing psychological turmoil, the struggle for further self-differentiation would persist, sometimes affording a gain and sometimes a loss to his inner sense of cohesion. It would take him the better part of his lifetime, if then, for a thorough repair of those injured parts of his personality that seemed to have been inadequately nurtured and insufficiently mirrored since early in life.[2]

Still, for the moment—as though he knew something certain about himself—his very next words of avowal exhibited a flash of prescience, like an equatorial line had suddenly been drawn across the canvas of his mind. He knew that the most important "break" had occurred within himself. He declared to Theo: "I am in for it now, and the die is cast. At an inconvenient moment but how can it be helped? . . . It is a risky affair, a question of sink or swim."

One thing was patently true. He had been impelled to take a significant leap of faith. He wrote to Theo on December 29, 1881: "As you can imagine, I have a great many cares and worries. But still it gives me a feeling of satisfaction to have gone *so* far that I cannot go back again; and though the path may be difficult, I now see it clearly before me" (CL 166).

By February 4, 1883, after an interval of approximately one year and a month, something far less prescient though far more predictable, and nearly fatal to a lark still learning how to maneuver the sky, was in

---

2. Richard C. Schwartz' seminal work, *Internal Family Systems Therapy*, is helpful for understanding the functional distinctions and connections of the internal parts or subpersonalities within persons, and how those parts interact with one another and in relation to their counterparts in other persons, bearing the roles, burdens, and polarizations that exist within the families of origin.

the course of unfolding. In a long letter addressed to his artist friend Anthon van Rappard, who had become a great source of comfort and encouragement, Vincent asked: "Do you remember the woman we met when you visited me during the summer, whom I said was a model I had found, adding that I had discovered that she was pregnant, for which reason I was trying all the harder to help her"? After elaborating in copious detail, he explained: "My friend Rappard, I will tell you frankly, I am living with a poor woman and two children, and there are many who, for that or some other reason, do not wish to associate with me, which makes it my duty to write you in this way. Won't you come and look at the *Graphics* with me some day?"

The situation was even more "graphic" to the extent that, as a consequence, Vincent had experienced further "disagreement" with his father. But he rapidly added: "The disagreement I had with him when I left home did not last long—we had made it up before I began living with this woman. And then, even though I was living with this woman, my father came to see me once" (CL R20).[3] "This woman" was Clasina Maria Hoornik, known informally as "Sien"—a former prostitute.

Midway during this fated interval between December 1881 and February 1883, Vincent had said to Theo that he thought *Theo's* social standing in Paris—his "station in life," as he put it—had become the very opposite of his own. He had reminded his brother of the fact that, yes, he, Theo, had previously had an "illusion," as their parents called it, with regard to a certain "woman of the people." Then, with a twist of wry humor, if not insufferable pathos, Vincent added: "It was not because you *could* not have chosen that path in life that nothing came of it after all, but because things in general took another turn." He was referring to the fact that Theo had assumed a new position as a managing Parisian art dealer, thereby catapulting him into a more respectable social arena.

Vincent continued: "As I see it [now], it would not be at all the right thing for you to take a woman of the people—for *you* the woman of the people was the so-called *illusion*—for you reality has become finding a woman of the same station in life as Kee Vos. But for me the opposite is true; my *illusion (although I do not think this word or this definition the least bit appropriate or correct either in your case or in mine)* was Kee

---

3. *The Complete Letters*, vol. 3, "Letters to Anthon G. A. Ridder van Rappard," cited henceforth in text and numbered sequentially R1–R58a, with the symbol "R" standing for Rappard, in this instance "R20" being the twentieth letter to van Rappard.

Vos—reality became the woman of the people." Moreover: "What I want to explain is this—what exists between Sien and me is *real*; it is not a dream, it is *reality!*"(CL 212).

Looking ahead approximately four years, to February 14, 1886, from Antwerp, we find Vincent writing to Theo, saying that his health is "a ruin," that his desire is for both of them to "find a wife in some way or other before long," and, most important of all, that "in the intercourse with women one especially learns so much about art."

It is a Sunday, he notes, "almost a spring day." He has taken "a long walk alone all through the city, in the park, along the boulevards." And the weather is "such that I think in the country they will have heard the lark sing for the first time. In short, there was something of resurrection in the atmosphere."

He bemoans the economic depression that has stricken the country, but believes the labor strikes that have set "the laborer against the bourgeois" to have been "justifiable." He bewails the fact that "although it's spring, how many thousands and thousands are wandering about, desolate." He then acknowledges the gross contradictions of life, as though with his brush he were depicting their irony, visibly, for an illustrated cover of a magazine: "I see the lark soaring in the spring air as well as the greatest optimist; but I also see the young girl of about twenty, who might have been in good health, a victim of consumption, and who will perhaps drown herself before she dies of any illness."

In the same letter he mourns the fact that the "well-to-do bourgeois" may "not notice this so much perhaps, but if one has dined for years on la vache enragée [rabid cowhide, so to speak, roughing it], as I have, one cannot deny that great misery is a fact that weights the scale." And, "one may not be able to cure or to save," he observes, "but one can sympathize with and pity them."

Then, with biting wit he recalls reading about the late Camille Corot, the charitable bourgeois Parisian landscape and portraiture artist, "who after all had more serenity than anybody else, who felt the spring so deeply, was he not as simple as a workingman all his life, and so sensitive to all the miseries of others? And what struck me in his biography was that when he was already very old in 1870 and 1871, he certainly looked at the bright sky, but at the same time he visited the ambulances where the wounded lay dying" (CL 453).

And now, at the point where present realities—concerning labor strikes—coincide with past memories, he cannot help but recall his own experience of having tended the wounded and dying in the fiery coalfields of the Borinage. Nor, in hearing the news that "thousands are wandering about, desolate" in a desperate economy, can he forget what it was like when he took in someone who, likewise, was "wandering about, desperate"—"the woman of the people," his special sitting model, "Sien," hospitalized as she was in Leyden, with a young child at her arm and another in her belly—when he found her sick and "in a very bad way" and did not know what to do. For he had thrashed about to convey the pathos of the moment to his confidant, van Rappard, asking: "Could I—*should* I help?—I was ill myself, struggling to decide." And he followed that question with yet another question, a confounding one. For if a weather-beaten, older-than-his-years vagabond painter was worth at least as much as the very pigment in his paint, then he *had* to ask: "Are there moments in life when it is criminal to remain impassive and say, What business is it of mine?" (R 20).

Camille Corot had been not only a very fine painter, but also a model of charity because of his considerable compassion and empathy. Thus, when Vincent mentions to Theo his thought of Corot's visiting the ambulances where the wounded lay dying, he quickly adds: "Illusions may fade, but the sublime *remains*" (CL 453).

Kee Vos, Vincent remembers, had been his illusion. She had faded. The woman of the people had become his reality. She had been no "dream," but she remained. Illusions aside, that day—the day when he had to decide—had to ask himself: "What business is it of mine?"—had also been "almost a spring day" with "something of resurrection" in the air. He knows, instinctively, that on such a day "illusions may fade, but the sublime *remains*."

Vincent's sister-in-law, Johanna, long after Vincent's death, would say of him that by taking "this poor neglected woman approaching her confinement" into "his protection, partly from pity but also to fill the great void in his life," he was not only making a faulty connection that could not last, but his "unfortunate liaison deprived him of the sympathy of all in The Hague who took an interest in him" (Memoir, xxxii–xxxiii).

Dropping back to early 1882, Vincent had managed to receive from Mauve a solid year's worth of invaluable instruction in the development of his art. One could hear the elation in his voice: "Drawing becomes more and more a passion with me, and it is a passion just like that of a sailor for the sea. Mauve has now shown me a new way to make something, that is, how to paint water colors" (CL 170).

Vincent's greatest practical difficulty, however, lay in the need to locate and pay for the living models he wanted to draw. At times they simply failed to show up for appointments. At other times they posed for hours but went home empty-handed without compensation. All the while, Vincent's chronic anxiety and episodic depression festered. For a considerable while he did not reveal the state of his mind to either Mauve or Tersteeg,[4] the latter being his former employer at Goupil's gallery, who "for years" had considered Vincent "a kind of incompetent dreamer" (CL 180). Nor did Vincent divulge to them the nature of his relationship with Sien, even though, as he said, "They suspect me of something—it is in the air" (CL 192).

As the external and internal pressures mounted, he sought to shore up his guard. He said: "For though I still have a dose of courage left, it is sometimes very hard always to show a good face to Mauve and Tersteeg and others. Yet I must, for though I do not pretend to be carefree, I need not tell them all the details and particulars. But it happens often enough that I am at quite a loss as to what to do. Now this morning I felt so miserable that I went to bed; I had a headache and was feverish from worry because I dread this week so much, and do not know how to get through it" (CL 171).

His apprehension was compounded not only by his critics but also by the frequently strained relationship he had with Sien and her family, including Sien's mother, as he struggled with the possibility of a deepening commitment to Sien. He confronted the harsh reality of his failure to provide even a subsistence living for himself. Besides, how could he, or rather, how could Theo, who was Vincent's sole means of financial support and was also sending money to their parents, feed two or three additional mouths?

---

4. Stolwijk and Thomson, *Theo van Gogh*, 24, contains a photograph of the dapper and often reproving art dealer Hermaus Gijsbertus Tersteeg, upon whom Vincent necessarily depended and at times loathed.

Vincent complained to Theo of his "scarcity of funds," of the fact that his "drawing board warped like a barrel," that his "easel . . . got damaged," that his clothes were in ill repair, and that—heaven forbid, if heaven cared at all—"My underwear is also beginning to fall apart" (CL 171). "One involuntarily becomes terribly depressed, if only for a moment, often just when one is feeling cheerful, as I really am even now. That's what happened this morning; these are evil hours when one feels quite helpless and faint with overexertion" (CL 171).

Yet another ingredient, added to the mixture of his malaise, was a critical factor contributing to his lack of composure. Vincent remained significantly undernourished most of his adult life. He seldom ate a solid meal. "Every day," he wrote his sister Wilhelmina, "I take the remedy which the incomparable Dickens prescribes against suicide. It consists of a glass of wine, a piece of bread with cheese and a pipe of tobacco" (CL W11). He drank heavily at times. When wine was too costly, he turned to absinthe. Imbibing—which is to say, his "bottle"—became a "surrogate selfobject" for assuaging his ever-present infantile thirst for emotional soothing and succor. A decanter of spirits was also, no doubt, a "transitional object" for containment of his aggression.[5]

His most coveted palliative, however, was the unrelenting quest for a lover, preferably a wife. Without the solace of a woman, whose touch and tenderness could merge with the disquietude of his fragile soul, a woman who, like an adoring mother, could calm and temper his puerile angst, a pipe of tobacco was more than a mere pipe of tobacco, and a bottle of booze was more than a sheer bottle of booze.[6] "If I were to think of and dwell on disastrous possibilities," he mused, "I could do nothing. I throw myself headlong into my work, and come up again with my studies; if the storm within gets too loud, I take a glass too much to stun myself" (CL 513).

Vincent's work increasingly became his day-to-day salvation. It remained its own perpetual addiction. It bore the price tag of a diminished body, a frazzled mind, and a foreboding spirit, depleted at such a rate that by his mid-thirties his frayed emotions felt trapped inside an urn

---

5. "Transitional objects (Winnicott) may be used not only as 'soothers,' but for some . . . as containers for aggressive drives as well." This is consistent with "Winnicott's . . . discussion of the development of the capacity to 'use' an object." See Smith, "The Community as Object," 532.

6. A play upon Freud's quip that "A cigar is sometimes just a cigar."

of incurable dread and decay. The time was to come when the demons of desperation would at last play out the closing lines of their merciless script. In a draft letter he had written to Theo, and which was found on Vincent's body at the time of his death, the hopelessly dejected artist summed up the excruciating extent to which he had given himself over, in obeisance, to the insatiable deity of self-sacrifice. His detractors would say it was self-destruction.

"My dear brother," he wrote to Theo, "my own work, I am risking my life for it and my reason has half foundered because of it" (CL 652).[7] Just so, in 1882, while he was still living at The Hague, before his artistic achievements were to come to full fruition, Vincent openly acknowledged to Theo that "I think the success or failure of a drawing . . . depends greatly on the mood and condition of the painter. Therefore I try to do what I can to keep cheerful and clear-headed. But sometimes, like now, a heavy depression comes over me, and then it's hell." "The only thing to do . . . is to go on with the work; for Mauve and Israëls and so many others who are examples to the rest of us know how to profit from every mood" (CL 173).[8]

Another easily accessible and potent "medicinal" remedy, in addition to alcohol, carried Vincent to a limited extent through lonely and arduous days and nights of self-doubt and self-recrimination, in the absence of a stable domestic community of kindness and affection that could deliver him from his protracted loneliness and despair. Pouring out his thoughts to Theo, he declared: "I tell you frankly that in my opinion one must not hesitate to go to a prostitute occasionally if there is one you can trust and feel something for, as there really are many. For one who has a strenuous life it is necessary, absolutely necessary, in order to keep sane and well. One must not exaggerate such things and fall into excesses, but nature has fixed laws which it is fatal to struggle against. Well, you yourself know all you have to know on that subject. It would

7. For an analysis of this letter set side by side with the one that was actually mailed to Theo, see Wilfred Arnold's illuminating work, *Vincent van Gogh: Chemicals, Crises, and Creativity*, 267–71. It is a book worth reading for the significant light it sheds upon Vincent's medical and psychological diagnoses as well as his suicide.

8. Mauve and Israëls represented idealized selfobjects providing Vincent opportunity to learn from them how they were able for the most part to modulate the inner fluctuations of their emotions without being overwhelmed by them—a life-long task at which Vincent was only moderately adept.

be well for you, it would be well for me, if we were married—but what can we do?" (CL 173).

Meanwhile, Mauve, who himself was not feeling particularly well, had begun to change his attitude toward Vincent. So had Tersteeg, who remained an important broker to the local art trade. It was Tersteeg who went so far as to try to convince Theo that he should no longer support Vincent financially. Tersteeg informed Vincent of what he had advised Theo, and told Vincent brusquely to his face: "Mauve and I will see to it that there is an end to this" (CL 188).

Being a sensitive soul who had wagered that an "artist's work and his private life" were "like a woman in childbirth" (CL 181), Vincent deemed it important that his primary teacher and his most readily available business vendor should regularly offer him encouragement and support instead of harping criticism. In addition to what many others sooner or later would say about his relationship with Sien, he took it to be especially unhelpful that his Uncle C. M. became fretful, too. Vincent clearly sensed that C. M. "would be angry" over Vincent's apparent ineptitude at "earning bread" since the overall perception was that he remained hopelessly unemployed—an echo of when Theo had called his brother "idle." Vincent, however, had viewed the money he received from Theo to be a fair exchange for his artwork, which he was sending to Theo to sell to the public through the gallery. This was his thought in spite of the fact that Theo was in effect buying Vincent's paintings and keeping them safely stored throughout his house.

C. M. had spoken with Tersteeg, who had just received from Vincent the repayment of ten borrowed guilders. Tersteeg knew, of course, that Theo had been the source of the loan. When C. M. proceeded to cast doubt upon Vincent's "worth" as a productive person, Vincent posed a serious question to his father's well-heeled brother: "Earn bread—how do you mean? Earn bread, or deserve bread? Not to deserve one's bread— that is, to be unworthy of it—is certainly a crime, for every honest man is worthy of his bread; but unluckily, not being able to earn it, though deserving it, is a misfortune, and a great misfortune. So if you say to me, 'You are unworthy of your bread,' you insult me. But if you make the rather just remark that I do not always earn it—for sometimes I have none—well, that may be true, but what's the use of making the remark? It does not get me any further if that's all you say" (CL 181).

C. M. dropped the subject. But "the thunderstorm threatened once more" when their conversation turned to the private lives of artists. Vincent had mentioned the name of the artist Charles de Groux with respect to de Groux's particular artistic "expression." C. M. protested: "But do you know that in private life De Groux has a bad reputation?"

Vincent reported their ensuing conversation to Theo:

> As you can imagine, C M. touched a delicate point there, and ventured on slippery ground. I could not stand and hear this said of honest father [Charles] De Groux. So I replied, "It has always seemed to me that when an artist shows his work to the public, he has the right to keep the inner struggle of his own private life to himself (which is directly and inevitably connected with the peculiar difficulties involved in producing a work of art), unless he wants to confide them to a very intimate friend. I repeat, it is very improper for a critic to dig up a man's private life when his work is above reproach. De Groux is a master like Millet, like Garvarni." (CL 181)

It just so happened, eight years later, in January 1890, in a twist of irony—on the eve of the major Brussels art exhibition, "Les Vingt"—that a half-dozen of Vincent's paintings were to be displayed, by invitation, alongside those of Henri de Groux, the son of Charles de Groux. Just before the exhibit was to open, the short-statured Henri caused a virtual donnybrook among the exhibitors by nearly provoking "a duel with swords in hand," between himself and Henri de Toulouse-Lautrec.[9] For, Henri de Groux had announced that he was not about to have his own work shown next to that "execrable vase of sunflowers of Monsieur Vincent or of any other agent provocateur."[10] Toulouse-Lautrec, nicknamed "Low-Assed" among his peers, due to his reduced height—the result of a shortening of both legs from a childhood accident—was fond of Vincent's work, and, as a friend, immediately came to Vincent's defense by drawing his sword in the face of de Groux's venomous attack. Paul Signac, who was among the exhibitors, thereupon "declared coldly that if Lautrec were killed, he would take up the affair himself" in aid of Vincent. Though the duel was averted by less impetuous minds, the

9. Octave Maus, "The Lanterne Magique" Lecture, 1918," in Stein, *Van Gogh: A Retrospective*, 198.

10. Sweetman, *Van Gogh: His Life and His Art*, 315.

outwitted Henri de Groux had already exclaimed that Vincent was "an ignoramus and a charlatan."[11] De Groux, in fury, promptly "withdrew his entries" from the exhibition, and was shortly thereafter "obliged to resign his membership" in the society of Les Vingt.[12]

One can only imagine whether Vincent, upon hearing of this incident, recalled what he had said eight years before, when disputing with C. M. about the life of Henri's father, whose venerable public works, despite any private goings-on, were "above reproach." Certainly, son Henri's public display was of no credit to his father, Charles. And that, principally, was the concern that had many times invaded C. M.'s mind about Vincent's carryings-on with a live-in prostitute—private news that by going all too public had brought discredit to the entire van Gogh family. But, then, as a highly principled Dutch Calvinist might be wont to do, in the interest of keeping the discussion of such things as much of a "private" matter as possible—so private, in fact, as to have to be circumspect about it—it would be better to castigate the private reputation of a dead artist rather than one of a living artist standing right there before you, face to face. This would be especially true if the living artist were one who, contrary to Calvinist principle, in the interest of defending himself would have no scruple whatsoever about *talking back*. One had to be cautious when "reasoning" in public or private with Vincent, as to just how far one would want to take a conversation. After all, in C. M.'s eyes, Vincent's reputation was far less at stake than C. M.'s was, or that of the family business. It was one thing for a respectable van Gogh art dealer to sell a work of art at public auction to the highest bidder, for profit, regardless of the *private* reputation of the artist. It was quite another, however, for a public figure, such as a van Gogh with an astute Calvinist business acumen, to have to live down the public reputation of someone else in his own family whose private life, like a private work of art on display in a public gallery, could cost the art dealer a bundle of *private* money, not to mention the threat to his *public* reputation.

As there was little use in pursuing with C. M. any further discussion of Charles de Groux's reputation, and thereby of his own, Vincent changed the subject. He pulled out a portfolio containing "smaller studies and sketches" that he had done, in order to show them to C. M. However,

11. Stein, *Van Gogh*, 198.
12. Sweetman, *Van Gogh: His Life and His Art*, 315.

C. M. remained silent until they came to a particular one that Vincent had recently sketched while "strolling around" The Hague at midnight with a friend named Breitner.

"'Could you make some more of these views of the city?' C. M. asked.

"'Yes, I make them for a change sometimes when I am tired from working with the model—there is the Vleersteeg—the Geest—the Fish Market.'

"'Then make twelve for me,'" C. M. requested.

"'Yes,' said I, 'but this is business, so we must fix a price at once . . . at 2.50 guilders—do you think that unreasonable?'

"'No,' he said, 'but if they turn out well, I will ask you to make twelve more of Amsterdam, and then I shall fix the price myself, so that you will get a little more for them.'"

Having finished relaying this conversation in his letter to Theo, Vincent concluded: "C. M.'s order is like a ray of hope to me." Then in a postscript Vincent added that on that very evening he had been to see the painting of "The Stable at Bethlehem" by Nicholaas Maes. He judged it to be "very good in tone and color, but the expression was not worth anything. The expression was decidedly wrong." Expounding upon it, he recalled that "once I saw this in reality, not of course the birth of Christ, but the birth of a calf. And I remember exactly how the expression was. There was a little girl in the stable that night—in the Borinage—a little brown peasant girl with a white nightcap: she had tears of compassion in her eyes for the poor cow when the poor thing was in throes and was having great trouble. It was pure, holy, wonderful, beautiful like a Correggio, a Millet, an Israëls. Oh, Theo, why don't you give up the whole thing and become a painter? You can if you want to, boy; I sometimes suspect you of concealing a famous landscape painter within yourself."[13] Vincent

13. In the "twinship transference" between Vincent and Theo, Vincent wants Theo to become a reflection (a mirror) of himself. Heinz Kohut tells of the time a patient spoke of "a bottle on her bureau that she always kept stoppered, but that she had imagined some person to be living in this bottle—'my genie.'" Kohut "ventured the guess that . . . the captive in the bottle was none other than" the psychoanalyst replacing the lost "sustenance of the patient's grandparents." The patient said it was not so. She said the "genie" as the "captive was a little girl, a twin, someone just like herself to whom she could talk, who kept her company and made it possible for her to survive the hours of loneliness when she felt that no one other than her companion in the bottle cared for her" (*How Does Analysis Cure?*, 195–96). In the same manner, Theo became Vincent's "genie in the bottle."

then appended some sound advice: "Theo, do not become materialistic like Tersteeg. The problem is, Theo, my brother, not to let yourself be bound, no matter what, by a golden chain" (CL 181).

If Vincent, as non-materialistic as he was, had only had the chance, more than once or twice, to turn a work of art into working capital, at least for the moment he would have been wholly ecstatic. He subsequently wrote to Theo that "it is not unreasonable for me . . . that I no longer need be afraid that what is strictly necessary will be taken from me, nor always feel as if it were the bread of charity" (CL 191). For the record, if a comparison were to be made between himself and the materialistic Tersteeg, then Vincent had found just the right way to state it: "Well, Tersteeg is Tersteeg, and I am I" (CL 180). More than a year later, after having turned the age of thirty, Vincent would say to Theo: "I would rather have 150 francs a month as a painter than 1500 francs a month in another position, even as an art dealer" (CL 335). But for now, C. M. proceeded to pay Vincent thirty guilders for the twelve sketches. Vincent then painted six more for C. M., for which he received absolutely nothing. "And there it stopped" (CL 193).

There was little use to complaining. For, as Vincent had remarked: "I never heard a good sermon on resignation, nor can I imagine a good one, except that picture by Mauve . . . [which] seems to say knowing how to suffer without complaining, that is the only practical thing, it is the great science, the lesson to learn, the solution of the problem of life" (CL 181).

Complaint or not, it seemed, as always, that disappointment followed upon the heels of disappointment, as though Vincent were destined to spiral down a path of infinite regression, despite his commitment to his art. Even so, he continued to do his sketches, which remained like a poor peddler's wares at the close of a soggy business day, still dangling from the backside of a one-horse shay.

"I am so angry with myself now because I cannot do what I should like to do, and at such a moment one feels as if one were lying bound hand and foot at the bottom of a deep, deep well, utterly helpless" (CL 173).

THE PLIGHT OF DARKNESS

The plight of nearly every starving artist is such that the very notion of "plight" seems obligatory for giving birth to the art. The span of time from Vincent's first letter written to Theo in 1872 until that fateful hour

5 reason

in 1890 when he penned his last, consisted of seventeen years and eleven months. Despite the gloomy shadows that had hung over him for most of that time, he nevertheless managed to produce drawings and paintings by the thousands—of which he apparently sold only *one* from a public exhibition, shortly before his death.[14] Unlike a lark with its waddle of chicks, observing its little "portraits" from high in the sky while towering over the "landscape" with a melody in its breast and a twinkle in its eye, Vincent was forced, for the most part, to swallow his pride—and this despite what he said: *"My* aim in *my* life is to make pictures and drawings, as many and as well as I can; then, at the end of my life, I hope to pass away, looking back with love and tender regret, and thinking, 'Oh, the pictures I might have made'" (CL 338).

By midway through his sojourn at The Hague, Vincent's personal story had already posed a serious theological question: Must such thoroughgoing and extraordinary artistic potential, which for so long had been submerged beneath religious and interpersonal conflicts and struggles—a seed waiting to sprout—require a prolonged season of gestation within the deep darkness of monumental suffering, before it could spring forth into life?

The challenge, for Vincent—while always a practical one of personal survival—consisted of what the philosophers and theologians have called "the problem of the existence of God." For, with any luck, *somewhere*, blended into the "blues" and "yellows" of life, there was waiting to be found the "opaque," washed-out, flush portrait of God's face—dense, unintelligible, and obscure—but, *where*?

The big question, for Vincent, was this: Would his trial by fire so transform his nascent aesthetic talent into such heightened perceptual awareness and ascendant creativity that he could in fact *envision and portray* that very "face" that largely evades human eyes? To what extent might the profound anonymity of God tangibly permeate such an improbable endeavor, so as to make it possible not only for Vincent but for others to catch a glimpse of the "Holy Grail"? The average person might not be quite so troubled about such impractical questions. But then Vincent, if in no more than this one respect, was not the average person. He said:

14. Stein, *Van Gogh*, 197. His painting of "The Red Vineyard" sold in 1890 to the Belgian artist Anna Boch.

One's real life begins at thirty, in fact, that is to say, its most active part. Friends and family may consider you old, or I don't know what, but you can feel a renewal of energy for all that. But then it is necessary to reflect well, and to have a will, and to be wide-awake. But in that period, a change is really necessary; one must wipe out the whole thing and start anew. *Just as one does when a boy*—but more maturely. Tom, Dick and Harry, who drowse away in the same old way, think this foolish, and say they don't see any good in it; all right, leave Tom, Dick and Harry alone, as long as they don't attack you; they are as little awake as a somnambulist. For one self one must not doubt that it is the way of nature, and that one works against nature only by *not* changing. There is an old saying, They have ears but they hear not, they have eyes but they see not, they have a heart but feel not; their heart is hardened, and they have closed their ears and eyes because they *do not want to hear and do not want to see.* (CL 335)[15]

Consider, by way of parallel, Jesus' vision of the Kingdom of God as he underwent his solemn test in the wilderness through drastic self-denial and dire self-renunciation—the self, emptied of itself—by means of which the vision and spirit of the Holy One took deep root in his life. And, if for Jesus, then why not also for Vincent? Why *not* the winnowing wind of the wilderness? For the wind, wild and tempestuous, whipping beneath the thrashing sun, strips and parches the land in order to wrest it of all pretense to self-generation and self-invention. As the sun rises from darkness, then returns to it, does not the artist's true vision require of the artist that self-absorption be relinquished to self-abnegation? —It is, at best, an impossible assignment.[16] Yet, what else could possibly account for Vincent's astounding achievement as an artist? Something solely human? Something composed of mere dust and ashes?

Vincent's astonishing rendering of a sparkling "Starry Night over the Rhone,"[17] emitting its festival of fireworks encircling a pair of lovers— could it have been so readily captured in the eyes of one preoccupied exclusively with himself? Certainly not by the near-sighted couple of old

15. A paraphrase of numerous Old and New Testament passages, playing upon the physical attributes of inanimate idols, subsequently applied to those who do not trust God. See, e.g., Jeremiah 5:21 and Matthew 13:15.

16. The metaphor should not be taken literally since the sun emits light constantly. The metaphor works only from the perspective of being earth-bound, from which the sun has the "appearance" of light arising from and receding into darkness.

17. Walther and Metzger, *Vincent Van Gogh: The Complete Paintings*, 431. Hereafter Walther and Metzger, *Van Gogh* = WM.

lovers who are painted into the picture—except in as much as all love is a festival of starlight descending from above the darkened firmament.

What of Vincent's vibrant, life-teeming, yellow-green "Café Terrace on the Place du Forum," set beneath a starlit sky with "topmost . . . gable . . . pointing into the blue infinity"?[18] Or, what of that solemn "landscape"— the wistful gaze in the countenance of an ordinary peasant by the name of "Patience Escalier"[19]—in so many respects a mirror image of the peasant's faith residing deep down in Vincent? Where, in all of these "pictures," does one catch a glimpse of the dance of Mystery twirling and spinning at the *center* of a stunning, sometimes sordid universe? Posed another way: Did Vincent's artistic "genius" emanate from the basement of his soul—correlative to a darkened world—as the place of paradox from which light bursts forth onto his canvases of lively oils—in likeness to the "blue infinity"? Perhaps so. For this was an artist bent upon seeing *beyond* what to most people in the middle of their muddle is the merely mundane—until at night, with moon and stars enshrouded by the deep, murky secrets of life's billowing storm clouds, there comes forth the thundering bolt of lightning that asks: Does God have anything at all to do with this? With me? With the present trouble I'm in? With the fact that death has hemmed me in like a feral cougar stalking its prey?

Vincent's imaginative backgrounds of roiling clouds and blackened skies are no less than symbols of the mammoth order of suffering that repeatedly besieges the palette of human existence as well as the panoply of mother nature. Such "darkness" is specifically what heightens the perceptual awareness so that pedestrian eyes may obtain a chance of "seeing" within the ordinary stuff of life an inkling of the "sublime." Even, in the gloomy shadows and grief-stricken fissures lining the weathered face of a poor, bare prostitute whose name is "Sorrow," we are left to ponder one of the most demanding questions: Can we see through the deep shadows of her destitution to the presence of the divine splendor that dwells at the heart of *her broken self*? It is as though Vincent is inviting the spectator of his "Lady" to unravel the same conundrum that riddles his own life: Does the Ineffable One reside, if at all, somewhere distantly remote—far, far away, out of sight—*behind* the canvas of human distress and anguish? Or does this Palpable One adhere *close-in, deep down within* the canvas of the "dark night of the soul"

18. Ibid., 425.
19. Ibid., 403.

Vincent's Sketch of Sien, Entitled "Sorrow"

wherein the silence of its Name is "spoken" to life? —Spectator, it is *your* art. *You* must answer the questions.

It is just so with the arresting images of diggers digging[20]—sowers sowing[21]—reapers reaping[22]—planters planting[23]—ploughmen plowing[24]—and coal miners mining.[25] They are each and all composed of the

20. "Two Peasant Women Digging," WM, 112 and114.

21. "The Sower," WM, 350 and 452.

22. "The Reaper," WM, 547.

23. "Potato Planting," WM, 48–49.

24. "Enclosed Field with Ploughman," WM, 532; "Field with Ploughman and Mill," WM, 556.

25. Brooks, "Miners in the Snow: Winter," F1202, JH 0229; "Miners' Women Carrying Sacks (The Bearer's of the Burden)," F0832.

same basic amalgam of which the drooping Christ was composed when, having suffered, he died, and, for the time being, remained dead[26]—until, like Lazarus, he came forth (leaping?) from his grave.[27] If one looks carefully, one can see Vincent's face, and the faces of *all* humanity, in these expressionist "portraits"—unless the eyes refuse to see, and the ears refuse to hear, and the heart refuses to feel.

Vincent said of "The Sower" and "The Reaper": "I see in this reaper—a vague figure fighting like a devil in the midst of the heat to get to the end of his task—I see in him the image of death, in the sense that humanity might be the wheat he is reaping. So it is—if you like—the opposite of that sower I tried to do before. But there's nothing sad in this death, it goes its way in broad daylight with a sun flooding everything with a light of pure gold" (CL 604). Such was the poor painter's true faith. For such renderings of the human condition—its "plight"—could not possibly have emerged from any canvas other than from one whose gleams of light cascade and glisten across the backdrops of dashed hopes and fallen dreams—those infinite chasms that surround the twinkling stars of night.[28] Ordinary folk, who live out their days solemnly acquainted with the sodden caverns of sorrow, and who spend their nights lonely with eyes fixed upon the crystal diamonds of heaven, *do believe so.*

How near to the present Darkness is the far-reaching Light? One thing is for sure. No one who is the slightest bit interested in the question stands around "idle" in pursuit of it. In search of "light," Vincent wrote his letters and painted his pictures partly to complain and cajole, but mostly, and more profoundly, to celebrate the fact that every brilliance forms a shadow, and every shadow in due time yields itself up in a blaze of brilliance. Accordingly, said Vincent: "Sainte-Beuve said, 'In most men there exists a poet [the light] who died young, whom the man [the shadow] 'survived.' And Musset said, 'Know that often a dormant

26. "Pietà" (after Delacroix), WM, 542.

27. "The Raising of Lazarus" (after Rembrandt), WM, 626.

28. For examples, see "The Potato Eaters," WM, 96; "Self Portraits," WM, 262–68, 534; "Seascape at Saintes-Maries," WM, 353; "The Mulberry Tree," WM, 556; "The Good Samaritan," WM, 627; "Landscape with Couple Walking and Crescent Moon," WM, 629; "Road with Cypress and Star," WM, 631; "The House of Père Pilon," WM, 638; "Chestnut Trees in Blossom," WM, 638; "Thatched Cottages in Cordeville," WM, 650; "The Church at Auvers," WM, 652; "Portrait of Adeline Ravoux," WM, 667; "Wheatfield under Clouded Sky," WM, 678; "The Grove," WM, 682; and "Wheat Field with Crows," WM, 690.

poet [the light] is hidden within us' [the shadow]—'always young and alive'—[the light]" (CL 31). "The passions are the little ship's sails, you know. And he who gives way entirely to his feelings in his twentieth year catches too much wind and his boat takes in too much water—and he sinks—or comes to the surface again after all" (CL 157).

Like all who wander in wonder, the texture of ordinary events, relationships, and passions, bore for Vincent the distinctive mark of sacrifice that belongs to nature within all its spheres and cycles. For him this meant that nearly every propitious forward motion implied a subsequent regression. His momentary gain, in joy, incurred a protracted loss, in sorrow. He was the roving, famished prodigal who partook of the pods of human tribulation in the company of a few "saints" who, by the measure of lesser artists, were called "swine." Limping homeward toward life, like Lazarus, with smudged face and rasping lungs, dredged up from the dust and sweat of the bowels of the "Marcasse," Vincent proclaimed: "Experience has shown that the people who walk in the darkness, in the center of the earth, like the miners in the black coal mines . . . are very much impressed by the words of the Gospel, and believe them, too" (CL 126).

Tersteeg had exclaimed: "You failed before and now you will fail again—it will be the same story all over" (CL 190). Even Mauve, almost as close as blood kin, once a considerate friend whose genuine welcome had been received by Vincent like the captive Hebrews' greeting of Cyrus the Persian as liberator—*pure Godsend*—yes, even Mauve turned out to be suddenly narrow-minded and partisan. "Mauve's sympathy," said Vincent, "which was like water to a parched plant to me, ran dry" (CL 191).

Not only did Mauve cast his officious vote squarely against Sien, and finally banish Vincent from his company altogether, but on one particular occasion Mauve insisted that, if Vincent ever wished to succeed, he must adhere to the tried and true ways of the artful academy—whereupon Vincent flew into one of his "artful" fits of rage. Venting about it to Theo, Vincent grumbled: "I had to draw from casts, that was the principal thing, [Mauve] said. I hate drawing from casts, but I had a few plaster hands and feet hanging in my studio, though not for drawing purposes. Once he spoke to me about drawing from casts in a way such as the worst teacher at the academy would not have spoken; I kept quiet, but when I got home I was so angry that I threw those poor plaster casts into the coal bin, and they were smashed to pieces. And I thought, I will draw from those casts only when they become whole and white again, and when there are no more hands and feet of living beings to draw from" (CL 189). The breach with Mauve was devastating. "I gave up painting and water colors for a time only because I was so shocked by Mauve's deserting me, and if he came back, I would begin again with new courage. I cannot look at a brush now, it makes me nervous" (CL 192).[29]

The collective opposition to Vincent's liaison with Sien ("Christine" was her Christian name) stampeded from every direction: "Mauve, Theo, Tersteeg, you, have my bread in your hands, will you take it from me, or turn your back on me?" he wrote to Theo in blistering reprisal (CL 192). In his ensuing letter, he declared: "I am between two fires. If I reply to your letter: Yes, Theo, you are right, I will give up Christine, then first I tell a lie in agreeing with you and second, I commit myself to doing a vile thing. If I contradict you and you act like T. and M. [Tersteeg and Mauve], it will cost me my head, so to speak." —"Well, for heaven's sake, off with my head, if that's the way it has to be. The other thing is even worse" (CL 193).

He recalled his final attempt in Amsterdam to see Kee Vos at her home. Upon being promptly refused by her father and mother, he placed his hand in the flame of the table lamp and said: "Let me see her for as long as I can keep my hand in the flame" (CL 193). —Their reply? —*You will not see her.* —And he did not.

Until his dying day Vincent contended with inner shadows. When, at last, he befriended the outer darkness, drifting asleep into the final night of all nights, the only question remaining was whether, or whether not, there would dawn for him a day flooded with the light of resurrection.

In his painting of the "Olive Trees with Yellow Sky and Sun,"[30] it is possible to view the scene as Walther and Metzger describe it: "the sun is merciless and the trees look as if they are trying to flee—but a dragging shadow is holding them back. This is an existence of slavery and mere endurance: there is not a trace of free, green burgeoning. Quite the contrary, the knotty trees look as if they are engaged in a wearisome

29. Vincent's loss of Mauve underscores the critical importance of "sustaining selfobjects" in the growth and development of persons. The loss of a significant selfobject—be it a friend, parent, lover, or spouse—often has a serious fragmentary effect upon the self. Continual losses of primary selfobjects can result in despair accompanied by an overwhelming sense of inner emptiness.

30. "Olive Trees with Yellow Sky and Sun," WM, 574.

struggle for a place in the sun. They are gnarled, almost deformed: their suffering lies within their own natures."[31]

This interpretation notwithstanding, it is also possible to see this painting precisely as a portrait of the human condition at the point of its greatest travail: the olive trees leaning, not only at the brink of death but also at the precipice of resurrection. Witness the risen "sun" towering majestically over the olive grove and embracing the land. The struggle of the gnarled trunks and branches—symbol of Christ's and of all human suffering—is equivalent to the pathos in Vincent's painting of "The Raising of Lazarus" (after Rembrandt),[32] completed just prior to his suicide. The risen sun, in both settings, promises resurrection.

Kathleen Powers Erikson wrote:

> It is with the lavish use of the color yellow . . . that van Gogh creates a sense of the same sacred, divine presence represented in the Rembrandt etching [of "The Resurrection of Lazarus"]. The yellow encircling Lazarus' head is reminiscent of the halo surrounding the head of Christ in Delacroix's *Christ Asleep During the Tempest*, which van Gogh had previously cited as an artistic source for his rendition of *The Sower*. The yellow light is symbolic of the divine presence as well as the resurrection in van Gogh's *Pietá*, which he completed about a year before his painting of Lazarus. The color yellow, which van Gogh often used to represent love, particularly the sacred love of God, is here suggestive of the rayon d'en haut (light from above). Van Gogh said that he was painting a rising yellow sun, often symbolic of rebirth and renewal, and here symbolic of healing as well as resurrection.[33] The sun becomes the symbol of the life-giving Christ.[34]

Figuratively, the sun is the daytime counterpart of the evening star, symbolic of the point through which eternity enters time, and time is imbued with eternity. Vincent wrote: "Just as we take the train to get to Tarascon or Rouen, we take death to reach a star. One thing undoubtedly true in this reasoning is that we *cannot* get to a star while we are *alive*, any more than we can take the train when we are dead. So to me it seems possible that cholera, gravel, tuberculosis and cancer are the celestial means of locomotion, just as steamboats, buses and railways are

31. WM, 527.
32. Ibid., 626.
33. Erickson, *At Eternity's Gate*, 155.
34. Ibid., 156.

"The Sower"

the terrestrial means. To die quietly of old age would be to go there on foot" (CL 506).

Yet, there is another distinct possibility: that a celestial means of locomotion would make its terrestrial way toward us. For—*where the sun rises, it cannot help but shine.*

THE CRADLE OF VISION

Given the prospect of "rebirth" on any given day, Vincent's "union" with Sien became for him a psychological merger of meanings with her act of giving birth to a "tiny infant boy" not of Vincent's making; and thus it was the occasion for an internal re-identification of himself. As he said . in his sermon at Richmond, "there is only a constantly being born again, a constantly going from darkness into light." His relationship with Sien, filled as it was with genuinely heartfelt empathy for "The Great Lady" of "Sorrow," as he called her, turned out to be for him a timely source of empowerment. In addition to the emotional and psychological benefits provided the two of them in support of one another, his connection with Sien—whom he also referred to as "the woman"—seemed to meet his primal need for someone besides his brother—or, God bless her, his mother—to give nurturance to his dream of becoming the best artist he knew how to become.

Vincent voiced to Theo that "if Tersteeg and others had their own way, they would of course tear Sien and me apart . . . [but] I will not leave Sien; I should be a broken man without her, and then I should also be ruined in my work and everything; then I should never get over [being] . . . a broken man, and everything [would be] lost. . . . *Living with the woman*, I have good courage" (CL 216).

Sien had her own dreams, too—which included a roof over her head, food on the table, a partner who cared for her personal worth, since few, if any, ever had (the natural father of the newborn had abandoned her)—and a desire for a man to devote himself lovingly to her children. Vincent, with his capacity for empathy and his love for children, was in many respects the right person. His sympathies were extensive; his gratitude was vast: "I have a feeling of being at home when I am with her, as though she gives me my own hearth, a feeling that our lives are interwoven. It is a heartfelt, deep feeling, serious and not without a dark shadow of her gloomy past and mine, a shadow I have already written you about—as if something evil were threatening us which we would have to struggle against continuously all our lives. At the same time, however, I feel a great calm and brightness and cheerfulness at the thought of her and the straight path lying before me" (CL 212).

What about that "straight path"? With Mauve having blatantly deserted Vincent because of his relationship with Sien, and, just as bad, or worse, having cast doubt upon the worth of Vincent's art—and, on top of that, with Theo's disapproval of Sien added, to boot—Vincent was in no mood to allow his serenity to be disturbed by anyone who wished, yet again, to meddle in his personal affairs and knock him off course.

In a lengthy, tersely worded, and blistering letter to Theo, in which he tried as best he could to explain his relationship with Sien, Vincent minced no words:

> Theo, you say that if I had really loved Kee, I shouldn't have done this. But do you understand better now that I couldn't go any further after what happened in Amsterdam—should I have despaired then? Why should an honest man despair—I am no criminal—I don't deserve to be treated in such an inhuman way.

> Well, what can they do this time? It's true they got the best of me,
> they thwarted me there in Amsterdam. But I'm not asking their
> advice any more now, and being of age, I ask you, Am I free to
> marry—yes or no? Am I free to put on a workman's clothes and
> live like a workman—yes or no? Whom am I responsible to, who
> will try to force me?

To underscore his point, in the very next sentence he let fly with a good
Old Dutch dictum: "To hell with anyone who wants to hinder me."[35] "Is
my path less straight because somebody says, 'You have gone astray'?"
(CL 193).

He had, indeed, heard the accusation more than once—from father, mother, uncles, siblings, employers, lovers, and the councils of
the church. The lovely Eugenie Loyer of London, whose engagement to
another he had sought to break, had left him dejected and mournfully
depressed. In Amsterdam he had reached for the hand and heart of Kee
Vos, only to have his own hand and heart seared in the flame from a
lamp. But now, at The Hague, in the city in which his mother had been
born, raised, and married—which is to say, had "come to life"— Vincent,
at long last, had found a place to lay his hand, his heart, and his head—
next to Sien's.

Despite the gloomy shadows of his past—judged, of some, to have
gone far "astray"—his feet were now planted, for once, it seemed, on a
path that was straight *enough*—and from which no one dare to hinder
him. For, as the Holy Scriptures had declared: "God maketh his sun to
rise on the evil and on the good, and sendeth rain on the just and on the
unjust."[36] Just so—from behind the clouds from which the shadows had
fallen, the heavenly "sun" had risen to warm the earth, and the "rain" of
God to quench the thirst of two lovers who had found one another—*just
as God had found them.*

In the fall of the previous year, after he had turned twenty-eight, with
Kee Vos still in his heart, and shortly before being introduced to Sien,
Vincent had raised the question:

35. Shades of Vincent's reaction to his father, with the grandiose sector of the self
(Kohut) standing in defiance of whatever threatens to reduce the self to a pile of ashes—
a defense against further wounding of the self, such as when it was said to the prodigal,
Vincent: "You have gone astray."

36. Matthew 5:45, KJV.

What kind of love did I feel when I was twenty? It is difficult to define—my physical passions were very weak then, perhaps because of a few years of great poverty and hard work. But my intellectual passions were strong, meaning that without asking anything in return, without wanting any pity, I wanted only to give, but not to receive. Foolish, wrong, exaggerated, proud, rash—for in love one must not only give, but also take; and, reversing it, one must not only take but also give. Whoever deviates either to the right or to the left falls, there is no help for it. So I fell, but it was a wonder that I got up again. . . . Gradually I began to love my fellow [humans] again, myself included, and more and more my heart and soul—which for a time had been withered, blighted and stricken through all kinds of great misery—revived. And the more I turned to reality, and mingled with people, the more I felt new life reviving in me, until at last I met *her*. (CL 157)

That was *then*, when he was still smitten of unrequited love for Kee. But this was *now*, when he was *dug in* with compassion for Sien—*struck* with a "calm and brightness and cheerfulness at the thought of her and the straight path lying before" himself. For, if being "revived" meant to be redeemed from being "withered, blighted and stricken" with a kind of living death unto oneself, then right now, in the present moment—regardless of what others said or thought—Vincent was *alive*. The hope and promise of Sien—"the woman"—midwife to Vincent's rebirth—consisted of the fact that it was she, like unto none other, who unfurled "Vincent, the artist" from the belly of "Vincent, son of the manse."

He made it clear to Theo that "what exists between Sien and me is *real*; it is not a dream, it is *reality!* Look at the result. When you come, you will not find me discouraged or melancholy; you will enter an atmosphere which will appeal to you, at least it will please you—a new studio, a young home in full swing. No mystical or mysterious studio but one that is rooted in real life—*a studio with cradle*, a baby's crapper—where there is no stagnation, but where everything pushes and urges and stirs to activity" (CL 212). To be sure, this newfound studio of "real life" was not to be furnished with just *any* old baby's cradle, because an artist's studio deserved to be appointed with one that was *a cradle for art*, from which would push, urge, and stir all manner of life. "I have started a new life, not purposely," he said, "but because I had a chance to begin anew and did not refuse it" (CL 193). Something good had been handed him, even though in the past, with respect to women, his reach had far exceeded his grasp.

Contrary to their wishes, for those who knew him it would come as a surprise that Vincent's relationship with Sien might endure for so much as a month, much less for as long as a year, after their decision to live together as husband and wife without benefit of ceremony. Had there actually been so much as a ceremony, it certainly would not have taken place in a church. "As she is Roman Catholic, the wedding will be even simpler, for then of course the church is out of the question; neither she nor I want to have anything to do with it" (CL 193).

But then, there was this: Apart from their mutual disdain for ceremonious institutions of religion, and in spite of their having "made life" together, as opposed to having only "made love" for a substitute, there was, for Vincent, an overriding consideration: "I only know one thing—drawing; and she has only one regular job—posing." "She knows what poverty is, so do I." A shortage of funds, in the one hand, is a great "pooler" of resources; in the other hand, it is a great "divider" of alliances. Their poverty called for the exercise of plain Old Dutch determination: "Fishermen know that the sea is dangerous and the storm terrible, but they have never found these dangers sufficient to keep them ashore," he said. "Let the storm rise, the night descend—which is worse, danger or the fear of danger? Personally, I prefer reality, the danger itself" (CL 193). But with the reality of the storm rising, and the night descending, close at hand, the danger of being at sea was plenty enough to make for a high degree of consternation. To put it in plain and simple Dutch, Vincent was fearfully worried.

As was already clear enough, he had every reason to be concerned that his relationship with Theo was permanently on the rocks. Despite being the elder of the two brothers—and for that reason supposedly the wiser—Vincent had been discovered, in Theo's mind (not alone), to be not so wise at all, but rather to have shipwrecked himself on the reefs of paradise in the company of some maiden of the city whose naked charms would bring him to no good at all, if not to everlasting ruin. And, worse still, in Vincent's mind, so far as shipwreck was concerned, he worried even more about the undue influence of Mauve and Tersteeg—and Theo. "I am prepared for the worst—what's it to be? Speak plainly," he wrote to Theo (CL 193). "You have me at your mercy, you particularly, along with many others, none of whom can agree with me. *And yet you will not be able to force me to renounce her*, whatever your financial power" (CL 193a). "What I experienced last winter at Mauve's hands has been a lesson to me; it has kept me prepared for the worst—a death sentence from you" (CL 193).

Notwithstanding Theo's waning patience and the threatened loss of his financial support, the conflict over Sien was being waged on more than one front, adding further anxiety to an already boiling pot of "stew." Vincent did not get along well with Sien's family. "I think the saying is true," he said, "'if one marries, one doesn't marry only the woman herself, but the whole family in the bargain'—which is sometimes awkward and miserable enough when they are a bad lot" (CL 279).

Sien's mother was a charwoman who had raised eight children of her own. Vincent, now needing to carry his worrisome thoughts beyond himself, complained to Theo of the larger family system in which he found himself: "As to what I wrote you about the relations between women and their mothers, I can assure you, in my case nine-tenths of the difficulties which I had with the woman originated directly or indirectly therein" (CL 281). "When the woman does wrong," he said, "it is sometimes the mother's fault; and when the mother does wrong, sometimes the family is in back of it" (CL 284). Yet, he conveniently failed to mention the "man," and thereby avoided implicating himself.

Insurmountable differences, nonetheless, had surfaced between him and Sien—obstacles they had little hope of overcoming. These included rising expenses and deeper debt, despite Theo's standard monthly provision, which kept them all a few days from starvation. And then there was Sien's alcoholism, along with her continuing flirtation with prostitution. Furthermore, he said, "the woman has certain faults and shortcomings in her behavior—how could it be otherwise?" And Vincent, who for a long time had been no stranger to prostitutes himself, and drowned many a sorrow in a bottle, was in no position (nor did he want to be) to cast the first stone. Yet, too much of a good thing, like love—which had become too much of a bad thing—swiftly became intolerable. "Habits of slovenliness, indifference, lack of activity and ability, oh, a lot of things. But they all have the same root: bad education, years of quite wrong views on life, fatal influence of bad company" (CL 284).

Constant quarreling, combined with a dwindling resonance of positive emotion, strained the bond between them. Neither one was able to provide the other with consistent or stable mooring. "At times," he said, "her temper is such that it is almost unbearable even for me—violent, mischievous, bad. I can tell you, I am sometimes in despair" (CL 284).

His own temper had met its match. In addition, his work presented him with relentless frustration, leaving him with the fear that—worst of all—he might never finally attain his ambition to be a painter, or, worse than worst of all, he might remain an average, misunderstood painter—like the preacher who, for the life of him, no matter what, no matter how, simply could not sing like a lark with a song in its heart. After the sun has risen: how fast the shadows of the night can fall and the voice of the lark go silent!

Vincent pondered his dilemma: "There is a similarity between art and love, it is like swinging between, 'je l'ai depuis longtemps' and 'je ne l'aurai jamais' [I have had it for a long time, *and* I shall never have it], as Michelet expresses it, and one passes from melancholy to animation and enthusiasm; and this will always remain so—only the oscillations become stronger" (CL 259). True, he was suffering from fluctuations between a convulsive mania, on the one hand, and an unspeakable depression, on the other—the extremes of which the connection with Sien ideally could have modulated. Such hope may have provided him with an unconscious motivation, and a powerful one, for their remaining together. Nevertheless, his ups and downs were getting to be *too little up* for the cost of *too much down*.

To avert further dithering about what to do, Vincent finally came to terms with himself. "The work is an absolute necessity for me," he declared. "I can't put it off, I don't care for anything but the work; that is to say, the pleasure in something else ceases at once and I become melancholy when I can't go on with my work" (CL 288).[37] His work became the only consistently sustaining, mirrored object of himself, in which he could see himself—except for Theo as a (wavering) distant support. Vincent "was made alive through the actual process of painting—by profoundly entering into a relationship both to the world that is painted and to the work itself."[38] Yet his longing was for the mirroring of himself by someone else. "It does me so much good when people feel some sympathy for my work," he said. "For it is so discouraging and dispiriting,

37. Heinz Kohut wrote: "The psychology of the self is needed to explain the pathology of the fragmented self . . . and of the depleted self (empty depression, i.e., the world of unmirrored ambitions, the world devoid of ideals)—in short, the psychic disturbances and struggles of Tragic Man" (*Restoration*, 243). Vincent had struggles with both pathologies of the fragmented and the depleted self, the latter of which he referred to as his empty depression.

38. Howard Baker, "Vincent van Gogh: Selfobject Factors," 208.

and acts like a damper, when one never hears, This or that is right, and full of sentiment and character. It is so cheering to realize that others feel something of what one has tried to express" (CL 208). Yet, despite this need, he seldom received such positive confirmation.

Re-commitment to his work was, nevertheless, of paramount importance. It overshadowed even the "great calm and brightness and cheerfulness at the thought" he had formerly held of Sien (CL 212). What she had once provided him by way of being a midwife to his rebirth as an artist, he must now provide for himself. Consequently, there came the inevitable moment of truth.

> Today I had a quiet day with her. I talked it over with her seriously, explaining to her fully what my situation is, that I *must* go away for my work, and *must* have a year of few expenses and some earnings in order to make up for the past that has been rather too much for me . . . that I should soon be unable to help her any more . . . so that, in short, she and I must be wise and separate as friends. That she must get her people to take the children, and that she must look for a job.
>
> So I said, "As long as I know that you are trying your best and are not losing hold of *everything* and that you are good to the children, as you know I have been to them—if only you act so that the children always find a mother in you, though you are just a poor servant, though you are just a poor whore, with all your damned faults, you will always be *good* in my eyes. And though I do not doubt for a moment that I have the same kind of faults, I hope I shall not change in this respect, that when I see a poor woman with a swollen belly, I shall always try to do what I can to help her." I said, "If you were in the same condition as when I found you, well, you would find a home with me—a shelter in the storm as long as I have a piece of bread and a roof over my head; but now it is different, the storm is over, you can go straight without me, I think—well, you must try to. For my part, I must also try to find a straight path, I must work hard; you do the same." That's the way I said it. (CL 318)

That straight path: If there were ever to be such a thing as his "Pilgrim's Progress," as he had so strongly believed there once had been, then there could be no turning back—no removing his hand from the plow while remaining true to himself. "All right," he said. "Once I am so far, it won't be by halves, for I don't work by halves" (CL 339). He had previously proffered that "an artist's work . . . [is] like a woman in childbirth and her baby" (CL 181).[39] In more ways than she could possibly have known, Sien had served as a living "model" for Vincent's giving birth to his art as his progeny.[40] Not only had she sat many times before his palette and posed, but when she was recovering from her own childbirth it was Vincent who had sat beside her and seen her through her depression and persistent weakness. She had drawn out the nurturing aspects of his character. If not for the first time in his life, Vincent had taken up closely into his arms a little boy, someone approximately "his own," and held him there to see and to touch, perhaps even to envision what promise such a child might have—*like that of an artist.*

Vincent had once so touchingly and tenderly said of his beloved:

> You see, a cradle is not like anything else—there is no fooling with it—and whatever there may be in Sien's past—I know no other Sien than the one of this winter—than that mother in the hospital whose hand pressed mine when we both felt tears in our eyes as we looked at the little baby for whom we had been working all winter. And just listen, entre nous soit dit [this is said just between us], without preaching a sermon, it may be true that there is no God here, but there must be one not far off, and at such a moment one feels His presence. Which is the same as saying, and I readily give this sincere profession of faith: I believe in God, and that it is His will that man does not live alone, but with a wife and a child, when everything is normal. (CL 213)

The qualifier, "when everything is normal," served but to underscore the fact that, for Vincent, at least, things were rarely normal, if "normal" meant having a wife with child without disruptions of one's calm and composure. Sadly, yet also happily for Vincent, calm and composure were best known, not within the company of a woman, but within the

39. This is a fascinating phrase (i.e., "like a woman in childbirth and her baby") in light of D. W. Winnicott's observation that "there is no such thing as a baby" since "infant and mother together form an indivisible unit" (Lee and Martin, 88). This conclusion implicitly raises the question as to what extent Vincent's artwork was an unconscious embodiment of the relationship he had with his mother, who as an amateur artist gave Vincent his first drawing lessons. More is said about this subject later in this chapter with respect to Vincent's last letter to his mother.

40. In D. W. Winnicott's terminology, the living model was what Winnicott would call a "transitional object" as symbolically "a concrete icon that designates the ghost of the umbilicus and the placenta, the important linkage between mother and infant during that special time just immediately prior to birth" (Grotstein, "Winnicott's Importance in Psychoanalysis," *Facilitating Environment*, 137).

friendship of the wafting wheat fields and the sunny skies of the heath, with the lyrical song of the lark in the air.

At one point, as had been the case all too often, it was Tersteeg who had befuddled Vincent's graces. "If Tersteeg were to get his way . . . I believe he would look on quite cold-bloodedly while Sien was drowning or some such thing, not lifting a finger, and say it was beneficial to civilized society. As long as I drown at the same time, I don't care. But we felt distinctly enough that her life and my life are as one, when we met . . . in that hospital by the side of the baby's little cradle" (CL 216).[41] It was plainly difficult for Vincent to work around someone so disapproving as Tersteeg, who had come to block Vincent's every move whether it was for receiving financial aid from his brother or for offering private charity to a prostitute. Tersteeg complicated Vincent's life like a bee in a bonnet, but only to the extent of prompting Vincent to have the charitable thought of drowning himself for the one right reason. Short of that, Tersteeg could not, for long, diminish Vincent's eye for drawing. Nor could the inconvenience of three weeks spent in the hospital, recovering from the acute effects of gonorrhea, bring Vincent down for good.[42] He said: "I promised myself something, that is, to consider my illness, or rather the remains of it, as nonexistent. Enough time has been lost, the work must continue. So, well or not, I shall start drawing again, regularly from morning until night. I do not want someone to say to me again, 'Oh! These are just old drawings.' Today I made a drawing of the baby's cradle with a few touches of color in it. . . . I will go out and work in the open air, even if it should cause my illness to return. I cannot keep from working any longer" (CL 218). By cradling his art, he cradled himself in the only way he knew how.

So long as he was about his work he made sure that Theo understood his "conception of art." "One must work long and hard to grasp the essence," he wrote. "What I want and aim at is confoundedly difficult, and yet I do not think I aim too high. I want to do drawings which *touch*[43] some people. 'Sorrow' is a small beginning" (CL 218). Sorrow,

41. The mirror transference was experienced as a merger between them.

42. Vincent had been hospitalized for three weeks in 1882 for treatment of gonorrhea, the symptoms lingering for some months. For elaboration, see Winfred Arnold, *Vincent van Gogh*, 75–76.

43. Vincent is referring to the emotional effect his art will have upon the viewer. From a psychological perspective it is worth noting that a work of art as a selfobject may take upon itself projected human qualities. The art "touches" just as a person as

of all the human emotions, was the one with which he had become all too familiar. For not only was "Sorrow"[44] the woman who had taken her name from Vincent while posing in his studio, and subsequently when lying beside him in their bed, but "Sorrow" was also the lament in the crest of the lark whose song had fallen too many times to the ground. "'Sorrow'—at least, I think it's the best I've done," he pointed out to Theo in a triple *entendre*, referring to the painting, his relationship with "the woman," and his own pure sorrow itself (CL 219). And when all was over with Sien, he said to Theo: "Of course the woman and her children were with me to the last, and when I left, the parting was not easy" (CL 323).

Portraits of people belonged to the first order of artistic magnitude. Landscapes came next. "The landscapes are also a small beginning," he said. "In those there is at least something straight from my own heart. In short, I want to progress so far that people will say of my work, He feels deeply, he feels tenderly—notwithstanding my so-called roughness, perhaps even because of it. It seems pretentious to talk this way now, but this is the reason why I want to push on with all my strength. What am I in most people's eyes? A nonentity, or an eccentric and disagreeable man—somebody who has no position in society and never will have, in short, the lowest of the low. Very well, even if this were true, then I should want my work to show what is in the heart of such an eccentric, of such a nobody" (CL 218).[45]

Vincent spoke of the years of his youth as having disappeared "irrevocably," and as having had a feeling arising from within "that there is some good in life, and that it is worthwhile to exert oneself and to try to take life seriously" (CL 219). Even as he was living with Sien, consciously though not consistently he had felt a great surge of energy and purpose, a decisive movement toward the realization of his vision in a way he

selfobject touches or is touched. Exhibitions of Vincent's art have proven to be deeply moving experiences for the many people who have seen them. Possibly more than any other single Western artist he has consistently captured the emotional heart and soul of the human condition. This, I believe, is what accounts for his enormous popularity. He "touches" those places deep in the heart where one knows both "sorrow" and "joy."

44. His depiction of Sien.

45. Here Vincent indicates how his works of art are extensions of his need for mirroring, displaying as they do the lifelong longings of his heart. Through his "heart-art" he hopes to recover the self-regard and dignity that he had lost not only before others but also within himself, and perhaps, most seriously of all, before God.

had not experienced before. Just as every propitious forward motion had implied a subsequent regression, so had a substantial regression become the occasion for a significant forward motion. As the darkness had come forth from the light, so had the light come forth from the darkness. Thus were his letters replete with luminous affirmations:

- "Drawing becomes a passion with me, and I throw myself into it more and more; and where there's a will, there's a way" (CL 195).

- "Great things are not accidental, but they certainly must be willed" (CL 237). And he added: "I had often suppressed the desire to paint" (CL 224). But "now I have *launched my boat*" (CL 223).

- "This much I want to tell you—while painting, I feel a power of color in me that I did not possess before, things of broadness and strength" (CL 225).

Thanks to Sien, and the grace of the rising sun, Vincent had unleashed his "nuclear self"[46]—that "artistic sense," as he said, "in the very marrow of my bones." Henceforth, his art was destined to remain in the center of his vision and at the core of his being—which is what he meant when he said, "I have a painter's heart" (CL 224).

From the artist's "cradle" of pain and suffering, from the "plight" of his darkness and the "shadows" of his doubt—there had come forth a "babe," who, indeed, could coo like a lark.

46. Heinz Kohut believed that the "nuclear self" is "composed of derivates of the grandiose self (i.e., of the central self-assertive goals, purposes and ambitions) and of derivatives of the idealized parent imago (i.e., of the central idealized values)" (*Self Psychology*, 10). The nuclear self is the part of the self most resistant to change, though it "is not immutable" (ibid., 11). "There are other, broad areas of the personality outside the nuclear self. But once it has been laid down, the nuclear self strives to fulfill itself. It moves, from the time of its consolidation, toward the realization of its ambitions and ideals, which are the ultimate descendents of the child's grandiosity and exhibitionism and of his strivings to emerge with an idealized selfobject. And if an individual succeeds in realizing the aims of his nuclear self, he can die without regret. He has achieved the fulfillment of the tragic hero—not the painful death of guilty man who strives for pleasure—but a death which is 'beyond the pleasure principle'" (ibid., 49).

"Self-Portrait in Front of the Easel"

THREE

"Such a Nobody"

"SORROWFUL YET ALWAYS REJOICING"

L IFE'S MOST SIGNIFICANT TURNINGS arise not so much from conscious awareness of obvious destinies as from unconscious streams of necessity to which we are irrepressibly drawn. Painting, like poetry, song, or dance, is vocation—a "calling forth," a "summoning"—and in that sense a "birthing" of something deep from within, tied to a transcending future with primal roots in a grounding past.

"We are so much attached to this old life," wrote Vincent, "because next to our despondent moods we have our happy moments when heart and soul rejoice—like the lark that cannot keep from singing in the morning even though the soul sometimes sinks within us and is perturbed. And the memories of all we have loved stay, and return to us in the evening of our life. They are not dead but asleep, and it is well to gather a treasure of them" (CL 98).

Amid those treasures, it is one thing to discover sorrow. It is quite another to find that sorrow has a companion by the name of joy. Alluding to the sentiment of the Apostle Paul, Vincent used to say a thousand times over: "God hath made me sorrowful yet always rejoicing" (CL 39b; *passim*).[1] It is impossible to know for certain which of those human emotions carried more weight in Vincent's heart on any given day.

---

1. Vincent was quoting St. Paul from 2 Corinthians 6:10.

69

When you read his letters you think it may have been sorrow. When you see his paintings you believe it could well have been joy.

Vincent had bestowed upon Sien the name of "Sorrow." But what name might Sien have bestowed upon Vincent, if *not* "Sorrow"? And what would have become of his joy in the midst of his sorrow, had he remained with Sien and there had been for him no "post-partum" life *alone* as an artist? Would he have known even less of joy, of which there was already a dearth, or more of sorrow to the point of not being able to paint at all?

Certainly—Vincent, the poet, would have perished considerably younger, buried within the shadow of "the man," being given up for dead—*bone dead to himself, as well as to his art*—had he not emerged rising and shaking off the dust from the crypt of Vincent, the "son of the manse." To that end there was still the spirit of Eliot's rebellious Felix Holt within him, who refused to succumb to the verdicts of so many eagerly attending "coroners" who, with scalpel in hand, were ready to pronounce him a lifeless sack of bones.

Six months before the day when Vincent had made the decision to rise from the shackles of domesticity with Sien, he re-read Eliot's *Felix Holt, the Radical* and Victor Hugo's *Les Misérables*. Of the latter he wrote: "It is good to read such a book again, I think, just to keep some feelings alive. Especially love for humanity, and the faith in, and consciousness of, something higher, in short, quelque chose la-haut [that something on high]" (CL 277).

Six years before his farewell to Sien, that very same spirit of hope and idealism had come upon him when he was about to turn the age of twenty-four, and he had spent an altogether joyful day alone with Theo, just the two of them walking side by side around the city of Amsterdam. Vincent recalled: "I stood watching your train until it was out of sight. We are such old friends already—how many walks have we taken to-gether since the time at Zundert, during this season, when we went with Father to hear the lark singing in the black fields with the young green corn" (CL 89).

Sorrowfully, though, it would not be until after his leaving Sien, and, even more significantly, after his father's death, that Vincent would flourish like that selfsame lark taking flight in the "Netherlands" with wings ascending high above the Brabant wheat fields with its poor peasants hunched over tilling the soil. But, for the moment it could be said of Vincent that he was at least *well off the ground.*

There is simply no straight path to a compelling vision that does not involve sacrifice of one order of magnitude or another. Sorrow may not issue in joy, apart from joy dissolving into sorrow. A child is not born to itself except having departed from the womb of its mother *and* sooner or later the house of its father and mother.

Having said a tearful goodbye to Sien and her children, followed by three months of living in Drenthe, where he painted dark and dismal scenes of peasant life, Vincent fell into "bitter loneliness and lack of money" that "put too heavy a strain on his nerves," enveloping him in a state of emotional stupor. With nowhere to turn he "hastened back to the parental vicarage" at Nuenen, which in December 1883 was "the only place where he could find a safe shelter" (Memoir, xxxv).

The preceding August he had written to Theo: "My firm resolve is to be dead to everything except my work. But it is very hard for me to speak about those things, simple in themselves, but which are unfortunately connected with much deeper things" (CL 313). Deeper things are invariably so deep as not to be noticeably connected. Vincent's mother was also an artist who to some unknown extent modeled the possibilities for her young son when giving him his first drawing lessons. Yet her own artistry, of itself, was no guarantee of her giving birth to an artistic genius, though she may have carried the genes. That said, the odds were greatly in favor of *someone* in Vincent's generation taking up the painter's brush, given the longstanding artistic proclivities within the two sides of his family.

After Vincent's father's death the widowed Anna moved away from the manse at Nuenen, packing up what belonged to her son, including "all" the "Brabant work" he had painted and had left behind when he headed out to Antwerp. She gave it to "the care of a carpenter in Breda and—forgotten!" After several years the canvases were sold to a junk dealer (Memoir, xxxix).

To die to one's own work is one thing, for it invariably happens. But for one's work to die at someone else's hand is quite another. In many cases the worker *and* the work, and all the evidence of it, die together. During his lifetime, however, Vincent eventually died to all things *except* for his work, which in significant measure still survives, including a vast number of his personal letters that fall into the category of great literature.

To Theo he said: "The main thing is to create; I would rather have a few years of that than years of brooding over it and putting it off. And I said to Rappard . . . for my part I thought there was truth in the mysterious saying, 'Whosoever will save his life shall lose it, but whosoever will lose his life for the Gospel's sake shall find it'" (CL 310). "My own future is a cup that will not pass from me unless I drink it" (CL 313).

There was no secret to the fact that Vincent could not sustain an intimate relationship with a woman, or for that matter an abiding friendship with a man without scrapping over their differences. Except for the connection with his youngest sister, Wil, in whom he confided by letter between the summers of 1887 and 1890—and the virtually inseparable yet severely tested bond that he had with his younger brother Theo—there were no other bonds that had beneath them a strong enough foundation upon which to construct a home that could withstand the winds of conflict. Given his fragile emotions, every trifling tremor produced at least a minor quake. While Sien had been at his side he seemed temporarily, if tenuously, fortified against collapse of the insecurely cemented walls of his innermost self. But something besides "the woman of Sorrow" was needed to strengthen securely the chambers of his heart.

Parenthetically, it was vital to his growth that during his time at The Hague he learned not only to work in water colors but focused additionally upon painting human figures as he sought to portray the essences of the persons who sat before his easel. As he gave life to their portraits, he also gave life, inch by inch, to the maturing artist within himself. Three years prior to his death, Vincent wrote to his sister, Wil: "In the years gone by, when I should have been in love, I gave myself up to religious and socialistic devotions. . . . You see what I have found—my work; and you see too what I have not found—all the rest that belongs to life" (CL W4).

Now that he had found himself living once more under the same roof with his parents, this time in the parsonage at Nuenen to which they had moved, it was only to be expected that old familial entanglements and disagreements would arise again. The vocal fisticuffs with his father continued—and this, despite a renewed opportunity for conciliation and a chance for his parents to observe his work in a new way. Neither he nor they, however, seemed constituted for the colossal reconstruction of the family that such change would require. At the outset of his arrival Vincent wrote to Theo: "There is a je ne sais quoi [I don't know what] in Father which I am beginning to look upon as incurable and which makes me listless and powerless."

In rejoinder to Theo, he challenged Theo's opinion that Vincent himself had become "more and more like Father." He did so by turning the tables on Theo:

> If this were true—that is to say, if you were to become more and more a "Van Gogh," a character like Father or C.M., and if by always being in business you should acquire a conception of life entirely different from mine—namely a commercial spirit—more or less a political personality—well, putting it bluntly, in that case I should prefer to have no intimate relations with you; then, instead of strengthening the ties between us, I would rather part company, both understanding that we are not well matched. At the moment I am right under Father's nose—I see, I hear, I feel, what Father is, and I do not approve of it, decidedly not—if you are like that and getting more and more like it, then it would be wise to part company. (CL 345)

Recalling how he had been locked out of the house on that especially ugly Christmas Day two years before, he evoked the image of "standing before a barrier of implacability" present in his father's attitude, which he immediately threw up to him: "'Pa, here I am faced by your self-righteousness, which was and is fatal, for you as well as for me.' Then Father said, 'Do you expect me to kneel before you?'" In exasperation Vincent said he thought it was "coarse" of him "only to look at it in that way," as though kneeling before him should solve anything. Then he roundly declared: "I should not waste my breath on the subject any longer."

Vincent explained to Theo: "There is no need for Father to say that he committed an error in my case, but Father should have learned what *I* have learned in these two years—that it was an error in itself, and that it should be rectified immediately, without raising the question of whose fault it was." What Vincent had received from his father, as he saw it, was his father's "forever lapsing into *narrow*-mindedness, instead of being bigger, more liberal, broader and more humane. It was clergyman's vanity that carried things to extremes at the time; and it is still that same clergyman's vanity which will cause more disasters now and in the future."

Clergyman's vanity to blame or not, Vincent had not forgotten the tone of his father's words—the sound of self-serving self-justification, despite the benevolent intent: "I have always done for your own good, and I have always followed my sincere conviction" (CL 345).

Vincent had held to the belief that the "burden" of what had happened between himself and his parents simply "did not weigh on them," as though they thoughtlessly possessed no empathy for him. So, when he sought to excuse himself for what *he* had so thoughtlessly voiced in the heat of argument, he did so by divorcing his actions from his words: "One *acts* as one *feels*—our acts, our ready compliance or our hesitation, they are what people may know us by—not by what we say with our lips, kindly or unkindly." Of course, the proverb stood for immediate correction: "Sticks and stones may break my bones, but words can never hurt me" should now be "sticks and stones may break my bones, *and* words can *ever* hurt me." Father's words to son, and son's to father, were proof *enough*.

Clearly, the protagonists in the present war of the "roses"[2] were not yet ready for a truce. The ramparts of self-justification on all sides of the conflict remained armed and ready for combat. Vincent led the charge: "I see now what I saw *then*—then I spoke *flatly against Father*—now I speak, and in all respects I speak, however it may turn out, flatly *against* Father again, because he is *unwilling*, because he makes it *impossible*" (CL 345). One can justifiably draw the conclusion that Vincent's father and mother felt the same way about Vincent. Vincent had also made it "impossible." To make matters interminably worse, it would not be long before yet another one of Vincent's "developmental disruptions" would tear to shreds what little cohesion was left between him and his parents.

In the meantime, and to his credit, as evidence of the sort of compassion of which he was quite capable, Vincent busied himself nursing his mother back to health after she suffered a fractured thighbone. No doubt, his focused attention upon his mother's infirmity may have had all manner of unconscious overtones for both mother and son, given the fact that once upon a time she surely had coddled him as an infant, and now it was he who was coddling her. It would be only sheer speculation to say just what those unconscious overtones might have been for them. Yet, in a general sense one might surmise that certain subliminal motiva-

2. "Their coat of arms was a bar with three roses, and it is still the Van Gogh family crest" (Memoir, xv).

tions could have been operative between an emotionally distant mother and her customarily rebellious son when a role reversal had taken place. Sigmund Freud might have said that Vincent was compensating for the pain and suffering he had caused his mother by his past behaviors, including a desire to assuage any guilt he might have felt within himself. Or, also in keeping with Freud's theory of the unconscious, and for the sake of a son's present pleasure, Vincent might have been engaging in something as neurotic, even perverse, as psychic Oedipal possession. Heinz Kohut, on the other hand, would have disagreed with Freud, to conclude that it would be far more likely that the most recent dynamic between mother and son was an attempt to restore between them a *pre-*Oedipal bond that had been prematurely disrupted or perhaps had never solidly formed from the beginning.

It would have been reassuring for Anna to have received even a modicum of the affection that for so long she had coveted from an *adoring* son, instead of from one whose tempests had been a source of constant heartache and embarrassment. And, for Vincent, it would have been redeeming to have had a chance to experience her reciprocal affection and to prove himself *worthy* of sonship. Incestuous, as their relationship surely was *not*—it was nevertheless far better under the circumstances, for all concerned, that Vincent demonstrate his attachment to a woman named "Anna," his mother, rather than to a dubious character named "Sien," "the woman of the people."

Vincent appeared to have granted his mother a more charitable understanding and respect than he had his father. "With Mother," he said, "I am quite sure that, at least at times, there is a substratum of deep thoughts (for her inner, mental life is rather complicated, and has different floors or layers) which she neither would nor could talk about. In many cases she used to be rather chary of speech, so I for one prefer to say that I don't know everything about her" (CL 433).

Family conflict notwithstanding, all the while that Vincent remained in Nuenen, he continued to paint feverishly during his jaunts into the countryside, depicting with increased sophistication the life of the peasants and weavers.[3] To bolster the pride he had taken in his work, he enjoyed the added bonus of having received a commission to produce some sketches of rural life for a local jeweler by the name of Hermans. Yet, the question persisted as to how long would be too long for a man

3. See examples in WM, 31–98.

well past his chronological adolescence, yet still trapped in a mostly regressive phase of his life, to expect to be "nursed" by his mother when her unconditional affection, for which he had yearned, remained decidedly uncertain. Perhaps it was no longer indispensable for his further progress. If there had been any lingering doubt in his mind as to the extent of her present fondness for him, Vincent eventually would have put the matter to a solemn test.

The time was fast approaching, and was mounting to a swift climax, when Vincent would jeopardize every positive good that had come of his return home, about which his father had every right to say they all should have afforded more thought before agreeing to it. The time was coming, too, for the sake of Vincent's maturation in selfhood, when he would need to disengage ever further from the overhanging clouds of father, mother, siblings, aunts, uncles, and cousins, who did not know exactly what to do with this obdurate sheep of the flock who was constantly fowling the family's reputation.

As a child he had made up enthralling games for his brothers and sisters to enjoy. As an adult, however, he seemed to be chasing the rightful inhabitants away from the chicken coop and inviting a bunch of "stray hens" to come make their nests instead. Just so, once again young Oedipus was back in town, romping around on his proverbial "playground," not far from the church, where he was up to his old tricks again. But this time he was chasing, of all people, not a woman of the night but one who was visible to all within sight, a neighborly spinster lady ten years his *senior*.

Aside from any lingering thoughts he might have had of returning to Sien, a move that was exceedingly unlikely, Vincent was now pushing his luck to the brink of disaster. Quite impulsively, he fell in love again. This time it was with Miss Margot Begemann, who had come along one day with the thought of providing an act of charity—and also with the possible thought of seduction. She came in the company of two of her sisters to visit Vincent's recuperating mother. To say the least that can be said, Vincent and Margot *connected*. The scandal broke out all over Nuenen. One can only imagine the ensuing rattle-chatter of jabbering jaws, heard from behind every mulberry bush.

This is the way we wash our clothes, This is the way we dry our clothes, This is the way we mend our shoes, This is the way the gentlemen walk, This is the way the ladies walk!

This is the way Mister Vincent talks, This is the way Miss Begemann talks!

This is the way we children laugh, and laugh, and laugh, and laugh, and play!

Did you hear? Did you hear that the good Reverend's son has taken up with the homely Miss Margaretha Begemann? Did you know about that? Why, yes, it's true!

The opposition was like the force of a hoard of ten thousand cannons and mortars aligned against two make-believe conspirators with but one bow and arrow feigning Cupid's defense—*except that Vincent and Margot were not feigning.* How better to set the wheels of state in motion than to disturb the peace by announcing *marriage*? This was the stuff of which Shakespearean comedy could be made. Yet, for their families, who sat closest to the stage, it was no laughing matter. Even Theo gave Vincent a good piece of his mind. "Sanity" finally prevailed, but only after it had first "lost its marbles." Vincent explained:

> She had often said when we were quietly walking together, "I wish I could die now"—I had never paid any attention to it. One morning, however, she slipped to the ground. At first I only thought it was weakness. But it got worse and worse. Spasms, she lost her power of speech, and mumbled all kinds of things that were only half intelligible, and sank to the ground with many jerks and convulsions. . . . It was different from a nervous collapse, though there was a great similarity, and suddenly I grew suspicious, and said—Did you happen to swallow something? She screamed "Yes." Well, then I took matters in hand and [make] no mistake—she insisted on my swearing that I should never tell anybody—I said, That's all right, I'll swear anything you like, but only on condition that you throw that stuff up immediately—so put your finger down your throat until you puke, or else I'll call the others. Well, now you understand the rest.

> That vomiting only partially succeeded, so I went to her brother Louis, and I told Louis what the matter was, and got him to give her an emetic, and I went to Eindhoven immediately to Dr. Van der Loo. (CL 375)

Margot had made a less than courageous attempt at committing suicide. She had consumed strychnine and perhaps something else along with it as a "counter-poison." She had done so "in a moment of despair"—in, of all places, the company of her "starry-eyed" Vincent. What made it so "*un*comical," dare to say, tragic, especially for Margot, whose family turned against her as soon as she was warded off for a stay in the hospital, was that Margot in all her life "had never really loved before" (CL 377). "It is a pity," said Vincent, "that I didn't meet her *before*, for instance, ten years ago. Now she gives me the impression of a Cremona violin which has been spoiled by bad, bungling repairers"—an unthinking remark on his part, which only piled further humiliation upon an already ill-fated situation. As for their intended marriage, Vincent asked Theo: "Was it foolish . . . ? Perhaps so, *if you like*, but aren't the *wise* people who never do a foolish thing more foolish in my eyes than I am in theirs?" (CL 378). Shakespeare would have had several good picks from which to have a "heyday" naming this one: "A Midsummer Night's Dream" (*Theseus*: "Lovers and madmen have such seething brains, / Such shaping fantasies, that apprehend / More than cool reason ever comprehends.") and "Romeo and Juliet" (*Juliet*: "Well, do not swear: although I joy in thee, / I have no joy of this contract to-night: / It is too rash, too unadvised, too sudden; / Too like the lightening, which doth cease to be / Ere one can say 'It lightens.' Sweet, good night!" and, *Romeo*: "O, wilt thou leave me so unsatisfied?"). And then the sequel to an old one: "Much Ado about Nothing: 'Part' Two."

Time is said to heal most things, but sometimes it simply brings matters to a grinding halt. Margot was *not* going to become Vincent's wife, if anyone in either family had anything to say about it—which they did—and which caused Romeo and Juliet promptly to dive into a lake of bottomless despair. As if that were not enough to plague the days of their lives in the van Gogh family—following upon the heels of two years of constant disputation between Vincent and his father—on March 26, 1885, four days before Vincent's birthday, and without a split second's warning after returning home from a walk, Theodorus dropped dead at the front doorstep.

One can only conjecture as to the multitude of things that weighed heavily upon his mind during those last, unsuspecting moments—and, not least, what in the world would become of his hopelessly lovelorn son, Vincent the prodigal. Vincent's flirtation with Eugenie Loyer, his proposal to Kee Vos, his league with "the woman of the street," and his most recent dalliance with the neighborly spinster lady, not to mention the surplus of one-night stands, had all had the effect of a whip-slap to his parents and a jab at the gossiping folk in the community. To say that all of this was more than a little comical would be to falsify the record. To say that every bit of this was tragic would be to stick to the truth. In either case, and in all cases, the combined consequence of his taboo "alliances" over the years, along with the internecine feuds they produced, had led Vincent to take up his artist's brush once again, to repaint his own self-portrait, and to redefine himself anew.

Vincent produced more than forty self-portraits in the course of his lifetime, many simply because he had no other model from which to work. But, as has been suggested, these self-portraits "confirmed, explored, or exploited some or other aspect of his ego. . . . Few men have shown so painstakingly in their writings and in their paintings, the search for the nature of their identity."[4] By the same token, his relationships with women did the same in as much as these, too, "confirmed, explored, or exploited some or other aspect of his ego." Some days there were haunting doubts as to which came first—the women or the work. Other days there was an unsullied certainty: "I *must* go away for my work," as he announced so plainly to Sien when preparing to tell her farewell. (CL 318).

His quest for the one thing that made for meaningful work, like his quest for satisfying relationships, was rife with the theme of leaving home in order to find home. Albeit with the aid of family, lovers, and fellow artists, who played a significant role in helping him along the way en route to maturation both as a person and as an artist, he was also bound to find home where he had always found it—within himself, within nature, and within the *pursuit of his art*. Whatever semblance of meaningful community he was able to enjoy with others, however limited, was secondary to his work.[5] In addition to his art, his closest friends

4. Bernard Denvir, *Vincent: The Complete Self-Portraits*, 9–10.

5. As a counterpoint to "modern psychological thinking," which may tend to overlook the need for retreat of the self into the self, preferring, instead, to hold that to be "normal and healthy [is] to be intimate with each other and to communicate well," thus viewing "flight from intimacy as neurotic, abnormal, and practically immoral," Thomas Moore concludes: "Rather than judge each other and ourselves for our failure to be sociable, we might reconsider our biases and assumptions, even our sentimentality, about relationship. Perhaps some of our narcissism is a symptomatic attempt to recover a strong *unrelated* sense of self. How can we reach out to another, anyway, if we don't have strong devotion to our individuality?" (Moore, *Original Self*, 45; italics added).

were his books. One of his favorite poets, Henry Wadsworth Longfellow, had captured in verse, about as well as anyone had ever said it, the twin loves that dogged Vincent all of his life—*his women and his work.*

> By his evening fire the artist / Pondered o'er his secret shame / Baffled, weary, and disheartened, / Still he mused, and dreamed of fame. // 'T was an image of the Virgin / That had tasked his utmost skill; / But, alas! His fair ideal / Vanished and escaped him still. // From a distant Eastern island / Had the precious wood been brought / Day and night the anxious master / At his toil untiring wrought; // Till, discouraged and desponding, / Sat he now in shadows deep, / And the day's humiliation / Found oblivion in sleep. // Then a voice cried, "Rise, O master! / From the burning brand of oak / Shape the thought that stirs within thee!" / And the startled artist woke, – // Woke, and from the smoking embers / Seized and quenched the glowing wood; / And therefrom he carved an image, / And he saw that it was good. // O thou sculptor, painter, poet! / Take this lesson to thy heart: / That is best which lieth nearest; / Shape from that thy work of art.[6]

Vincent's rehabilitation, to the extent that it was possible during the two years he lived with his parents at Nuenen, was followed by a short stint as a student at the Antwerp Royal Academy of Fine Arts, where, once again, he re-enacted an ancient curse: *never in his mind enough motherly nurturance, never enough fatherly acceptance, never enough money on hand, never enough models he could afford to pay, never enough strength to curb the aberrant appetites that adversely affected his health—and, all else said and done, never enough hours seated before his easel.*

Regardless of the litany of his "never, nevers," there was one major difference between the *there and then* of the fading past and the *here and now* of the present moment: If through the years he had simply "had enough" of his father and mother, or maybe *not* enough of them in the manner he wanted, then, either way, he must now resolve within himself the lingering conflict between whatever it was that he most of all desired and whatever he would actually settle for—given his own peculiar traits and the limitations of those who had "parented" him.

6. Henry Wadsworth Longfellow, "Gaspar Becarra," *The Seaside and the Fireside,* 70–72.

Despite his deficiencies, wherever from this day forward he hoped to find his "home," and whatever he sought to become as "a nonentity, or an eccentric and disagreeable man . . . to show what is in the heart . . . of such a nobody," as he said of himself, he would always manage, throughout his ups and downs, to muster the determination to keep one sure fire burning: "I have no other wish than to live deep, deep in the heart of the country, and to paint rural life. I feel that my work lies there, so I shall keep my hand to the plow, and cut my furrow steadily," he wrote shortly after he had buried his father (CL 398). To that end, from the last of November 1885 through February 1886, he put his tender roots down in Antwerp, where he swore a pledge to himself: "A great deal may depend on my being able to stick to my guns" (CL 438).

While reflecting upon several of a multitude of paintings by others that he had closely studied over the years, several enchanting portraits drew his attention: one named "Fisherboy" by Frans Hals, another "Saskia" by Rembrandt, and then "a number of smiling or weeping faces by Rubens." "Smiling" or "Weeping"—"Joy" or "Sorrow"—were consistently captivating themes within his own art, of which he said: "Ah, a picture must be painted—and then why not simply? Now when I look into real life—I get the same kind of impressions. I see the people in the street very well, but I often think the servant girls so much more interesting and beautiful than the ladies, the workmen more interesting than the gentlemen; and in those common girls and fellows I find a power and vitality which, if one were to express them in their peculiar character, ought to be painted with a firm brush stroke, with a simple technique."

Signing off at the end of one of his letters to Theo, he added a postscript about the relatively new art of photography, which did not especially impress him. "The painted portraits have a life of their own, coming straight from the painter's soul, which the machine cannot reach" (CL 439). And as for the virtues of the painted art, he said: "There is, relatively speaking, higher and lower art; *people* are more important than anything else, and are in fact much more difficult to paint, too" (CL 444).

Apart from philosophizing, Vincent's time in Antwerp became an interim for absorption of grief and consolidation of ambition, both of which, like sun and moon rising and falling over the horizon, defined his days and nights. There in the midst of melancholic heartache, situated in a lonely room rented above a paint shop, like a miner crouching in the dark asking for someone to hand him a torchlight, Vincent petitioned Theo: "Send me much or little, according to what you can spare, but remember that I am literally starving" (CL 441).

He was steadily losing weight. He was in need of new clothes for his work at the academy, having worn the ones on his back for two years. His teeth were rotting, of which he had already lost or was about to lose "no less than ten." He mentioned that when he coughed he would "expectorate a grayish phlegm," and he feared that if he continued to neglect himself "it would be the same with me as with so *many* painters (*so very many* if one thinks it over), I should drop dead, or worse still—become insane or an idiot" (CL 448). Remarkably, at the same time, he managed to maintain "a certain calmness and serenity, notwithstanding everything" (CL 449). He acknowledged the welcome "feeling of compensation" derived from turning his attention to novelists and painters like Turgenev, Daudet, and Delacroix—and, as always, to the subject of women: "Sensitive, delicate, intelligent, like women," these "great thinkers" were, and "also sensitive to their own suffering, and yet always full of life and consciousness of themselves, no indifferent stoicism, no contempt for life. I repeat—those fellows, they die the way women die. No fixed idea about God, no abstractions, always on the firm ground of life itself, and only attached to that. I repeat—like *women* who have loved much, hurt by life" (CL 451).

In early 1886, still in a desperate circumstance and unsettled as to where to be in order to rekindle his health and re-energize his art, he moved in February to the northern part of Paris called Montmarte, where Theo was overseeing a branch of Goupil's gallery. Together they rented a nearby apartment. For several months Vincent frequented Fernand Cormon's studio in the company of Emile Bernard, Paul Signac, and Paul Gauguin. He attended numerous art exhibitions and expositions, traveled about Paris and beyond, continued to meet with and learn from the Impressionists and Post-Impressionists, as well as many who belonged to the lively and controversial Paris avant-garde art scene. He exchanged works of his own with fellow artists. He read insatiably—Maupassant, Voltaire, Tolstoy, to name a few—collected hundreds of Japanese woodcuts, interacted with art dealers and found camaraderie with the thoughtful Émile Bernard, one of the few friendships that lasted. As always, he turned to his easel where he painted still-life poppies, roses, and chrysanthemums when affordable real-life models could not be found. True to his disposition, he often engaged in intense or heated conversations with artists about various subjects of art, and from time to time got himself into fights, usually associated with having imbibed too much alcohol.

The year after his death, his friend Bernard, who had first met Vincent at Cormon's, vividly described the person he came to know so well:

> Red-haired (goatee, crude moustache, shaved cap of hair), with an eagle's gaze and an incisive mouth set as if to speak; of medium height, stocky without the usual excess, quick-gestured, with an abrupt gait—such was Van Gogh, always with his pipe, a canvas, an engraving, or a portfolio. Vehement in discourse, interminably explaining and developing ideas, little inclined to controversy, yet always involved in it. And such dreams, ah!—giant exhibitions, philanthropic artists' communities, the foundation of colonies in the Midi and, elsewhere, a progressive invasion of the public spheres in order to ably re-educate the masses in support of the art that they knew in the past. . . . A Dutchman, a Protestant, a pastor's son . . . excessive in everything, he doubtless caused an affront to the narrow doctrine of his masters! Smitten with art . . . Enamored by the art of the Japanese, Indians, Chinese, with everything that sings, laughs, vibrates, he found . . . astounding technique for achieving harmonies and the extraordinary flights of his drawing, [and] just as deep within himself he found the delirious nightmare with which he oppressively bears down on us without respite.[7]

There in Montmarte, Vincent placed a few of his works on display with Père Tanguy, a socialist paint shop owner whose communitarian views eventually resulted in his exile, and whose lively and colorful portraits Vincent affectionately painted.[8] All the while in Paris, Vincent managed brotherly excursions and intimate late night conversations, as well as incessant arguments, with Theo. Most importantly, from these experiences he garnered new insights into his artistic style and technique. And—in the midst of it all—yet once again—Romeo fell in love.

7. Stein, *Van Gogh*, 282.
8. "Portrait of Père Tanguy," WM, 282.

However briefly "the tie that bound" may have lasted, this time it was with an Italian restaurant matron, Agostina Segatori. Her Paris establishment, called Le Tambourin, was the setting in which Vincent painted at least one of her brilliantly striking portraits.[9] In addition, "The only nudes he ever painted in oil were of her."[10] Of the painting entitled "The Italian Woman,"[11] for which she posed in gala Japanese costume, the art historians Walther and Metzger said: "If there is one Paris work that points the way forward to the future, it is this. Here, and here alone, van Gogh has removed all trace of the other isms that had influenced him. Even in the portraits of Tanguy his brushwork still had an Impressionist quality."[12]

The record is conflicting as to whether or not it was in exchange for anything specific, possibly including the provision of meals, that Agostina Segatori appeared to have permitted Vincent to display some of his canvases upon her walls, which would have been good for his prospective sales. Yet, the paintings, for reasons not altogether evident, became a bone of considerable contention. For as Vincent informed Theo: "I said to Segatori . . . I had torn up the receipt for the pictures, but that she ought to return *everything*" (CL 461). The relationship had become noticeably problematic, perhaps in connection with Agostina's illness from a possible miscarriage or abortion, with which Vincent, from beneath the bed sheets, may or may not have had anything to do. His unyielding and callous ambivalence about her included the fact that, as he said, "if she refuses in cold blood to give me what belongs to me or does me any wrong once she is well, I shall not spare her—but that will not be necessary. I know her well enough to trust her still. And mind you, if she manages to keep her place going, from the point of view of business I should not blame her for choosing to be top dog, and not underdog. If she tramples on my toes a bit in order to get on, well, she has my leave. When I saw her again, she did not trample on my heart, which she would have done if she had been as bad as people said" (CL 461). As things turned out, whether or not *she* had actually trampled on Vincent's toes or his heart, or something else—*someone*, if not she, had trampled on his art. The benefit of having his works displayed on her

9. "Agostina Segatori Sitting in the Café du Tambourin," WM, 206.

10. WM, 287. For the paintings, see 202–3.

11. Ibid., 293.

12. Ibid., 298.

walls had literally come to naught when Le Tambourin was shut down, and, without any consideration given to the artist, his paintings were seized, then "piled up into a heap" and "auctioned for a derisory sum."[13] Vincent was not even so much as reimbursed for a single brush stroke. This regrettable development was most certainly an instance in which Shakespeare's sympathy for Vincent would have far outweighed that of the auctioneer. For as *Helena* said in the play: "ALL'S WELL THAT ENDS WELL yet, / Though time seem so adverse and means unfit." And then, she added: "I do beseech you, whither is he gone?"

Vincent soon thereafter wrote his sister Wil: "As far as I myself am concerned, I will go on having the most impossible, and not very seemly, love affairs, from which I emerge as a rule damaged and shamed, and little else" (CL W1). Two years later, two months before Theo was to wed his fiancé, Johanna, Theo penned a letter to her in which he said of his wild and wacky brother: "There's something in the way he talks that makes people either love him very dearly, or unable to tolerate him." Moreover, as to the general topic of "unhinged" artists, and the one in particular that Theo knew best, he concluded: "Genius roams along such mysterious paths in the mind that a spell of dizziness can bring it hurtling down from its heights."[14] As for those dizzy spells, poor Vincent surely knew where to obtain a "screw" in order to hang a good picture, but when it came to the one *being* "screwed," an auction fared about as well as a brothel.

In hindsight, after leaving Paris for Arles in February 1888, burned out from city life, wanting no longer to be deprived of fresh oxygen that could be better found in the warmer climate of the south, and still struggling with his health, he wrote to Theo, reflecting upon the things that weighed heavily upon his heart. These included the subject of homosexuality—about which he had thought deeply, as was his custom on most matters about which he thought at all. He had read a French novel, *The End of Lucie Pellegrin* by Paul Alexis, which was about a Paris prostitute whose life had ended badly, abandoned to disease and left dying alone.

13. From Bernard's recollections, *Vincent van Gogh: The Letters* (Museum Letters Project), letter no. 571, footnote no. 3, http://vangoghletters.org/vg/letters/let571/letter.html.

14. *Brief Happiness*, 160–62.

Vincent thanked Theo for sending the book, and said some things pertaining directly to himself. Of Alexis' story he wrote descriptively:

> *Lucie Pellegrin* is very fine, it is quick with life and is still exquisite and moving, because it keeps the human touch. Why should it be forbidden to handle these subjects, unhealthy and overexcited sexual organs seek sensual delights such as da Vinci's. Not I, who have hardly seen anything but the kind of women at 2 francs, originally intended for the Zouaves.[15] But the people who have leisure for love-making, they want the da Vinci mysteries. I realize that these loves are not for everyone's understanding. But from the point of view of what is allowed, one could write books treating worse aberrations of perversion than Lesbianism, just as it would be permissible to write medical documents on this sort of story, surgical disquisitions.
>
> At all events, law and justice apart, a pretty woman is a living marvel, whereas the pictures by da Vinci and Correggio only exist for other reasons. Why am I so little an artist that I always regret that the statue and the picture are not alive? Why do I understand the musician better, why do I see the raison d'être of his abstractions better? (CL 522)

With the "da Vinci mysteries" thoughtfully decoded, Vincent penned yet several more paragraphs having to do with the artist Paul Gauguin and himself. Little did he know at the time that his words presaged unpredictable events looming in the not so distant future. To wit: "With regard to Gauguin, however much we appreciate him, I think that we must behave like the mother of a family and calculate the actual expenses. If one listened to him, one would go on hoping for something vague in the future, and meantime stay on at the inn, and go on living in a hell with no way out. I would rather shut myself up in a cloister like the monks, free as the monks are to go to the brothel or the wine shop if the spirit moves us. But for our work we need a home" (CL 522).

The primary reason Vincent did not find a "home" in Paris was that there were too many distractions and unpleasantries. Living in close proximity to Theo proved to be especially trying for both of them, resulting in yet another round of estrangement. Vincent literally wore his brother out with endless argument, numerous demands upon Theo's time and resources, and with a florid temper that kept the air charged

---

15. French infantrymen.

with negative electricity. Having said farewell to Theo, and with his art-ist's rig in hand, Vincent made peace with Paris as he boarded a train in February 1888, traveling to Arles in the south, seeking new friendship with the countryside. There in the brightness and warmth, and within the studio of what he lovingly called his "Yellow House," rented for the purpose of establishing a colony of like-minded artists who would live and paint together in mutual support, he went to work again on his art.

Within ten months of having established his residence in Arles, the experiment in communal living commenced, enthusiastically, with the arrival of Paul Gauguin in October. In late December, it ended sud-denly, and predictably, with Gauguin's departure. As had been the case between Vincent and his father, and Vincent and Theo, the sparks had flown, and the two, who argued as much as anything over how to create their art, finally came to blows. Besides, Gauguin was himself entirely too egocentric and authoritarian ever to make a go of it with Vincent, and Vincent's explosive reactivity was more than Gauguin could handle. This time, with yet another lapse into psychological regression, his worst to date, Vincent suffered the loss not only of a significant part of his dignity and spirit but also the loss of a delicate portion of his ear, which gained him the one ineffaceable fact that solidified his reputation as a painter, perhaps forever. For there are still many who continue to ask: Is he the famous painter who cut off his ear?[16]

Following several hospitalizations due to debilitating seizures and psychotic episodes involving delusional thinking, and with the neighbors complaining and harassing him, calling him "the redheaded madman,"[17] Vincent admitted himself in May 1889 to the asylum of Saint-Paul-de-Mausole at Saint-Rémy. He did so after the police commissioner placed him "under lock and key . . . without [his] guilt being proved or even open

16 Winfred Arnold offers a lengthy analysis of the probable causes of Vincent's depleted state of body and mind (Arnold, 139–217). He notes that "the psychoanalysts have had a field day with Vincent's ear-cutting. Although there is nothing inherently wrong with psychological interpretations, such theorists have unfortunately wrapped the artist with thick tissues of imaginative but ill-founded verbiage. The effects of their speculations are still being felt because the press, films, and other popular media reflect their views of Vincent. Vincent's ear-cutting affair certainly must be addressed because it was a bizarre act by any standard. However, it may be one of the least important aspects when properly considered within the total picture of this great artist's unusual life" (ibid., 255).

17. WM, 714.

to proof" (CL 579). During the next year of confined convalescence, he continued to paint as much as he could, amid the debilitating depression and recurrent psychosis that added further insult to the injury of his physical and mental suffering.

Subsequent to Gauguin's departure, and during Vincent's time of hospitalization, the local postman, Joseph Roulin, and his family, befriended Vincent, who said: "When I came out of the hospital with kind old Roulin, I thought that there had been nothing wrong with me, but *afterward* I felt that I had been ill. Well, well, there are moments when I am twisted by enthusiasm or madness or prophecy, like a Greek oracle on the tripod" (CL 576). For Vincent, Roulin had become like a surrogate father, who in disposition was the kind of father that Vincent had always wanted.

> Roulin, though he is not quite old enough to be like a father to me, nevertheless has a silent gravity and a tenderness for me such as an old soldier might have for a young one. All the time—but without a word—a something which seems to say, We do not know what will happen to us tomorrow, but whatever it may be, think of me. And it does one good when it comes from a man who is neither embittered, nor sad, nor perfect, nor happy, nor always irreproachably just. But such a good soul and so wise and so full of feeling and so trustful. I tell you I have no right to complain of anything whatever in Arles when I think of some things I have seen there which I shall never be able to forget." (CL 583)

In retrospect—back in 1882, before these subsequent events in Paris and Arles had unfolded, and while he was still living at The Hague, on the verge of taking one more modest step forward before taking yet another confounding one backward, Vincent parted company with Sien, hoping that the "gestating" artist inside himself would come to full term. The question then was this: What name—if not the name of "Sorrow" or "Joy" or "such a nobody"—would Sien, or anyone else, have bestowed upon this precocious, struggling "artist within the man," upon the occasion of his "rebirth" as the one who would become known everywhere as the legendary and renowned "Vincent van Gogh"?

"The Postman, Joseph Roulin"

BENEATH THE SHADOW OF A NAME

It was by no means merely co-incidental to his personal evolution that Vincent would live his entire life beneath the shadow of another Vincent Willem van Gogh, a stillborn, whose short-lived "birthday" fell exactly one year to-the-day before March 30, 1853—the day upon which the artist-to-be was born.

The unborn Vincent's fetus was buried in the graveyard of the church[18] at Zundert, adjacent to the family home in the parsonage

18. As to Vincent's disenchantment with the church, the "objective genitive" phrase "graveyard of the church" signifies not only the place where corpses are buried, but also the plot where a dead church might itself be buried—"the graveyard of the *church.*"

where Theodorus and Anna van Gogh and their children lived until they moved to Helvoirt in 1871. Off and on, for portions of those eighteen years, Vincent had more than a passing opportunity to stop in front of the tombstone to contemplate the ghostly remains of his elder brother. Just who, then, would be the likely one to assume the legacy of this unborn first child? More precisely—who would be the one to fulfill the *ecclesiastical* birthright?

Without question, a first-born male of the manse was favored in the eyes of Vincent's father and mother to carry on the pastoral charge that had been so well ensconced within at least four generations of van Gogh clergymen. These men of the cloth included a certain "remonstrant" Arminian[19] by the name of Cornelius van Gogh, whose particular brand of watered-down Dutch Calvinism harkened back to the day when "Arminius nearly ruined" the older and stricter Calvinism, until the Synod of Dort came along in 1619, meeting for a total of one hundred fifty-four sessions, and "restored it."[20] Cornelius must have had the purest of "rebel" blood in his veins, because he continued to remonstrate long after two hundred or so of the Arminian faithful had lost their pastoral charges, one of whom was imprisoned and another beheaded.

Complementing this slightly less than maximally austere Calvinist heritage of clergy—which was austere enough, nevertheless—there existed within the illustrious genealogy of the van Gogh patriarchal lineage the following persons.

In the family tree, moving downward from the branches toward the trunk, and skipping below Vincent, then skipping again, below Vincent's father, Theodorus, we find the distinguished clergyman grandfather of Vincent, also named Vincent. Below him was his father, Johannes, who was the son of Jan, who, in turn, was the son of David—the latter three all having been gold wire-drawers whose artistry had provided the finest of regal embellishments for the likes of the royal embroidery. The middle one of these three generations, Jan, had a brother named Vincent, who belonged to the famous Cent Suisses of the Swiss Guard—contractual mercenaries and household guardians of kings and queens—who had left his art and fortune to his nephew, the aforesaid Johannes, the great-grandfather of Vincent, the artist.

19. A follower of the teachings of the Dutch Reformed theologian Arminius (1560–1609).

20. Bangs, *Arminius*, 21.

Beneath the three eighteenth-century generations of gold wire-drawers (here the record states that the social standing of the family was somewhat diminished by the early 1700s), there resided a physician at Gouda by the name of Mattias, subsequently a clergyman at Moordrecht, whose own father was Cornelius, the aforementioned "remonstrant" clergyman at Boskoop, who, in turn, was a descendant of Michel van Gogh, consul general to Brazil and later a member of the state embassy that welcomed Charles II of England upon the occasion of his assent to the throne in 1660.

Proceeding further down the line, Michel's august ancestor, Johannes, was an esteemed magistrate and high treasurer of the Union, whose own thoroughly dutiful, thrifty, and pious ancestor was Jan, a wine and bookseller and captain of the civil guard who hung out "in the Bible under the flax market." Then, as far back as memory served, during the turmoil and tribulation surrounding the somewhat remote Protestant Reformation, Jan, who had been the one so fortunate as to hang out "in the Bible under the flax market," was born the son of the distinguished and notable Jacob van Gogh of Utrecht, Holland, who could be found (lounging around?) "in the Owl behind the Town Hall."

All of these distinguished van Goghs were of celebrated European descent, having hailed from the small town "Gogh" (possibly meaning "red," or "Gogh" knows what) on the German frontier, then having established themselves in Holland in the 1500s under their legendary coat of arms bearing a golden seal of approval in the form of a hefty gold bar (or bar of gold) emblazoned across the center of a red shield embellished with a Trinitarian arrangement of perfectly proportioned and stately embossed gold roses.[21] Apparently, gold was of sufficient abundance as to warrant a position of regal, if not absolute, prominence within the decorum of the helm, the shield, the mantle, and triangle of those Trinitarian roses, not to mention the other places that it would eventually come to adorn the laudatory heraldry of generations unborn. To be a "gold wire-drawer" was but a natural consequence of possessing a golden pedigree (even though someone else was paying for the gold), and thus to be in a "chain" of descent from which come such things as an appointment to the office of honorable magistrate and high treasurer of the Union, or consul general, or state ambassador bowing and scraping in deference to the king, or member of the Swiss Guard whose contractual obligation is

21. The genealogy is according to the Memoir of Johanna van Gogh-Bonger.

to guard the king, and as the king's mercenary to go marching forth in the name of the king to *obtain the gold*—to prevent too much of it from being frittered away in such places as "the Owl behind the Town Hall."

Just how all those most saintly and consecrated clergymen managed to fit into such a lush entourage of van Goghs was anybody's guess—though it could have had something to do with the untimely misfortune of the one so-called Jan, who, in the midst of selling his delectable wine and urbane books "in the Bible under the flax market," got hold of the Bible one day, and that was the beginning of all manner of "remonstrance" and holy mischief from that day on.

Then—*above them all*—in the uppermost branches of the ancestral tree there emerged an entire generation of van Gogh art dealers, who knew beyond a shadow of a doubt how to turn a priceless work of art into a pricey pot of gold. It bears repeating: Vincent's three distinguished uncles were all prosperous art dealers: Uncle Hein, Uncle Cent, and Uncle Cor, the latter having been introduced, affectionately, as "C. M."

And then—at the very *top of the heap* (some would have preferred to say, at the very bottom)—there stood an assorted (some would have preferred to say, "sordid") array of brotherly and sisterly parson's kids, including the woebegone, penniless Vincent—frenzied, to say the least, and "dizzyingly" brilliant, to say the *most* that only a few, if any, of the then living or dead would ever have said of him.

On the whole, Vincent's siblings did not fare much better either. His youngest sister, Wil, lived out her adult years in a mental hospital with "an incapacitating psychosis," until she died at the age of seventy-one. His youngest brother, Cor, committed suicide ten years after Vincent did the same. Theo, Vincent's beloved alter ego, died six months following Vincent's death, of grief, exhaustion, and paralytic dementia, the latter having been the horrid consequence of syphilis.

Somewhere—sometime—since the good-old-days-of-gold in "the Bible under the flax market" and "the Owl behind the Town Hall," an aphid or a worm had gnawed its way beneath the bark of the old "Gogh" tree and *struck gold*.

A twentieth-century student of ecclesiastical and family studies, the late Rabbi Edwin Friedman, in his investigation of intergenerational family life, opined that "a sibling system can . . . create herd-like panic, as when the marriage of one daughter triggers the marriage of all of her sisters within a year. This can look as if the houseboat is sinking."[22] So, what, then, when one brother's death triggers the death of two more? Would it be fair to say, in retrospect, that something, or someone, lodged far back within the van Gogh line of descent was in need of a "remonstrant" redemption? And also that, in prospect, something far forward in the line could have used the therapeutic services of a psychiatrist, if not a wise and astute clergyman?

If the unrelieved burdens of the past are visited upon the generations to come, as the Scripture says they are,[23] then it is sometimes helpful, or thought to be at any rate, that an especially tolerant and supportive wife or husband be acquired. Or, in lieu of the compensatory accoutrements of marriage, then the wearing of the mantel of a certain religious order might be considered salutary for relieving the interminable burdens of the past that otherwise, over time, tend to multiply like rabbits, or aphids, or worms.

Who was it that said, quite perceptively, that family secrets are the portals through which ancestral demons pass from one generation to the next? As Edwin Friedman claimed, whenever this happens someone becomes the family scapegoat.[24] One can always posit a theory as to just how such things may have happened among the van Goghs, although the available evidence does not warrant a watertight hypothesis. That said, a brave attempt to explain things might go something like this:

- Vincent's paternal grandfather, also Vincent van Gogh,[25] was the distinguished Dutch theologian who conducted the service of "confirmation into the ministry" for Vincent's father, Theodorus.[26]
- Vincent's mother, née Anna Cornelia Carbentus, of The Hague,[27] was the daughter of Willem Carbentus, the "bookbinder to the King," who bound the first constitution of the Netherlands (Memoir, xix).

22. Friedman, *Generation to Generation: Family Process in Church and Synagogue*, 55.

23. Numbers 14:18.

24. An essential tenet of family systems theory as developed by Murray Bowen, his student, Edwin Friedman, and others.

25. See photograph of Vincent van Gogh, pastor and theologian, Vincent's grandfather, Stolwijk and Thomason, *Theo van Gogh*, 18.

26. Ibid., 17.

27. Photograph of Anna Cornelia van Gogh-Carbentus, Vincent's mother, ibid.

"Books and reality and art are alike to me," Vincent once wrote with considerable understatement (CL 266). Yet, why did Vincent not explicitly include theology within the scope of such "reality"? It is likely that his very next words betrayed the answer: "Somebody out of touch with real life would bore me" (CL 266). And who might that have been? Vincent had written to Theo that he very much wished Theo could "persuade Father and Mother to be less pessimistic, for they are awfully pessimistic" (CL 155). So, was it then an air of chronic pessimism—not much of a secret, to be sure, but a portal for demons, nonetheless—that prompted Vincent to become bored, if not totally perturbed with his familial situation?[28] Or, perhaps there was something else more furtive or sinister at work. "Well, I dare not allow myself any illusions," he lamented to Theo, "and I am afraid that Father and Mother may never really appreciate my art. This is not surprising, and it is not their fault; they have not learned to look at things as you and I have learned to look at them. They look at different things than we do; we do not see the same things with the same eyes, nor do the same thoughts occur to us" (CL 226).

In spite of how his parents may have looked curiously upon, or modestly interested in, or even totally askance at his artistic endeavors, there was something else besides Vincent's artistic bent that stirred their puzzlement and outspoken disdain for what he was doing with his life. And that "something else," besides his women and his art, yet indicative of both, was his *contrary worldview.*

Vincent was a devotee of French naturalist literature, which by the family's standards was not viewed to be compatible with the ideology of moderate to conservative Dutch Reformed Calvinism. Then too, to make matters worse, Vincent had strong leanings toward political and economic socialism (CL W1). Émile Zola's *La Joie de vivre* was Vincent's

28. Such pessimism would not have been conducive to the increase of Vincent's self-confidence, but would have functioned as a deterrent to his optimal self-mirroring and self-idealization, retarding his ability to experience positive self-regard, and leading to the devaluation of his emerging ideals, especially where those ideals were not coincident with the ones his parents held for him. The disheartening effect would have been to compound his feelings of defeat as he internalized their pessimism as his own. Theirs may well have been aimed at him, given their perception of his incorrigible attitudes and behaviors. A cloud of pessimism, in addition to exhibiting a sense of hopelessness, contains elements of the self's shame and disgrace. Tersteeg's pessimism about Vincent's constant failure to remain productively employed may have reflected the same pessimism that the parents and the extended family had directed toward Vincent. While he was for the most part exhilarated whenever he was engaged in his work, near the end of his life he confessed to Theo: "As for myself, I feel a disgrace and a failure" (CL 610).

"Still Life with Bible, Extinguished Candle, and French Novel"

"secular Bible." It influenced his thinking probably as much or more than any other single book, aside from *The Holy Bible*, Thomas à Kempis' *The Imitation of Christ*, and John Bunyan's *Pilgrim's Progress*, although there were numerous others of sizeable influence, too many to mention, some of them all covered with dust and stacked over in the corner of the room "in the Bible under the flax market."

Immediately following his father's untimely death, Vincent painted "Still Life with Bible, Extinguished Candle, and French Novel" in memoriam. The Bible shown in the painting was his father's, opened specifically to the suffering servant passage of Isaiah 53. The novel, which was set at the edge of the table and squarely at the forefront of the painting, was Emil Zola's *La Joie de vivre*.

Vincent's father considered Zola to be anathema. So outlandishly secular did he believe the book to be, in contrast to the bedrock teachings of Arminius and Calvin, that it was hardly worth going to the trouble to set it afire, much less to read it. Judy Sund described how the novel, through the lives of its two protagonists, reflected the contentiousness that existed between Vincent and his parents.

> The travails of Pauline Quenu . . . are readily compared to those
> of Van Gogh perceived at Nuenen: An outsider looking in, she

is forced to live in rural isolation with family members who are exploitative and mean-spirited. Loving, and yearning to be loved, Pauline encounters hardship and disappointment but keeps steadfastly on. Her fortitude in the face of difficulties and hopefulness in the face of death doubtless appealed to—and perhaps encouraged—Van Gogh. On the other hand, his situation also bears comparison to that of Lazare, a young man who constitutes one of Zola's several renderings of the creative persona at odds with the world. A longtime pianist, Lazare is—at the book's beginning—completely caught up in music, despite the dismissive attitude his mother takes toward his work. Like Van Gogh's father, Mme. Chanteau is a damper on her son's artistic impulses; as Lazare works on a symphony he is determined to write, for instance, his mother insists, "You would do better . . . not to waste your time on foolishness." She urges him to find an "honorable career" and Lazare, "furious, violently closed the piano, while screaming that she was 'a dirty bourgeoisie.'" Though Lazare pronounces himself willing to kill himself before abandoning his music, he eventually gives in and goes to medical school, but when he fails to succeed in the career his family advocated, he returns to their home at loose ends and unable to support himself—much as Van Gogh had returned to Etten and, two years later, to Nuenen. Lazare, however, feels his talent and dreams desert him as the reading of Schopenhauer shapes his increasingly morbid outlook. His mother's death provokes fear and a feeling of powerlessness in Lazare, as does his wife's childbirth; Pauline, by contrast, attends to both with courage and skill.[29]

The parallels to the painting are so obvious as hardly to need mention, since "in this pictorial context *La Joie de vivre* suggests rebellion, contemporaneity, and—by virtue of its title—life in the face of death."[30] Sometimes it takes the eyes of a visual or literary artist to see exactly what is going on in the *big* picture. Heinz Kohut wrote: "The great artists of any period are in touch with the currently preeminent psychological tasks of a culture. I call this the anticipatory function of art. The artist is thus ahead of the scientist in responding to [humankind's] unfolding needs. Through his work [the artist] leads [humanity] to a dawning conscious awareness of preconsciously experienced psychological conflict or of an only preconsciously experienced psychic defect. The artist prepares the

29. Sund, *True to Temperment*, 113. *La Joie de vivre* translates as "The Joy of Life."
30. Ibid., 109.

way for the culturally supported solution to the conflict or for *healing of the defect*."[31]

In Vincent's case, just what might be said to have been the apparent *defect*?

"Van Gogh probably identified to some extent with each of Zola's protagonists," Sund continued. "*La Joie de vivre* presents several situations and relationships that can be seen to mirror those he faced at Nuenen: isolation in a closed community, a love affair sabotaged by 'well-meaning' outsiders, the striving to create [his art] in discouraging surroundings, [and] the death of a parent who is at once hated and esteemed."[32] In Vincent's case, the combination of all of these factors made for a condition that was ripe for the exposure of a defect. If there had ever existed some *secret of prodigality*, a long-standing one perhaps—a family defect hidden "beneath the covers," so to speak, or tucked away in an envelope at the back of the family vault—then such a secret would have been no secret at all to the extent that it was repeatedly whispered among some of the "mature" adults who otherwise sought to keep it under wraps, lest it see the larger light of day.

Most illicit love affairs that are "sabotaged by 'well-meaning' outsiders" are just that—they are sabotaged. They have taken place in isolation or discouraging environments. Sometimes the hush-hush surrounding someone's mysterious death or appalling moral demise has complicated the matter. But such secrets, despite all efforts to contain them, can spread like wildfire, smoldering first here and there, and then breaking out into open flame. Vincent, the isolated eccentric, living in down-beat surroundings and being endlessly talked about behind his back, while flagrantly exhibiting his amorousness on the avant-garde side of the street, was a shoe-in for sabotage by "well meaning" outsiders and *insiders*.

This was true in spite of the fact that Theo—figuratively speaking, the fair-haired one—had undertaken a few escapades of his own, on the same side of the street. One potentially torrid affair, whose embers quickly died out, was with an unnamed, clingy prostitute, referred to clandestinely as "S."—of whom Theo declared: "Either she gets out or I will." Vincent straight away proposed that he could solve the "S. problem" for Theo. He said that "an amicable arrangement . . . could be reached by your passing

31. Kohut, *Self Psychology*, 88–89, italics added.
32. Sund, *Op. Cit.*, 113.

her on to me. So much is certain that, if you could reconcile yourself to it, and S. too, I am ready to take S. off your hands, *i.e.* preferably *without* having to marry her, but if the worst comes to the worst *even* agreeing to a marriage de raison [marriage of convenience]" (CL 460).

Johanna described Theo to be "more tender and kind than his brother, who was four years older. He was more delicately built and his features were more refined, but he had the same reddish fair complexion and the same light blue eyes which sometimes darkened to a greenish-blue" (Memoir, xx). And, for good measure, Theo was his parents' favorite son. "They clung fondly to him because he more than any of the other children repaid their love with never-failing tenderness and devotion, and grew up to be, as they so often said, 'the crowning glory of their old age'" (Memoir, xxiii).

Yet, Theo was fair-haired in another respect. He was highly invested in the art business, and the art business was highly invested in him. He was on his way up the ladder of ascent to inherit his uncles' lucrative international art trade. Hence, a golden watch chain was more than a golden watch chain. It was an emblematic link attached to the "chain" of the generations—past and future. As Vincent had once so cleverly cautioned his brother: "Theo, do not become materialistic like Tersteeg. The problem is, Theo, my brother, not to let yourself be bound, no matter what, by a golden chain" (CL 181)—*which was tantamount to saying*: Don't forget what that golden chain meant to some of our esteemed and celebrated ancestors, including those closest to the throne of the king. Since it is the king who *controls the gold* (which, in turn, controls the king), the first obligation of those who serve the king is to *fetch the gold* for the king. And the second obligation is to make sure that nobody *steals the gold* from the king. So, brother, if you are the high treasurer of the king, then you *hold the king's gold in your hands*. And if you are the "bookbinder" to the king, you are "hide-bound" to "bind" the king's Bible to the king's golden interests. And—'Gogh' help you—you are also the guardian and "repairer" of the king's royal hymnal, which means you shall "bind" the people to the "authorized version" of the hymnody (*not* the psalmody) from which the king permits his congregants in the assembly of the king's church to sing. Last, and anything but least, you are dutifully ordained by the king to put "the spine and pages" of the people's "constitution" back together should they ever fall apart. Otherwise, the king may have to spend his royal gold to dispense his royal army—and blood will flow on the avant-garde side of the street.[33]

Vincent posted a letter to Theo, in which he said:

> Listen—Father has felt *suspicious* of me *very* often and *to a high degree*. For that matter, you know something about it, and I for my part know perhaps ever more about it. But—for all that—the man really thought he was in the right, and he was unable to take any other view of things, and—after all is said and done—he meant well, that is to say, if you want to take it that way—but one fine day I told him flatly: Don't call yourself my friend as long as you think such and such things of me. People who think that way about me *are not my friends but my enemies*, and as sure as 2 x 2 = 4, they are my worst enemies. (CL 388)

Vincent's iconoclasm and his ribaldry were every bit of an open book. Everyone within a snail's length of his obstinacy knew that he frittered away too much of his time in the "Owl behind the Town Hall"—and not always reading art books, either. More often he was simply preoccupied with sitting in his room and reading the pages of the Bible, among other *less* controversial books. Then again, he would take up a Victor Hugo novel, and draw a sketch or two of whatever came to mind, followed by an exhaustingly long letter describing how he felt about what he had learned from reading the novel. And then when he completed his sketching, his reading, his thinking, and his writing, he would set up his easel and seriously get to work. Finally, when all the day's seriousness was over and done with, he would return to the "Owl behind the Town Hall" and finish out the night with some after-hours "conversation" with any who would listen.

"They will hardly be able to understand my frame of mind, and they will not know what urges me on. When they see me doing things which

33. In 1816, under the royal decree of King Willem I, as the "ecclesiastical law of the land," the Hervormde Kerk (Reformed Church) was "reestablished as the only state-supported religious body and public monies again flowed to support it, but it was no longer Presbyterian in form, with authority flowing upward from the local congregations. Rather, power flowed from the top down, and the church shared with the government the task of nurturing loyal subjects. Given the ever closer bond between church and state, this change meant that any future church conflict would inevitably become a threat to the political order" (Swierenga & Bruins, *Family Quarrels*, 11–12). Moreover, "the revised structure *mandated* pastors in each worship service to select one or more hymns from the new hymnal, *De Evangelische Gezangen*, which included 192 gospel songs to augment the traditional Genevan psalms" (ibid., 12).

they think strange and eccentric, they will ascribe them to discontent, indifference, or carelessness, whereas in reality there is something quite different at the bottom of it, namely, the wish to pursue, coûte que coûte [cost what it may], what I need for my work." And, as for that: "there is something infinite in painting—I cannot explain it to you so well—but it is so delightful just for expressing one's feelings" (CL 226). "Believe me, I work, I drudge, I grind all day long, and I do so with pleasure; but I should get very discouraged if I could not go on working as hard or even harder. . . . I feel, Theo, that there is a power within me, and I do what I can to bring it out and free it" (CL 171).

Deep therein lay the great burden of his being a descendant of generations of renowned politicians and conscientious clergy, on the one hand, and of royal bookbinders and servants of the king, on the other. From among them all, there had arisen this prickly thorn upon the roses, this *supreme defect*, named Vincent. For, in his nonconformity he was determined to "remonstrate" yet again, that they all might become free from the sins of the fathers and the mothers passed down from generation to generation. *To them*, however, who were the whole thundering herd of venerable van Goghs, he appeared to be nothing less than the one bleeding cow that had bloodied the entire creek. Yet, as is usually the case, there are at least *two* bleeding cows—*defects*—submerged beneath the water for every one bloody secret that floats to the top.

On a cold winter's day in January 1886, Vincent bewailed to Theo about having "always to be in a state of exile, forever having to make great efforts, always half measures! But never mind—the family stranger than strangers is one fact—and being through with Holland is a second fact. *It is quite a relief*" (CL 443). If any of his ancestors had been wondering just how they might manage to rise up from their graves to prevent the indelible color of rebel-red ink from swamping the entire helm, shield, mantle, crest, and trinity of gold roses painted on the venerable van Gogh coat of arms, then they were in for a rude "awakening." Of the manifold generations of Vincents, Johanneses, Matthiases, Jacobs, Michels, and Corneliuses, the majority of whom had been bred high and born mighty, little did any of them know that *one* of their hearty stock would outdistance all the rest of them as the most notorious and prominent of the bunch. Any telltale family secrets hidden away within the basement of a gallery filled with old warped and cracked Dutch paintings sooner or later would see the light of day when all seventeen hundred pages worth of the juicy details finally made it into print.

Had Theodorus and Anna, Uncle Hein, Uncle Cent, Uncle Cor, Uncle Jan, Cousin Mauve, and Boss Tersteeg only known what that scoundrel had said about them when they were still alive, they might have put a stop to it. As it was, it was too late.

> In my eyes Father is a man who, when he ought to have had it, did not possess any knowledge of the intimate life of some great men. What I mean to say is that in my opinion Father never knew, and does not know now, and never will know what the soul of modern civilization is. What is it? The eternal quality in the *greatest of the great*: simplicity and truth. Dupré, Daubigny, Corot, Millet, Israëls, Herkomer—as well as Michelet, Hugo, Zola, Balzac, and many another master of older and newer times. Father is too much circumvented by his prejudices to understand this; all through life he applies them with a punctiliousness worthy of a better cause. For me he is the rayon noir [black ray]. Why isn't he a rayon blanc [white ray]?—this is the only fault I find in Father. True, it is a great fault—I cannot help it. And listen to what I say: Try to find the rayon blanc, but blanc, do you hear? (CL 339a)

Vincent customarily did not see the world so evenly divided between "black ray" and "white ray." Yet, in the case of how he perceived his father and certain others whom he undertook to name, he sometimes "split" them off into bitterly opposing realities. At an unconscious level this could have demonstrated his projection of a similar divide within himself: devoid of self-esteem on the one hand—as he said, "lowest of the low"—and desperately seeking a sense of self-worth on the other. The redeeming fact, however, was that he also sought, if with a tad of sarcasm, to "find the rayon blanc [the ray of white light]," as though he knew it might well be hiding somewhere in his father, waiting to be found. There were even times when he spoke compassionately of both of his parents, such as when he remarked to Theo: "I shall never forget Mother at Father's death, when she said only one little word: it made me begin to love dear old Mother more than before. In fact, as a married couple our parents were exemplary, like Roulin and his wife, to cite another instance" (CL 573).

Vincent's "dear old mother" was less confrontational than her son, to be sure. In fact, she may have been more expressive of her endearing and better self when she was not around Vincent. Johanna said that her mother-in-law was faithful in making pastoral calls with her husband, and she kept in touch with people by letter, "tell[ing] of all the small events of daily life at the parsonage; what flowers were growing in the garden; and how the fruit trees bore, if the nightingale had been heard yet, what visitors had come, what the little sisters and brother were doing, what the text of Father's sermon was, and among all this, *many particulars about Vincent*" (Memoir, xxiii, italics added).

She had sought to instill in Vincent the faith that was worthy of a proper Dutch Reformed Calvinist. Yet, her view of the faith sometimes vexed Vincent, as did her perceptions of his work. "Mother is unable to grasp the idea that painting is *a faith*, and that it imposes *the duty* to disregard public opinion—and that in painting one conquers by *perseverance* and not by making *concessions*—and that 'I cannot give thee the faith'—that is exactly what is the matter between her and me—as it was with Father, and remained so. Oh dear" (CL 398).

Furthermore, Vincent's mother's sister, Cornelia Carbentus, was married to the Vincent van Gogh known as "Uncle Cent," the prosperous art dealer who had taken the greatest interest in Vincent and Theo, *until Uncle Cent discovered what the young Vincent was really up to*. All the van Goghs and Carbentuses had strong opinions of him. Another of Anna's sisters, Willemina Carbentus, became the wife of Johannes Stricker of The Hague, the pastor and scholar with whom Vincent had studied in preparation for taking up theological studies at the university. Johannes was the one who on that most infamous of all occasions told Vincent in no uncertain terms that he would *not* get to see his daughter, Kee Vos.

Some of the relatives had given considerable thought as to how to be rid of Vincent. There is no evidence that "murder" was ever mentioned, at least in public. Yet, Anton Mauve, who was married to Anna's niece, finally tossed out Vincent as though he were a cracked plaster of Paris bust headed straight for the wastebasket. There was just no getting around the fact that Vincent was the one "family secret" that the entire family could not keep secret. Art and theology were inextricably intermarried within the constellation of the two families, van Gogh and Carbentus, if not with a vengeance then at least as tight as the jaws of an iron vice screwed together. And Vincent was caught royally in the middle of the vice, just where a family scapegoat belonged.

There is simply no straight path to a compelling vision that does not involve sacrifice of one order of magnitude or another. This great theological truth was exactly what Vincent had unconsciously set out to prove. In 1881, when he escaped from the parsonage in Etten to find "sanctuary" at The Hague—his mother's ancestral home and birthplace—fleeing, as he was, his father's scorn and nursing wounds that for so long had been inflicted upon his tormented "inner exile"[34]—the little "remonstrant" in him was headed straight for the "temple of revenge" to make his atoning sacrifice. It was to be a sacrifice of the highest order. For the reputation of the entire Carbentus clan (and with it all of the van Goghs) was to be offered up as an oblation to the goddess of "naturalism"—and that in the center of The Hague, *of all sacred places*. And the name of that goddess to whom he was to devote himself was no less than "the woman," "the woman of the people," the "Great Lady of Sorrow" ("Christine" being her Christian name). *And the ancestors were furious!* No dancing around the mulberry bush *this* time. This time they were going to dance around a funeral pyre! The situation, to say the least, was highly combustible. For when the "tribal parts" of any family go *all out* to war, someone becomes the bloody scapegoat *for the entire system*.[35]

34. In Richard Schwartz's *Internal Family Systems Therapy*, the "exiled parts" of a person are those "neglected, abandoned, needy, lonely, desperate, hopeless, helpless, ashamed, guilty, worthless, unlovable, scared, empty, and hollow" parts that are "burdened by extreme ideas about themselves and are stuck at some extreme point in the . . . past," feeling "neglected" and "chronically disapproved of and criticized internally," which "only confirms the negative beliefs they have about themselves that come from the past." Corresponding to the exiles are the "managers" (controlling parts) that want to keep the exiled parts "shut off," "dissociated," and "frozen in time," while the "firefighters" (the addictive and "rash, destructive" parts) sound "an alarm, ready to jump into action if these child-like parts are activated, so as to quickly distract from or anesthetize these parts" (95–97). One of the common "firefighters" is rage. "Whenever a firefighter symptom exists, one or more managers are likely to be fueling it." (162). Dysfunctional families are characterized by highly polarized internal parts that, in turn, become polarized with parts in other members of the family. At the center of this internal "tribe of parts" is the responsible Self compassionately differentiating itself from its own parts and the system of parts within the "larger tribal nation of many parts and several Selves" that constitute a family (160). It is the goal of the responsible Self to heal and lead its parts into constructive harmony.

35. The phenomenon of "displacement" or "scapegoating" occurs when a family system has lost its internal balance or homeostasis in the context of high anxiety related to extremes of polarization between members of the family. Edwin Friedman wrote: "In a family emotional system, when an unresolved problem is isolated in one of its members and fixed there . . . it enables the rest of the family to 'purify' itself by locating the source of its 'disease' in the disease of the *identified patient*. By keeping the focus on one side of its members, the family, personal or congregational, can deny the very issues that contributed to making one of its members symptomatic, even if it ultimately

What better way for the descendants of the king's bookbinder to be compelled to surrender their *pride,* their *honor,* and their *"station in life,"* than for all three of these seeming virtues to be subjected to Vincent's crowning blow to the family's golden heraldry, by "skirting," as he did, all the rules of regal rank and protocol, flagrantly asserting himself to be of "the lowest of the low" with respect to his own and *their* "station in life"? Somewhere down the long line of illustrious ancestry, the parade of dignitaries was bound to stumble all over itself. As has already been said (from the Book of Numbers 14:18), the iniquity of the parents is visited upon the children to the third and the fourth generation. Somewhere, in every spoiled pedigree there can be found at least one common horse thief or one quarrelsome crapshooter who knows exactly how to throw the dice. Vincent qualified for both honors.

Under the circumstances, just what systemic principle might have been at work with respect to the prodigal's return to the veritable "womb" of his Carbentus parentage? Might it have been no less than the furtive principle of incest, merrily at work, at least according to the considered opinion of Dr. Sigmund Freud? Had the goddess's name been Kee Vos, then maybe so. But her actual name was Sien, and she was not the only one of Vincent's numerous night visitors whose means of livelihood represented the singular worldly disgrace that was *more disgraceful* than the sin of incest. Yet, theologically and artistically—since theology and art were the two distinguishing hallmarks—it was happy for Vincent, if not for the rest of the kin, that a little debauchery should take place "in the Owl behind the Town Hall" in the hope of finding a smidgen of grace in an otherwise oppressive and graceless situation. It seemed to Vincent that there was nowhere else much to find it, perhaps least of all in the church. Thus did the "Great Lady of Sorrow" become the "midwife" to Vincent's "second birth."

We do not know precisely what happened "in the beginning of the eighteenth century" to have caused "the social standing of the family" to have become, as the record states, "somewhat lower," economically or otherwise (Memoir, xvii). But we can assume that whatever great misfortune befell the family between the time of Matthias (the physician at

---

harms the entire system" (*Generation to Generation,* 20). It is worth noting that within the larger societal context of the period of time before and during which Vincent lived, the church was highly polarized into ideological camps struggling with one another, not only with respect to basic Christian doctrines, but also over the relationship of the church to the state. Scapegoating was common among all parties to the conflict.

Gouda and clergyman at Boskoop) and the three generations of gold wire-drawers, it was significant enough to have left its mark upon the family folklore. Perhaps it had something to do with what sometimes happens to the children of clergy. They become a little restless with the sufferance of clergy wages and decide instead to go panning for gold. We do know, however, that there is more than one way in which a family may suffer from the ill effects of "prostitution." Sometimes it is due to the fact that Tom, or Dick, or Harry gains a sleazy reputation for having absconded with the family fortune. In other words, the "love of mammon" becomes the "harlot" of prostitution because neither Tom, Dick, nor Harry ever learned the difference between philanthropy and philandering after the "golden goose that laid the golden egg."

Then again, there is another way to interpret the business of prostitution, by asking a simple question: Was Vincent conducting himself in such a way that all might see, flat out in the open, just how some of the aforementioned "gentlemen van Gogh" might have conducted themselves privately and only within the shroud of secrecy? And in that sense, had Vincent become the family scapegoat for unconsciously and involuntarily exposing that "second bleeding cow" that had rather thoughtlessly "bloodied the entire creek"? By making no pretence to keeping his numerous affairs a secret, he did them all a favor by preparing the way for the *"healing of the defect."*—Which is to say: *Truth*, not deception, heals what is ailing. "Man is born broken. He lives by mending. The grace of God is glue."[36]

From where we dwell on "this mortal coil" we cannot know what truths are to be revealed on the far side of "Starry Night." It is quite possible that, by the time the entire world arrives at its celestial destination, all mortal sin shall have been totally and forever forgiven (Gospel of Mark 3:28). In the meantime, memories are long and frayed tempers can be *un*forgiving.

"Father, for instance, said to me at the time, 'There is something immoral in a liaison with a woman of lower station in life'" (CL 290). But what if Vincent's liaison had taken place secretly with a woman of "higher station"? Would that have made it not quite so immoral? Or, would such a "miscreant affair" have been sufficiently rationalized and hushed up so as to permit no light to shine upon such a mortal deed and defect—this side of heaven?

36. Kohut, *Self Psychology*, 169. From Eugene O'Neill's drama, "The Great God Brown." See the prologue to this book.

At one point, Vincent's father went so far as to consider having his prodigal son placed under legal guardianship. "Alas, yes—Father is capable of it—but I tell you, if he dares attempt anything of the sort, I shall fight him to the limit" (CL 204). And, in a sense, that is exactly what Vincent did.

Yet, there is one final consideration regarding all prodigals who for one reason or another get locked up into themselves or locked out of the family. Beneath the shadow of a name there is always more to the story than the name itself conveys.

Whoever would have guessed that a poor prodigal by the name of Vincent van Gogh —"such a nobody," who rarely invested a dime in anything except in his paint, his easel, and a few glorious moments in the "the Owl behind the Town Hall"—would in all his wildest dreams have become associated with the highest price ever paid for a single work of art?[37] Or, for that matter, that a lowly prostitute named "the Great Lady of Sorrow" would have become a saintly sitting model for anyone, except for her children, her mother, herself, her Vincent, and some other stray "dogs" and "cats" that, like Vincent, were hungry for a "home-cooked meal"?

Who knows just what secrets lurked beneath the shadows of *all* those names? Does anyone know now—did anyone know then—other than God—*for certain, and in every respect?*

Theodorus? Anna?

C.M.? Cent? Hein? Jan? Tersteeg?

Theo? Johanna?

Anna? Elizabeth? Willemina? Cor? Kee?

Vincent, Theologian? Willem, Bookbinder to the King?

Vincent, Sculptor and Member of the Cent Suisses?

David, Jan, and Johannes, Gold Wire-Drawers?

Matthias, Physician at Gouda and Clergyman at Moordrecht?

Cornelius, Remonstrant at Boskoop?

Michel, Consul General and Envoy to the King?

Johannes, Magistrate and High Treasurer of the Union?

Jan, Wine and Bookseller "in the Bible under the flax market"?

Jacob (lounging around?) "in the Owl behind the Town Hall?"

---

37. In August 1989, Vincent's "Portrait of Joseph Roulin" sold for a record sum of $58 million, plus the exchange of other works. In May 1990, Vincent's "Portrait of Dr. Gachet" sold for a record sum of $82.5 million.

And, Vincent himself, who said: "That is exactly the fault of the Dutch, to call one thing absolutely good and another absolutely bad. Nothing in the world is as hard and fast as that" (CL 555).

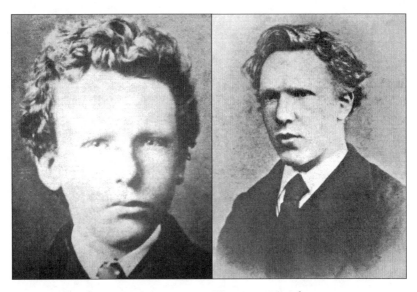

Vincent at age thirteen   Vincent at age eighteen

Vincent's wash drawing of his   Vincent's mother, Anna (Carbentus)
grandfather, Vincent van Gogh   van Gogh

Vincent's father, Theodorus van Gogh   Vincent's brother, Theo van Gogh

Vincent's sister, Anna van Gogh   Vincent's sister, Elizabeth van Gogh

Vincent's sister, Willemina van Gogh   Vincent's brother, Cor van Gogh

Vincent's uncle, Johannes van Gogh   Vincent's uncle, Vincent van Gogh
("Uncle Jan")   ("Uncle Cent")

Vincent's uncle, Cornelius van Gogh ("C. M.")

Johanna van Gogh-Bonger, Theo's wife and Vincent's sister-in-law

FOUR

The Prodigal

"THE LITTLE CULPRIT"

ACCORDING TO HIS SISTER-IN-LAW Johanna, when Vincent was a youngster his Grandmother van Gogh "witnessed one of 'Vincent's naughty fits.'" "She took the little culprit by the arm and, with a sound box on the ears, put him out of the room" (Memoir, xx).[1]

One immediately sees a link between Vincent's problematic childhood when he was perceived to be a "little culprit," and his adult life

---

1. The action on the part of the grandmother, as a means of expressing her frustration and desire to control Vincent, could only have added further to Vincent's already wounded and fragile sense of self, of which his acting out was characteristic. The phrase "Vincent's naughty fits," as quoted by Johanna, presumably was the grandmother's spoken idiom or that of others in the family, giving a clue as to how Vincent's behavior was viewed to be shameful. When Vincent heard the word "naughty" as a description of himself, he would have internalized the criticism as shaming. The more he was shamed, the more he acted out as a counter-defense against further emotional wounding, which served then to feed into the vicious cycle of more shaming followed by more acting out. Repetitive shaming of a child by an adult indicates a deficiency of empathy on the part of the adult within the adult-child dyad, and likely is a repetition of how the adult was treated as a child. The grandmother, who had raised twelve children of her own, was evidently practiced in the application of stern and sometimes humiliating discipline, not hesitating to apply it to Vincent. This may also have been her way of exerting her authority relative to her son and daughter-in-law, thus re-enacting an old family script, serving to triangulate the grandmother between her son and his wife, which actually turned out to be the case when Theodorus became the mediator between Anna and her mother-in-law over this very incident.

when people took his insolence to be that of an eccentric and obstrep-
erous rebel. The Reverend J. Frits Wagener, pastor in the 1990s of the
Zundert congregation in which Vincent grew up as a boy, spoke of him
in an interview.

> The now very old granddaughter of a servant girl of Pastor van
> Gogh and his family at the time has told me of her grandmother,
> a Miss Honcoop, as often speaking about her time as a maid in
> the parsonage; she would always mention that the van Gogh chil-
> dren were sweet and decent, except for one . . . Vincent: he was
> always very troublesome, fond of teasing, and contrary.
>
> On the other side are people who testify to his gentleness, for
> instance, the oldest daughter of Mr. Van Aalst, who was then a
> grocer in Zundert. She has characterized Vincent as kind, oblig-
> ing and sweet. . . . The maid just mentioned as Miss Honcoop,
> called him in the typical dialect of Brabant, ''n orige,' which
> means something like 'the queer one.'"[2]

The appellation would again haunt Vincent in later life. The mu-
nicipal librarian in Arles, a Mr. Serret, had a colleague who observed
that "people did not like to associate with Vincent, as he was always
hanging about in the brothels. I knew him, too. He was my next-door
neighbor, so to speak. Along with other young people I used to poke fun
at this queer painter. Well, we were only children then. His appearance
made a highly comical impression on us. His long smock, his gigantic
hat, the man himself continually stopping and peering at things, excited
our ridicule" (CL 590b).

Reflecting upon the two years the brothers spent together in Paris,
Theo wrote to his wife, approximately a year before Vincent's death:
"Models didn't want to pose for him, he was forbidden to sit and work
in the street & because of his volatile disposition this repeatedly led
to scenes, which upset him *so* much that he became completely unap-
proachable & by the end of it all he'd had more than enough of Paris."

Being rewarded with profuse love for showing kindness and sweet-
ness, on the one hand, or being punished with ridicule for displaying a
volatile disposition, on the other, represents the externalization of an
internal "split" between good and bad "selfobjects" lodged within, which
every child must contend with, to one degree or another, in the course
of developing a predominantly positive or negative sense of self—for the

2. Masheck, *Van Gogh 100*, 198.

sake of which the forces of admiration and shame vie with each other for becoming "king of the hill."

Vincent's personality was no exception. As the oldest child he was expected to be the model child. But as he gradually acquired a more negative view of himself, as mirrored early in his life by parents and others, it was natural that any tendency toward self-deprecation would compete with a desire for self-enhancement in an ongoing struggle to claim a true self, as opposed to living out a false one. As has already been stated, tell a prodigal often enough that he is a prodigal, and he will believe he is a prodigal and act like a prodigal. Or, he will demonstrate that the meaning of "prodigal" is something quite different from how others characterize it. The suppressed parts of the self must assert their rebelliousness sufficiently to demonstrate themselves to be of equal if not greater value than the fawning parts of the self that submit to being humiliated. Predictably, the more the rebel in Vincent rebelled, the louder were the calls for his banishment.

It was said of Vincent that "at the age of eight he once modeled a little clay elephant that drew his parents' attention, but he destroyed it at once when, according to his notion, such a fuss was made about it" (Memoir, xx). It is not known whether his parents praised his clay elephant or disparaged it. He may have destroyed it due to an excessive amount of admiration or over-stimulation, which he could not emotionally tolerate. Or, more probably, his destruction of the elephant resulted from excessive belittling of his youthful artisanship, which he could tolerate far less than extreme admiration. Whether he was feeling overly admired or unduly shamed, either scenario could have induced a sense of disgrace coupled with a pre-existing and reinforced feeling of inadequacy. Given the preponderance of criticism about which he spoke in his letters, he had rarely considered himself worthy of praise at all. Smashing the elephant may have simply demonstrated at an early age the very thing he had come to expect from a parent, grandparent, or governess who was not able to abide his impish attempts to act out a compensatory grandiosity. It was as though he were saying of the elephant: "This is what they do to me, and this is precisely how I feel—*shattered!*"

"The same fate befell a very curious drawing of a cat, which his mother always remembered" (Memoir, xx). Just what could have been so "curious" about Vincent's drawing of the cat is uncertain. His mother may have remembered the incident, as if the cat symbolically represented the particularly ferocious, or, then again, occasionally cute and affectionate expressiveness of her son. Or, the drawing may simply have been an outstanding example of Vincent's precociousness seen as a product of his mother's tutelage, giving her reason to be proud.[3]

With regard to the smashed elephant, the overwrought grandmother's anxious response to her grandson's "naughty fit" would have deflated Vincent's ego, enraged his emotion, and crushed his heart. Most prodigals, in one way or another, have been crushed. Vincent stood in line for his first "crushing"—birth can be traumatic—on that ominous occasion of his own delivery into the world exactly a year to the day after his stillborn brother's sudden disappearance. The nature of Vincent's conscious or unconscious boyhood rumination about the stillbirth remains unknown. It may have been that every anniversary of his birthday became a reminder. As Vincent frequently walked by his brother's grave in the churchyard, one can imagine some of the thoughts that could have run through his curious, youthful mind.[4] It certainly would not be hard to conceive of Vincent's imagining the skeletal remains of his brother lying lifeless beneath the ground. A year's difference in age was little difference at all. A phantom twinship with his still-born sibling may easily have formed within his imagination as he carried on a fantasized conversation with him. Most haunting of all, he may have wondered, many times over, if his brother's premature fatality would some day befall him as well.

There remained a larger question. Did the knowledge of his elder stillborn brother's fate remain a significant subliminal force shaping Vincent's own subsequent "birthings," as well as his pre-mature death? It is impossible to know. We do know that he was preoccupied with thoughts of death, off and on throughout his lifetime. At the far end of the spectrum, in December 1889, but seven months before his suicide, Vincent wrote to his friend Émile Bernard. The subject was Vincent's work and what he should like to accomplish as a painter. He said: "My ambition is limited to a few clods of earth, sprouting wheat, an olive

---

3. Ana-Maria Rizzuto has written about the failure that occurs during the mirroring "when the mother exalts the child" so "that the mirroring reflects not the real child but what she fancies the child to be: that is, she uses the child for her own narcissistic balance. The child, then, is deprived of a more accurate mirroring of himself and deprived, too, of the mother as the mirroring person" (Rizzuto, *The Birth of the Living God*, 187).

4. See Humberto Nagera's discussion and reference to studies concerning theories about the "replacement child" (Nagera, *Vincent van Gogh*, 14).

grove, a cypress—the latter, for instance, by no means easy to do" (CL B21). Such were the objects of his art, but also symbols of the "quarantined" self and the hovering ghosts of death. One of his final paintings, if not in fact his last, was a harvest scene, the picture of a stormy wheat field containing pathways laid down in its midst in the sign of the cross, with ominous, dark midday clouds and a flock of crows hovering from beyond and from above, giving the viewer a sense of staring straight into the eyes and clutches of the grim reaper of death.[5]

So when Vincent, as a youngster, smashed his clay elephant to the floor, the action may have implied his own sense of the diminishment of his nascent self. His shattered self-esteem may have required an act of defiance to rectify appalling feelings associated with the specter of emotional annihilation.[6] For any artist, either young or old, there is the potential for a latent, or not so latent, grandiose exhibitionism to work itself into the art. In instances of extreme narcissism the artist may paint "self-portraits" as though the entire world were being summoned to focus its attention upon the proud or damaged visage of the self.[7] In the same way, a child such as Vincent may have constructed and then immediately laid waste to a great "elephant" that was a symbol and projection of the dimensions of his besieged and struggling self.

Many years after the events of his troubled childhood, Vincent wrote with substantial insight into himself concerning the pivotal Christmas incident of 1881, saying: "I was forced to leave the house. I said that for me this not only brought about considerable financial trouble, but also that it drove me to extremes, and that I was forced into a much more stubborn attitude than I should have adopted of my own free will." As he had said to his father, "*What one thinks one should do*

5. "Wheatfield with Crows," WM, 690–91.

6. Either during a lifetime or at the end of a lifetime, a person whose psychological equilibrium is appreciably off-balance in the direction of self-depreciation (or in the opposite direction of self-inflation) may create an epidemic of narcissistic grandiosities, including overpowering rage (and, in severe cases, atrocities), to assuage a pervasive sense of self-denigration. The result can be sadistic behaviors intended to punish others, or masochistic self-recriminations aimed to rebuke the self for not having lived up to those internal expectations derived from external demands and stipulations. It is as though the admiring gleams of parental approval—so desperately needed yet so sorely deficient (or, alternately, so utterly traumatizing and thoroughly abusive)—have turned inside out, replaced by the laser-beams of parental scorn and displeasure.

7. It is possible to view many of Vincent's self-portraits from this perspective, as though he were depicting multiple renditions of himself lying within himself.

may be diametrically opposed to *what one ought to do*" (CL 345a). He may have also been alluding to himself. For there were two "elephants," each seeking to make space for itself within the same house, and each reacting in extreme to the other. The younger "elephant" felt impelled to walk away licking its wounds, trying its best to hold its head high in order to keep its "big ears" from dragging the ground.

In view of the fact that the ear is the organ through which words of admiration or criticism are received, it is possible to conjecture unconscious motivations. When many years later Vincent sliced off a portion of his ear in response to the extreme criticism and rejection received from the artist Paul Gauguin, Vincent's act of apparent self-destruction or "partial suicide"[8] may have been a way of doubling back upon himself in self-flagellation, reinforcing the inner compulsion for further emotional wounding of himself. (Tell Vincent that he is no good to himself or to anyone else, and he will demonstrate to himself and the entire world that he is in fact no good.) He may have been saying, as it were: I can no longer tolerate hearing such criticism of myself. Thus will I punish the inner critic now deeply embedded within my psyche. And I will do so by "boxing" my ears, in effect, as my grandmother once did, and thus prove to myself and to others just how unworthy I am.

Two days before Christmas 1888 (a symbolically significant date relative to his ostracism on Christmas Day of 1881), having thus severely wounded himself, he presented his bloody earlobe to the prostitute Rachel, who promptly proceeded to faint. By looking immediately to a trusted woman as a source of consolation and nurturance, "he may have been saying subconsciously . . . 'Please hear me! Please accept me!'"[9] Accordingly, in the newspaper account of the incident, Vincent was reputed to have asked Rachel to "guard this object carefully."[10] That "object" was a stand-in for Vincent's very self. The tragedy behind the tragedy lay in the fact that "the maternal and paternal selfobjects lodged within the core of his being were apparently too weak, or too overbearing [more likely the latter], for Vincent to be able to employ them successfully in his own best interest."[11] This was not unlike the day he placed his fingers in the flame to draw attention to his quest for someone—someone

8. See discussion in Arnold, *Vincent van Gogh*, 245–55.

9. Davidson, "Vincent van Gogh," 254.

10. Arnold, *Vincent van Gogh*, 247.

11. Davidson, "Vincent van Gogh," 255.

like the beautiful, tender, motherly cousin Kee—to love him. "The soul is a mirror before it becomes a home."[12] In the process of becoming a home, many visages appear in the mirror, including the "mother-father-brother-sister-cousin-self," and even the image of a stampeding elephant or a squeamish cat.

In contrast to the "little clay elephant," the cat that Vincent's mother so vividly remembered may have had a slightly different role to play in Vincent's psyche. But first the proverbial cat must take into account the proverbial "dog." Recall again the fateful Christmas of 1881, when Vincent shared with Theo his extreme anguish.

> I feel what Father and Mother think of me *instinctively* (I do not say *intelligently*). They feel the same dread of taking me in the house as they would about taking a big rough dog. He would run into the room with wet paws—and he is so rough. He will be in everybody's way. *And he barks so loud.* In short, he is a foul beast.
>
> All right—but the beast has a human history, and though only a dog, he has a human soul, and even a very sensitive one, that makes him feel what people think of him, which an ordinary dog cannot do.
>
> And I, admitting that I am a kind of dog, leave them alone.
>
> Also this house is too good for me, and Father and Mother and the family are so terribly genteel (not sensitive underneath, however), and—and—and they are clergymen—a lot of clergymen.
>
> The dog feels that if they keep him, it will only mean putting up with him and tolerating him "*in this house*," so he will try to find another kennel. The dog is in fact Father's son, and has been left rather too much in the streets, where he could not but become rougher and rougher; but as Father already forgot this years ago, and in reality has never meditated *deeply* on the meaning of the tie between father and son, one need not mention that.
>
> And then—the dog might bite—he might become rabid, and the constable would have to come shoot him.
>
> Yes, all this is very true.

12. As quoted by Vincent from Alphonse de Lamartine's 1859 biography of Oliver Cromwell.

> On the other hand, dogs are guardians.
>
> But that is superfluous, there is peace, and there is no question of any danger, they say. So I keep silent about it.
>
> The dog is only sorry that he did not stay away, for it was less lonely on the heath than in this house, notwithstanding all the kindness. The dog's visit was a weakness, which I hope will be forgotten, and which he will avoid committing in the future. (CL 346)
>
> In character I am rather different from the various members of the family, and essentially I am *not* a "Van Gogh." (CL 345)

If Vincent was not a van Gogh, then who was he, besides a lonely and abandoned dog? There is a powerful sense in which he would need to draw pictures to find out. So, what if one of those pictures at the age of eight should happen to have been of a cat, the one that his mother remembered? A cat could simply be a cat. Or, if the elephant had been the "father" within the son, then the cat could signify the son's unconscious longing for connection with a depressed and emotionally unavailable mother (cat). As it were: "Here, look at me, Mother Cat! I am this little kitten for you to love! I should become the 'mirror' of your affection!" Then, too, the cat could have been a mirror in which the mother could see herself.

Marion Woodman wrote:

> Many people can listen to their cat more intelligently than they can listen to their own despised body. Because they attend to their pet in a cherishing way, it returns their love. Their body, however, may have to let out an earth-shattering scream in order to be heard at all. Before symptoms manifest, quieter screams appear in dreams: a forsaken baby elephant, a starving kitten, a dog with a leg ripped out. Almost always the wounded animal is either gently or fiercely attempting to attract the attention of the dreamer, who may or may not respond. In fairytales it is the friendly animal who often carries the hero or heroine to the goal because the animal is the instinct that knows how to obey the Goddess when reason fails.
>
> It is possible that the scream that comes from the forsaken body, the scream that manifests in a symptom, is the cry of the soul that can find no other way to be heard. If we have lived behind a mask all our lives, sooner or later—if we are lucky—that mask will be smashed. Then we will have to look in our own mirror at our own reality. Perhaps we will be appalled. Perhaps we

will look into the terrified eyes of our own tiny child, that child
who has never known love and who now beseeches us to respond.
This child is alone, forsaken before we left the womb, or at birth,
or when we began to please our parents and learned to put on our
best performance in order to be accepted. As life progresses, we
may continue to abandon our child by pleasing others—teachers,
professors, bosses, friends and partners, even analysts. That child
who is our very *soul* cries out from underneath the rubble of our
lives, often from the core of our worst complex, begging us to say,
"You are not alone. I love you."[13]

So, in view of the fact that Vincent was an unreconstructed prodigal and
a downright "dog" in the house, he had a chance as an elephant-maker
and cat-creator, as well as a sophisticated artist, to redeem his stance
before the mirror of self-respect—"especially as in my case I am not an
adventurer by choice but by fate, and feeling nowhere so much myself a
stranger as in my family and country" (CL 459a).

To reclaim himself, and thus free that part of himself that was severely suppressed due to harsh and unempathic parenting, he essentially
recast himself *as the prodigal* at the entrance to his mother's "womb"
in The Hague, and in a multitude of "similar" places. By doing so he
upended a "two-story" cultural universe in which he made no claim to
the upper level. He "leveled" his entire world and that of his parents
and ancestors into a horizontal plane where no one could remove the
privilege of his being exactly the person he was destined to become, and
where their pretension, of being more than *they* actually were, was laid
bare. It was reminiscent of Jesus engaging the scribes and Pharisees to
tell them that they were "whitewashed tombs, which on the outside look
beautiful, but inside they are full of the bones of the dead and of all
kinds of filth."[14] "You people do not understand me," Vincent said, "and
I am afraid you *never* will" (CL 346). So with his tongue only partially in
cheek, he declared: "I have found myself—I am that dog."

> This may seem exaggerated . . . but I will not take it back. Without
> being personal, just for the sake of an impartial character study,
> as if I did not speak about you [Theo] and me but about strang-
> ers, for the sake of analysis, I point out to you once more how it
> was last summer. I see two brothers walking about in The Hague
> (*see them as strangers*, do no think of yourself and me).

13. Woodman, *The Pregnant Virgin*, 25.
14. Matthew 23:27.

One says, "I am getting to be like a dog, I feel that the future will probably make me more ugly and rough, and I foresee that 'a certain *poverty*' will be my fate, but, but, *I shall be a painter*."

So the one [Theo]—a certain standing as an art dealer.

The other [Vincent]—poverty and painter.

I tell you, I consciously choose *the dog's path through life*; I will remain a *dog*, I shall be *poor*, I shall be a *painter*, I want to *remain human*—going *into* nature. In my opinion the man who goes *out of* nature, whose head is always stuffed with thoughts of maintaining this and maintaining that, even if this causes him to go out of nature to such an extent that he cannot but acknowledge it—oh— in this way one is apt to arrive at a point where one can no longer distinguish white from black—and—and one becomes the exact opposite of what one is considered and what one thinks oneself to be. For instance—at present you have a manly fear of mediocrity in the unfavorable sense of the word—why then are you going to kill, to extinguish, what is best in your soul? (CL 347)

Dare it be said that the working-through of infancy is a life-long project. For Vincent it took the greatest leap forward the day the "dog" was shooed away from the house ("this house is too good for me"). Rebirth—conversion—required an un-doing. As Marion Woodman said: "The possibility of rebirth constellates with the breakdown of what has gone before."[15]

"I cannot repeat to you often enough, boy," Vincent said, "that when one is thirty, one is just *beginning*. Look at the biographies of art-ists, even many who had painted from their earliest years changed only then, found their own personality only then" (CL 339). In his last letter to his mother, composed weeks before his death, he bore her the follow-ing message: "Dear Mother . . . Painting is something in itself. Last year I read in some book or other that writing a book or painting a picture was like having a child. This I will not accept as applicable to me—I have always thought that the latter was the more natural and the best—so I say, only *if* it were so, only *if* it were the same. This is the very reason why at times I exert myself to the utmost, though it happens to be this very work that is least understood, and for me it is the only link between the past and the present" (CL 641a). Vincent may just as well have been say-ing to her: "Dear Mother . . . I beg of you finally to see that I am yours, if

15. Woodman, *The Pregnant Virgin*, 24.

only through nothing more than the image of a single smashed elephant or a broken cat, or, for that matter, a desecrated dog"—*and now through these finely painted pictures*—as though he were repeating the words of the crucified Jesus looking upon his mother and the beloved disciple John, saying: "Woman, behold thy son!"[16]

To stare into the face of Vincent's "mother Mary" in his painting of the "Pietà" is to see her as detached in her grief, hovering above Vincent's own anguished soul depicted in the face of the mortal Jesus.[17] In that respect Anna was akin to "Rachel . . . weeping for her children,"[18] for all the lost children who *were* her world. And it was a world that included the "lost child" within Anna, who in a sternly Calvinistic, hierarchical, and patriarchal culture never managed fully to become her own woman. Sadly, Anna outlived all four of her sons, including the first Vincent, the "stillborn," and the second Vincent, who in a real sense was birthed to her as an "illborn."

In a letter that Vincent sent to Wil, the sister closest to him, he included a poem about which he said: "Whistler painted a picture of his mother which is like that [poem]. But we find this especially in our old Dutch pictures now and then. When I think of Mother it seems to me she is like that too" (CL W18).

Who is the maid my spirit seeks
Through cold reproof and slanders blight?
Has she love's roses on her cheek
Is hers an eye of calm delight?
No, wan and sunk with midnight prayer
Are the pale looks of her I love,
And if by times a light be there
That light was kindled from above.
I choose not her mine heart's elect
Amongst those that seek their maker's shrine

16. John 19:26, KJV. The Jesuit psychoanalyst W. W. Meissner sees in Vincent's painting of "The Raising of Lazarus" (WM, 626) "the angelic figure welcoming Lazarus from the grave and back to life" to be the same "woman who had stood for Vincent's mother" in Vincent's "La Berceuse" (Walther and Metzger, ibid., 481–83). Meissner concludes: "It was only through the Christlike torments of suffering and death that one could achieve the blessings of resurrection and loving acceptance from his mother—something that he had endlessly sought and always been denied" (Meissner, *Vincent's Religion*, 157–58).

17. "Pietà" (after Delacroix), WM, 542.

18. Jeremiah 31:15b

> In gems and garlands proudly decked
> As if themselves were things divine.
> No, heaven but faintly warms the breast
> That beats beneath a broidered veil,
> And they who come in glittering dress
> To mourn their frailty—yet are frail.
> Not so the form of her I love,
> And love because her bloom is gone,
> But ne'er was beauty's bloom so bright,
> So touching as that form's decay,
> That in the altar's wavering light
> In holy lustre fades away.[19] (CL W18)

Vincent had long before cried out: "I should like to be with a woman. I cannot live without love, without a woman. I would not value life at all, if there were not something infinite, something deep, something real" (CL 164). But despite suffering from shame, humiliation, and defeat, let alone from any deficiency of character within himself, or what may have been lacking of his mother's and father's actual or perceived love, he gave birth nonetheless to his art. And to that end he found himself a woman to become if not his wife then at least his permanent mistress.

"DAME NATURE"

"Now, in my opinion there are two kinds of mistresses. There is the kind whom you may love and be loved by, all the time being aware that on one side or on both it is nothing permanent, and that you do not surrender yourself completely, unconditionally and without reservation. . . . The mistresses of the second kind are of an entirely different variety. Collets montés [stiff collars]—female Pharisees—female Jesuits!!! These are women of marble—sphinx-like—frozen vipers—who would like to fetter me completely, once and for all, however, without on their part surrendering themselves unconditionally and without reservation. They are bloodsuckers, these mistresses, they freeze men and petrify them." Vincent compared them to the "academy." So, what a person must do, he said, is to "fall desperately in love with your real sweetheart: Dame Nature or Reality."

---

19. The author was the Irish poet, Thomas Moore (1779–1852).

Portrait of the Artist's Mother

"I fell in love the same way too—desperately, I tell you—with a certain Dame Nature or Reality, and I have felt so happy ever since, though she is still resisting me cruelly, and does not want me yet, and often raps me over the knuckles when I dare prematurely to consider her mine. Consequently I cannot say that I have won her by a long shot, but what I *can* say is that I am wooing her, and that I am trying to find the key to her heart, notwithstanding the painful raps on the knuckles" (CL R4).

Vincent had lived in lonesome solitude for as long as he could remember. His was the disposition of a monk who only occasionally went to a meeting of the order. "If it were not that I have almost a double nature, that of a monk and that of a painter, as it were, I should have been reduced, and that long ago, completely and utterly, to the aforesaid condition" (CL 556). While living in Dordrecht as an assistant at the Blussé and Van Braam bookshop, he had lamented: "I . . . am sometimes lonely and sad, especially when I am near a church or parsonage" (CL 88). Like St. Francis of Assisi conversing with the birds, Vincent found nature to be a more comforting sanctuary. For there he made friends with sprouting trees and budding flowers, with waves breaking upon the sea, with the heath spread out before him like a royal carpet, with the heavens hovering securely above, and with the sporadic pilgrim crossing his path to whom he occasionally gave a passing nod.

The visual world of art—*the world as art*—was his constant companion. Singing birds, croaking frogs, purring cats, and barking dogs added the dimension of music to his art. At one point he even sought to take piano lessons. Anton Kerssemakers, an artist who befriended Vincent in Nuenen, reminisced:

> In those days he was starving like a true Bohemian, and more than once it happened that he did not see meat (for the purpose of eating) for six weeks on end, always just dry bread with a chunk of cheese. . . . On the other hand he liked to have some brandy in his flask on his rambles, and he would not have liked to do without it; but as far as I know this was the only luxury he permitted himself. . . . He was always drawing comparisons between the art of painting and music, and in order to get an even better understanding of the values and the various nuances of the tones, he started taking piano lessons with an old music teacher who was at the same time an organist in Eindhoven. This, however, did not last long, for seeing that during the lessons Van Gogh was continually comparing the notes of the piano with Prussian blue and dark green and dark ocher, and so on, all the way to bright cadmium-yellow, the good man thought that he had to do with a madman, in consequence of which he became so afraid of him that he discontinued the lessons. (CL 435c)

Piano lessons aside, Vincent voiced a singularly profound truth, among his many profundities concerning the subject of art: "How rich art is; if one can only remember what one has seen, one is never without food for thought or truly lonely, never alone" (CL 126). For him, nature was at once the object of his love and the one "personification" that more than any other lover had loved him in return.[20] Despite the fact that

---

20. Couched in the language of Self Psychology, nature itself can be said to have served as a powerful selfobject that mirrored the ambitions and reflected the ideals of

painting was a solitary enterprise, as well as "like having a bad mistress who spends and spends and it's never enough" (CL 502), he made a point to say that "I prefer painting people's eyes to cathedrals, for there is something in the eyes that is not in the cathedral, however solemn and imposing the latter may be—a human soul, be it that of a poor beggar or of a streetwalker, is more interesting to me" (CL 441). The latter, like the sun or stars, was Vincent's most engaging conversation partner.

There were many "altars" at which he worshipped in nature's sanctuary. Among them was the leafy twig from which the lark's eye gazed godlike over the sweeping manifold of life, as well as the single blade of grass bending penitently in the wind like a hushed hermit praying at Compline beneath the setting sun's fading rays. Such altars of mystery were incomparably beautiful and frightfully elusive. In their own right these miracles were best understood when witnessed through the clarifying lens of a painter's mystic eye. For these, too, were among the great antiphony of saints. "*Omnes ergo in unum positi compleant*"—"All having assembled in one place, let them say Compline"[21]—until the night shall rest in silence.

Subsequent to painting the "Night Café,"[22] Vincent wrote to Theo of his "terrible need of—shall I say the word?—religion. Then I go out at night to paint the stars, and I am always dreaming of a picture like this with a group of living figures of our comrades" (CL 543). To van Rappard, he demurred: "We shall never be justified in secretly concealing the ideal and all that approaches the eternal, as if all that were none of our business" (CL R34). The same had been true when Vincent's eyes had encountered Sien's eyes—like four planets rising to greet one another on a rainy day from behind their veils of dense cloud—with the fog of self-doubt, self-reproach, and self-invisibility coating their pupils like thick cataracts. The search for the eternal made even such delicate attempts at mutual admiration seem a necessary exercise in myopia.

For Vincent, painting the human eye was an act of opening nature's grandest cathedral door, a luminary through which to enter the inner

---

Vincent's inner self. His self-selfobject relationship with nature offered a displacement as well as a replacement for the one with his parents and others. While nature at times is cruel, it is also calming and soothing for the soul, like a nurturing mother—thus, the conflicting aspects of "Dame Nature."

21. From The Holy Rule of St. Benedict, chapter 42.

22. See WM, 427–28.

sanctum of the holiest of holies. So when someone like himself, considered *persona non grata*, caught sight of a poor beggar's or streetwalker's eyes, there was every likelihood of his detecting far more than what others, from a more elevated position, could see within such caverns of misery. Yet when it came to painting the visage of Christ, he said: "I have scraped off a big painted study, an olive garden, with a figure of Christ in blue and orange, and an angel in yellow." For, on second thought, "I scraped it off because I tell myself that I must not do figures of that importance without [the living] models" (CL 505).

Vincent's father and mother, as living models, had done the best they knew how. With their own peculiarities, and those of extended family, culture, and church embracing a Dutch Reformed conception of God that focused overly upon the *frown* upon God's face, there was every good reason for Vincent not to paint stone cathedrals but to prefer instead those that were composed of flesh and blood.[23]

Kee Vos, at one time, but never so long ago as to be completely forgotten, had offered high hope and a certain promise for genuine certification of Vincent's pedigree. Kee was of his mother's breed. But she also represented the potential for *not* being the leveler of a two-story hereditary universe. Despite the fact that raised eyebrows cried "incest," it is true that she could have enhanced Vincent's fastly deteriorating social standing. But he never would have dressed the part. For one thing, he was an incurable dissident. For another, Kee belonged to the "right" order of the king's royal bookbinder, though not in the same sense that Vincent was "bound" to his books. For any number of reasons, she would have been a fool to marry him, and not least because of *her* elevated "station in life." Had she done so, it would have appeared as though the royal princess had wed the palace dog.

Consequently, Vincent had little recourse but to remain bound to his books, his pictures, and his fleeting acquaintances with prostitutes. The latter, it appeared, offered greater opportunity to wrest his world from the gods and goddesses of cultural affectation. Stripped of such

23. J. Grotstein set forth the concept of "the background selfobject of primary identification." He said, "There is a considerable difference phenomenologically between background objects and interpersonal objects which are impressed into service as selfobjects. The concept of selfobject, I strongly maintain, transcends far more than just simply the mother or father. It includes tradition, heredity, the mother country, the neighborhood, etc." (Lee and Martin, *Psychotherapy after Kohut: A Textbook of Self Psychology*, 173).

exaggeration, the elemental goodness and beauty of Dame Nature could prevail upon his portraits and landscapes, notwithstanding the paths of destruction that she sometimes left in the wake of her sudden tempests. "You see there is a blond, tender effect in the sketch of the dunes, and in the wood there is a more gloomy, serious tone. I am glad both exist in life" (CL 228). For Vincent, these were the basic hues from which all of life's "colors" were derived, irrespective of who wore them or what price happened to be paid, or legacy conveyed, to acquire them. Vincent knew how to catch both the "tender effect" and the "serious tone" with his brush. Sorrow and joy adhered as much in the eyes of the beheld as in the eyes of the beholder, regardless of whose eyes they were. At the end of the day, when a two-story cultural universe would once and for all collapse into one story, there would be no further need for distinction between those, on the one hand, who possess the "tender effect" and those, on the other, the "gloomy tone." In the meantime, the aspect of some appears to be more like the dunes, and others more like the wood.

At the relatively exuberant age of twenty-two, an air of adventure had attached itself to the ideal of his father's vocation. The strictures of his religious upbringing and the fear of dangers inherent in worldly literature had been instilled in him enough to pass along some judicious advice from an older to a younger brother. He asked: "Have you done as I suggested and destroyed your books by Michelet, Renan, etc.? I think that will give you rest." Then he quickly added: "I am sure you will never forget that page out of Michelet about the 'Portrait of a Lady' by Ph. de Champaigne, and do not forget Renan either; but destroy them all the same. 'If thou hast found honey look to it that thou eatest not too much of it, that it may not become loathsome,' is written in the Proverbs, or something like this'" [24] (CL 42).

Only two years *before*, at age twenty, Vincent had written to Theo: "Not everybody is capable of perceiving the good and the beautiful as keenly as you do. And now . . . I enclose another picture of autumn, this one by Michelet."

> From here I see a lady, I see her walk pensively in a not very large
> garden, bereft of its flowers early in the season, but sheltered, as

24. Proverbs 25:16. "Hast thou found honey? Eat so much as is sufficient for thee, lest thou be filled therewith, and vomit it" (KJV).

you see them behind our cliffs in France or the dunes of Holland. The exotic shrubs have already been put back into the conservatory. The fallen leaves reveal a number of statues. An artistic luxury which contrasts a little with the lady's very simply, modest, dignified dress, of which the black (or gray) silk is almost imperceptibly brightened by a lilac-ribbon.

But have I seen her already in the museums of Amsterdam or The Hague? She reminds me of a lady by Philippe de Champagne (. . . in the Louvre), who took my heart, so candid, so honest, sufficiently intelligent, yet simple, without the cunning to extricate herself from the ruses of the world. This woman has remained in my mind for thirty years, persistently coming back to me, making me say, "But what was she called? What has happened to her? Has she known some happiness? And how has she overcome the difficulties of the world?"[25] (CL 11)

By the end of his life, these were among some of the great questions that had haunted Vincent all along, not to mention the "Portrait of a Lady" whose actual name could have been any woman with whom he happened to fall in love. These included "Dame Nature" posing as Eugenie, Kee, Sien, Margot, Rachel, or even his mother Anna, when she was the object of his empathy more than the subject of his regret.

Dame Nature—"so candid," "honest," "intelligent, yet simple, without the cunning to extricate herself from the ruses of the world"—she wore many faces that could steal Vincent's heart. Any ruse discovered within himself would be taken to heart only from the clarifying distance of hindsight, many, many miles from home.

REVERIE

A prodigal's "way home"[26] remains steep, winding, and arduous.[27] Some days it is downright treacherous. "On the road walks a pilgrim, staff in hand. He has been walking for a good long while."[28] A "narrow path"[29] beckons him through "wheat field, olive grove, and tall-standing

25. A quotation from Jules Michelet's *Les aspirations de l'automne*.
26. "The Sower," WM, 434.
27. "Thatched Cottages in Jorgus," WM, 646.
28. Vincent's sermon (CL I, 91).
29. "Flowering Garden with Path," WM, 383.

"The Painter on His Way to Work"

cypress."[30] Not far from a faintly drooping "sunflower"[31] he passes a "peasant digging"[32] for buried treasure. He rounds a wayside "quarry"[33] where insiders bypass "an outsider" fallen into the hands of ravenous thieves, lifted up from destitution by yet another outsider whom the insiders accuse of having "fallen" by other means.[34]

30. "Wheat Stacks with Reaper," WM, 370–71; "Olive Picking," WM, 594–95; "Road with Cypress and Star," WM, 632.

31. "Two Cut Sunflowers," WM, 281.

32. "Man Digging," WM, 12.

33. "Entrance to a Quarry," WM, 529.

34. "The Good Samaritan," WM, 627.

The prodigal summons "fearful and timid hearts"[35] to "waiting fishing boats"[36] beached along the "threatening sea."[37] Bearing his own burden of "Sorrow"[38] in likeness to a broken-winged "sparrow"[39] fluttering and quivering in an unfriendly field, the "sufferer"[40] inches on, step by step. He scales the "hills."[41] He huffs and puffs and falters, upward, downward, sideways, then slips in the "rain."[42] He breaks his forward stride in order to contemplate a goldfinch's "nest"[43] perched within the forked green shoots of a budding "Mulberry tree."[44] The "eggs,"[45] all but a few, have hatched, and there is little sign of "life past"[46] except for the lice and ants foraging for the stale "leftovers."[47]

The prodigal, weary from the day's work, lies down on the ground to catch his breath, turns about, leans back, and stretches himself out against a high, golden haystack. He kicks his shoes from his feet, covers his face with his straw hat, and raises his arms and folds them behind his head. As he falls asleep, his anxious thoughts are carried away like a sack full of troubles into a "still life"[48] dream.

> Now as for me, I am doing very well down here, but it is because I have my work here, and nature, and if I didn't have that, I should grow melancholy. . . . For loneliness, worries, difficulties, the unsatisfied need for kindness and sympathy—that is what is hard to bear, the mental suffering of sadness, or disappointment

35. "The Schoolboy (Camille Roulin)," WM, 458; "Portrait of Armand Roulin," WM, 459.

36. "Fishing Boats on the Beach at Saintes-Maries," WM, 355.

37. "Seascape at Saintes-Maries," WM, 353.

38. "Self-Portrait with Bandaged Ear and Pipe," WM, 478; "Drawing of Sien as 'Sorrow,'" (CL 244).

39. "Studies of a Dead Sparrow," January-February 1885 (Brooks, # F1360v, JH 0621).

40. "Self-Portrait" while at the asylum in St. Rémy, WM, 536.

41. "Two Poplars on a Road through the Hills," WM, 557.

42. "Wheat Field in Rain," WM, 572.

43. "Still Life with Five Birds' Nests," WM, 127.

44. "The Mulberry Tree," WM, 556.

45. "Still Life with Three Birds' Nests," WM, 127.

46. "Avenue of Poplars in Nuenen," WM, 51; "Chapel at Nuenen with Churchgoers," WM, 53; "The Parsonage at Nuenen," WM, 129.

47. "Still Life with Clogs and Pots," WM, 63.

48. "Noon: Rest from Work," WM, 610–11.

undermines us more than dissipation—us, I say, who find ourselves the happy possessors of disordered hearts. (CL 489)

My own adventures are restricted chiefly to making swift progress
toward growing into a little old man, you know, with wrinkles,
and a tough beard and a number of false teeth, and so on. But
what does it matter? I have a dirty and hard profession—painting—and if I were not what I am, I should not paint; but being
what I am, I often work with pleasure, and in the hazy distance I
see the possibility of making pictures in which there will be some
youth and freshness, even though my own youth is one of the
things I have lost. (CL W1)

And I think that *if* we knew all, we might attain a certain serenity. Having as much of this serenity as possible, even though one
knows little—nothing—for certain, is perhaps a better remedy
for all diseases than all the things that are sold in the chemists'
shops. Much comes of its own accord; one grows and develops of
one's own accord. So do not study and grind away too much, it
makes one sterile; amuse yourself too much rather than too little,
and do not take art and love too seriously. One can do so very
little about it oneself; it is mainly a question of temperament. If I
were living in your vicinity I should try to make you understand
that it would perhaps be more practical for you to paint along
with me than to write, and that in this way you might sooner
attain the ability to express your feelings. At any rate, I can do
something about painting personally; but as for writing, I do not
belong to the profession. Otherwise that idea of yours of becoming an artist is not so bad, for if one has fire within oneself and
a soul, they cannot be hidden under a bushel, and—one prefers
being scorched to being suffocated. Because what one has within
oneself 'will out'; for me, for instance, it is a relief to paint a picture, and without it I should be more miserable than I am.

Sometimes art seems to be something very sublime, and, as you
say, something sacred. But this is also the case with love. And
the crux of the question is that not everybody thinks about it in
this way, and that those who feel something of it, and let themselves be carried away by it, have to suffer so much—in the first
place on account of not being understood, and quite as much
because so often our inspiration is inadequate, or work is made
impossible by circumstances. Besides there are times when it is
far from clear to us that art should be something holy or good.
For that matter, just think whether it would not be better to say
that, if one has a feeling for art and seeks to work at it, one does

this only because one is born with this feeling, and cannot help oneself, and follows one's nature—rather than to say that one does it for a good purpose. Isn't it written in *A la rechereche du bonheur* [the quest for happiness][49] that evil lies in our own nature—which we have not created ourselves? I think it such a fine thing about the moderns that they do not moralize like the old ones. Many people think it outrageous, and are scandalized, for instance, when they hear, Vice and virtue are chemical products like sugar and vitriol. (CL W1)

I *do not know* myself how I paint it. I sit down with a white board before the spot that strikes me,[50] I look at what is before my eyes, I say to myself, That white board must become something; I come back dissatisfied—I put it away, and when I have rested a little, I go and look at it with a kind of fear. Then I am still dissatisfied, because I still have that splendid scene too clearly in my mind to be satisfied with what I made of it. But I find in my work an echo of what struck, after all. I see that nature has told me something, has spoken to me, and that I have put it down in shorthand. In my shorthand there may be words that cannot be deciphered, there may be mistakes or gaps; but there is something of what wood or beach or figure has told me in it, and it is not the tame or conventional language derived from a studied manner or a system rather than from nature itself.[51] (CL 228)

I almost think that these canvases will tell you what I cannot say in words. (CL 649)

49. The name of a collection of stories by the Russian author, Leo Tolstoy, published in 1886.

50. "Self-Portrait in Front of the Easel," WM, 2, 298.

51. Robert Kegan wrote: "Not only does an understanding of 'natural therapy'— those relations and human contexts which spontaneously support people through the sometimes difficult process of growth and change—offer 'preventive psychology' a sophisticated way to consider a person's supports, it offers a new guide to therapeutic practice by exposing some of the details of those interactions which it is quite possible successful therapy is replicating, whether it knows it or not. From research on the outcomes of psychotherapy we have good reason for believing the success of therapy is not a function of the particular personality theory or identifiable therapeutic approach favored by the therapist. . . . [Rather,] since therapeutic processes are rooted not in theory but in nature, it was a mistake to use theories (and the approaches theories give rise to) as the hoped-for determiner of outcomes in the first place. Would it not have made more sense to try to understand how a therapeutic process works—all on its own, without the presence of professionals—and then evaluate which professions were able in some way to foster or replicate these processes?" (Kegan, *Evolving Self*, 256).

Awakened, with the pulsing heat of the summer sun pressing against his face, its intensity suddenly interrupted by a spritely song in the air, the pilgrim inquisitively attunes his ear to the call of the "Kingfisher."[52] Only minutes later does he become aware of a pounding disturbance spinning about in his forehead, which he caresses within the cup of his hands. He ponders:

> I have had in all four great crises, during which I didn't in the least know what I said, what I wanted and what I did. Not taking into account that I had previously had three fainting fits without any plausible reasons, and without retaining the slightest remembrance of what I felt.
>
> I am unable to describe exactly what is the matter with me; now and then there are horrible fits of anxiety, apparently without cause, or otherwise a feeling of emptiness and fatigue in the head. I look upon the whole thing as a simple accident. There can be no doubt that much of this is my own fault, and at times I have attacks of melancholy and of atrocious remorse; but you know, the fact is, that when all this discourages me and gives me spleen, I am not exactly ashamed to tell myself that the remorse and all the other things that are wrong might possibly be caused by microbes too, like love. (CL W11)

He stares down upon the wrinkles, creases, and abrasions in his "shoes." His "leathers," like his life, are frayed, worn, and profligate. His "strings are loose."[53] He shields his "eyes"[54] against the rays of the sweltering "sun."[55] "Thinking of this, but far away, I feel the desire to renew myself, and to try to apologize for the fact that my pictures are after all almost a cry of anguish, although in the rustic sunflower[56] they may symbolize gratitude" (CL W20).

He rises to his feet, secures his stance, then settles, taking his seat on the stool before the easel. His fingers take hold of his brush, with his elbow at his palette of oils and his eyes surveying the canvas."[57] Continuing to paint, he turns briefly toward an echo from the forest[58] and catches

52. "The Kingfisher," WM, 199.
53. "A Pair of Shoes," WM, 183.
54. "Self-Portraits," WM, 6, 262–71, 396–98, 534–37.
55. "Olive Trees with Yellow Sky and Sun," WM, 574.
56. "Two Cut Sunflowers," WM, 281.
57. "Self Portrait with Dark Felt Hat at the Easel," WM, 150.
58. "Trees and Undergrowth," WM, 277.

the hiss of the "cicada"[59] as it bemoans the fever of the noon hour heat constricting the flow of the midsummer air. By late afternoon as a thunderstorm brews[60] and the wind waggles his canvas, the prodigal abruptly seizes the brim of his hat to swat with all his might in the direction of an unwelcome intruder, as he argues vociferously with the bumblebee.

With thunder swelling like the drum-roll of a distant army approaching, Vincent notices that a delicate yellow "butterfly,"[61] having burst its moribund chrysalis, passes along a broad bed of orange "poppies," hovering for a split second, then descending upon the pistil and stamen in search of sweet nectar.

The artist draws his breath, fills his lungs, and releases pent-up tension as the refreshing breeze rakes against his stubbly "beard"[62] and flushes his furrowed "brow."[63] With a piercing gaze he glances across the "river"[64] and along its bank, long enough to obtain his perspective. He then lifts his brush and dips its tip into bright yellow pigment.

The storm soon passes without spilling its rain, and the minutes turn into hours as the day wears long and wanes. His stomach growls from emptiness, and the pilgrim asks of himself: What shall come of tomorrow's foraging of nature? Will yet another "mammoth bolder,"[65]—the ruins, say, of a church, one of the earth's many dry bones teetering on the "pinnacle of the big rock,"[66]—provide sustenance for this artisan who in his own "earthy" way still searches for God? Or, will the artist's eye converge upon that wee poking "blade of grass,"[67] the tiniest, most glorious of all slender creatures, so delicate yet so common in the ordinary as to be hardly noticed—and dare to believe even when bent in the wind as penitently as the monk is desolate in prayer that this blade of grass is capable of feeding a poor person's soul?

"What life I think best, oh, without the least shadow of a doubt it is a life consisting of long years of intercourse with nature in the

59. "Three Cicadas," 6 June 1889 (Brooks, # F1445, JH 1765).

60. "Landscape under a Stormy Sky," WM, 338.

61. "Poppies and Butterflies," WM, 622.

62. "Self-Portrait," WM, 534.

63. "Self-Portrait" (CL I, Frontispiece).

64. "The Banks of the Seine," WM, 245.

65. "The Old Cemetery Tower at Nuenen," WM, 102.

66. "Rocks with Oak Trees," WM, 377.

67. "Clumps of Grass," WM, 492.

country—and Something on High—inconceivable, 'awfully unnamable'—for it is impossible to find a name for that which is higher than nature" (CL 339a).

Even so—night is fast approaching and the sun is setting. And "Dame Nature" remains headstrong[68] and recalcitrant,[69] like the "beetle on the rose petal"[70] or the "the mistral" on the "heath."[71] The cry of a single, solitary reed of grass would make itself audible if it could, alongside the palpable sobbing of a lovely woman saturated in dark blue lament.[72] Both are aching to be heard above the clapping "storm"[73] of life rumbling into the distance. And the artist who for the moment stands still before his easel is the only person, short of God knows who in heaven itself, to be witnessing these weepings.

Should he, therefore, construe Dame Nature in all her moods to possess far more brave beauty in the face of adversity than all her fears and miseries combined could possibly steal from her? And how would he do that? How would he speak to those who someday may stumble upon his dry-rotted pigment—watching, as if there were something "higher than nature" to see—without his having to scribble its name in the corner of the canvas, which would say about as much of "God" as the scribble itself? When words have failed, how does an artist give, not a voice, but a *face* to the unnamable?

"Nature always begins by resisting the artist, but he who really takes it seriously does not allow that resistance to put him off his stride; on the contrary, it is that much more of a stimulus to fight for victory, and at bottom nature and a true artist agree" (CL 152).

For here is what the artist is granted to see: The sturdy "crocus,"[74] the amiable "sunflower,"[75] and the radiant "almond blossom"[76] desperately desire to be painted in their entire splendor in a world conditioned to

68. "Self-Portrait," WM, 262.
69. "Landscape under a Stormy Sky," WM, 338.
70. "Roses and Beetle," WM, 622.
71. "The Heath with a Wheelbarrow," WM, 28.
72. "Woman Sitting in the Grass," WM, 228.
73. "Wheat Field under Clouded Sky," WM, 678.
74. "Still Life with a Basket of Crocuses," WM, 230.
75. "Garden with Sunflower," WM, 257.
76. "Blossoming Almond Tree," WM, 615.

the laboratories of the "flat sciences"[77] and the deafening detonation of canons.[78] That same splendor also is what the artist wants to paint of himself. For that is how the artist and nature, at their best, agree—and, at their worst, suffer a devastating disharmony.

A single sapling, asserting its will in the face of whatever betides it, is what captures the imagination of the artist, as from its roots this newborn "pushes, urges, and stirs"[79] through the earth's abrasion, arching toward the sunlight. This, too, is where the artist and nature agree—since neither can do its respective work apart from the light, nor apart from the resistance to the light by the forces of darkness that work against it.

So, as for a "stimulus to fight for victory," the tender "crocus" so spitefully stepped upon and all but crushed to smithereens, like the artist whose art is judged severely or altogether ignored, remains stubborn enough to be revived of nature and poke its wee blades of color to rise again through the crusty cold ice of winter, and in its stride to become spring's first burst of laughter. "Something on High"—unnamable—unfathomable—demands it—justifies it. This is what the artist knows, and this is the stream of necessity to which he has been beckoned and called.

The "ravine"[80] into which the pilgrim must fall before the day is over, has a name—and that name is Obscurity. It is the place of deep shadows where all flesh must wither and all bones must crumble into the dust before being devoured in the mouth of unsearchable darkness. This, too, the artist knows to be true, and is capable of rendering it as true to his art. Does the Darkness devour the Light? the artist asks. Or does the Light embrace and illumine the Darkness? "Does the candle burn for the moth's sake?" asks Vincent. "If one knew that for certain—well it might be worth while to commit suicide in this way. But what if the candle itself should snigger at the burned wings . . . ?" "I was struck by it, whatever the truth of it may be. And—I firmly believe that there are things like that in the depths of our souls—and that they would cut us to the quick

77. "Bulb Fields," WM, 25.

78. "If you live in a time of war, you might have to fight; you would regret it, you would lament that you weren't living in times of peace, but after all the necessity would be there, and you would fight" (CL 542).

79. CL 212.

80. "Les Peiroulets Ravine," WM, 570–71.

if we knew about them. At times we are quite disenchanted by [human] kind—our own selves included, of course—and yet—seeing that we are going to pop off soon enough after all—it would hardly be worth while to stick to our displeasure, even if it were well founded" (CL R41).

The thoughtful painter is exhausted from his long journey into the infinite recess of his questioning. He declares: "I am an artist"—"Always seeking without absolutely finding." "It is just the opposite of saying, 'I know, I have found it'" (CL 192).

The pilgrim rears his head toward the "firmament."[81] The last hour is approaching. He tips his straw hat to the white ray of "sunlight"[82] cascading through the dense clouds as he loosens and swallows the lump in his throat. His eyes squint in the hunt for the crest of the "mountain."[83] His "shadowy gaze"[84] fastens to the thickening dusk like molten iron, and his temper is livid and then limp.[85]

Where goes the blazing "sun" when it travels beyond the horizon? Does it return to its home again? And whom does it carry with it?[86]

"Is the whole of life visible to us, or isn't it rather that this side of death we see only one hemisphere?"[87] From which side of fatality, then, do the "blackbirds" swoop?[88]

Whatever shall be, or not be—*Go for it, old boy!—Go for it!*

He reaches into his pocket[89] and whispers:

81. Wheat Fields at Auvers under Clouded Sky," WM, 688.

82. "Olive Trees with Yellow Sky and Sun," WM, 574.

83. "Mountains at St. Rémy with Dark Cottage," WM, 529.

84. "Self-Portrait," WM, 267.

85. "Wheat Field with Crows," WM, 690–91.

86. "The Raising of Lazarus" (after Rembrandt), WM, 626.

87. CL 506; "Enclosed Field behind Saint-Paul Hospital: Rising Sun," WM, 598.

88. "Wheat Field with Crows," WM, 690–91.

89. Hulsker, *Vincent and Theo*, 442. In a reputed though disputed incident involving Dr. Gachet, Vincent had a fit of "violent rage" and "put his hand in one of his pockets . . . to seize a revolver," but when given a stern and "domineering glance" by Dr. Gachet, "Vincent took his hand from his pocket, empty, went to the door and went out with a contrite air." Given the possibility of a father transference with Dr. Gachet, the incident raises the question as to whether Vincent unconsciously recapitulated the rage shown his father. Shortly thereafter Vincent shot himself with a pistol. In the last posted letter that Theo received, Vincent wrote: "Perhaps I'd rather write you about a lot of things, but to begin with, the desire to do so has completely left me, and then I feel it is useless" (CL

"If you ever fall in love and get the answer, 'No, never never,' do not resign yourself to it."[90]

"I am in for it now. And the die is cast."[91]

FLIGHT

The sower has finished his sowing, the reaper his reaping, and the painter his painting.

A golden orb appears on the horizon. The "crown of night" glistens as a "coronet of stars" in the sky.[92]

Soaring through the "grey clouds with their linings of silver and gold and purple"[93] a "wingéd lark"[94] sets forth into flight. Its song is the "sorrow" of its heart calling—for "joy."

I will speak to my Lord, I who am but dust and ashes. If I repute myself greater than this, behold, You stand against me, and my sins bear witness to the truth which I cannot contradict. But if I abase myself and humble myself to nothingness, if I divest myself of all self-esteem (as I really am) and account myself as the dust which I am, Your grace will favor me, Your light will enshroud my heart, and all self-estimation, no matter how little, will sink in the depths of my nothingness and there lose itself for ever.

—Thomas à Kempis, *The Imitation of Christ* [95]

---

651). In his final, unmailed letter to Theo, found on Vincent's body, he wrote these last words: "Well, my own work, I am risking my life for it and my reason has half foundered because of it—that's all right—but you are not among the dealers in men as far as I know, and you can still choose your side, I think, acting with humanity, but que veux-tu [what do you wish? / what can you expect?]?" (CL 652). Theo was considering leaving employment at Goupil.

90. CL 153. Death becomes the means, at last, of being relieved of interminable suffering, and also as a way of making a final sacrificial offering of himself.

91. CL 166.

92. "Starry Night," WM, 520–21.

93. From Vincent's sermon (CL I, 90).

94. "Wheat Field with a Lark," WM, 251.

95. Composite translation, Bruce (100), Burns (163).

"Old Man in Sorrow (On the Threshold of Eternity)"

PART TWO

The "Artist" within
the Art

FIVE

The Artist before God

THE HUMAN SELF WITHIN THE DIVINE CIRCLE

IT IS TRUE THAT throughout his lifetime Vincent endured a profound order of personal suffering that acquainted him with the deepest recesses of existential anguish. His despair was the principal medium for his thoroughgoing identification with the human Jesus. This, in part, explains the enormous appeal of his art to an ever-expanding audience. His popularity is certainly due to the ability he had to elicit the deepest of human emotions and religious sentiments, touching the hearts of those who contemplate the lushness and beauty of his art.

To restate the pervasive theological question that begs an answer throughout Vincent's life and work: *How near to the present darkness of human experience is the far-reaching Light of God—what Vincent called that "ray from on high"*? To pose it another way: To what extent, if at all, is the divine presence revealed in the bleakest moments of suffering and despair?

Aesthetically and existentially, Vincent sought the light of God's immanent presence within the natural order, even when it seemed impossibly obscured. He especially searched for the glow in the faces of persons sitting before his easel, whose eyes were openings upon the depths of the soul. He said: "If one feels the need of something grand, something infinite, something that makes one feel aware of God, one need not go far to find it" (CL 242).

Conversely, the eternal "ray from on high" is sufficiently concealed within the natural order and within the experience of the "dark night of the soul" to raise serious doubts about the existence and presence of God. Vincent quoted Victor Hugo: "God is an occulting lighthouse (the French call it an eclipsing lighthouse), and if this should be the case we are passing through the eclipse now" (CL 543). The person who can see no light of ultimate hope within his or her life dwells within an impenetrable darkness. For such an individual the apparent eclipse of God suffuses the agonizing experience of human despair.

As the nineteenth-century Danish philosopher-theologian Søren Kierkegaard wrote in *The Sickness unto Death: A Christian Psychological Exposition for Upbuilding and Awakening*, the archetypal meaning of despair is "to lose the eternal."[1] Or, we might preferably say, it is to lose *sight* of the eternal. For Kierkegaard, "the self is the conscious synthesis of infinitude and finitude that relates itself to itself, whose task is to become itself, which can be done only through the relationship with God."[2] But when the self, estranged from God, loses its sense of origin, grounding, and purpose in God, the self falls into an ultimate despair. In the words of Paul Tillich:

> The pain of despair is that a being is aware of itself as unable to affirm itself because of the power of nonbeing. Consequently it wants to surrender this awareness and its presupposition, the being which is aware. It wants to get rid of itself—and it cannot. Despair appears in the form of reduplication, as the desperate attempt to escape despair. If anxiety were only the anxiety of fate and death, voluntary death would be the way out of despair. The courage demanded would be the courage *not* to be. The final form of ontic self-affirmation would be the act of ontic self-negation.
>
> But despair is also the despair about guilt and condemnation. And there is no way of escaping it, even by ontic self-negation. Suicide can liberate one from the anxiety of fate and death—as the Stoics knew. But it cannot liberate from the anxiety of guilt and condemnation, as the Christians knew.[3]

1. Kierkegaard, *The Sickness unto Death*, 55.
2. Ibid., 29–30.
3. Tillich, *The Courage to Be*, 55.

Kierkegaard radicalized the meaning of despair by characterizing what lies at its root. For him it signified *the self as unconscious of itself as spirit and unconscious of itself before God.*

> Every human existence that is not conscious of itself as spirit or conscious of itself before God as spirit, every human existence that does not rest transparently in God but vaguely rests in and merges in some abstract universality (state, nation, etc.) or, in the dark about [its] self, regards [its] capacities merely as powers to produce without becoming deeply aware of their source, regards [its] self, if it is to have intrinsic meaning, as an indefinable something—every such existence, whatever it achieves, be it most amazing, whatever it explains, be it the whole of existence, however intensively it enjoys life esthetically—every such existence is nevertheless despair.[4]

> Insofar, then, as the self does not become itself ["conscious of itself as spirit or conscious of itself before God as spirit"] it is not itself; but not to be itself is precisely [to] despair.[5]

Approximately a year before his suicide, Vincent's mental condition had deteriorated from recurring bouts of psychotic seizures and chronic depression so debilitating that, for a few days to a week or two at a time, he was unable to work. He experienced the greatest despondency of his life, sunken into a pit of spiritual darkness. This threw him into the realization that his life had become virtually devoid of meaning except for the episodic, secondary capacity to create—which he called his "powers to produce." Yet, as Kierkegaard would have said, this alone could not sufficiently compensate for the aching of his soul.

Nonetheless, through the sometimes frenetic "medium" of his art he managed to portray intimations of the divine still present within the sphere of his consciousness, thereby counteracting his despair with vestiges of *"that something of the eternal"* that seemed so doggedly unwilling to come from behind the dense "cloud of unknowing."[6]

Paradoxically, despite its debilitating effect upon him physically and emotionally, for some time Vincent's despair had propelled him into the zenith of his generative creativity. In one sense he had lost himself and in another he had gained himself, hurled as he was into the great void

4. Kierkegaard, *Sickness*, 46.
5. Ibid., 30.
6. The name of a fourteenth-century anonymous work of Christian mysticism.

of the "self-emptying God." His desolation was like that of Jesus and the psalmist who cried out: "My God, my God, why have you forsaken me? Why are you so far from helping me, from the words of my groaning? O my God, I cry by day, but you do not answer; and by night, but find no rest."[7] Vincent had entered the space in which, as Ken Wilber said, "the dark night of the soul sets in, and the light of consciousness seems to turn back on itself and disappear, leaving no trace. All seems lost, and, in a sense, all is. Darkness follows darkness, emptiness leads to emptiness, midnight lingers on. But, as the Zenrin[8] has it: At dusk the cock announces dawn; / At midnight, the bright sun."[9] For this is the time of *kairos*[10] when the finite greets the infinite. While the Mysterious One does not unveil its face, it beckons the conscious self ever deeper into that unconscious stream of necessity to which it is irrepressibly drawn. This is simultaneously the time of not knowing and the time of desiring to be known. It is the time when the self cannot discern of itself what it wants to possess, yet is convinced of its being "possessed." Here Vincent's experience of the absence of God is paradoxically joined to his dependence upon the very transcendence of God to give intent to his will to create. Despite all that he doubts of himself and of God, he is driven to the heart and purpose of his painting.

> I can very well do without God both in my life and in my painting, but I cannot, ill as I am, do without something which is greater than I, which is my life—the power to create. . . . And in a picture I want to say something comforting, as music is comforting. I want to paint men and women with that something of the eternal which the halo used to symbolize, and which we seek to convey by the actual radiance and vibration of our coloring. Portraiture so understood . . . would be more in harmony with . . . a *real* [person]. Ah! Portraiture, portraiture with the thoughts, the soul of the model in it, that is what I think must come. (CL 531, italics added)

7. Psalm 22:1–2.

8. The Zenrin-kushu is a seventeenth-century Japanese collection of earlier passages and sayings from Buddhist scripture and Zen masters.

9. Wilber, *No Boundary*, 156–57.

10. Of *kairos* (qualitative, fulfilled time), Tillich wrote: "[Human]kind is never left alone. The Spiritual Presence acts upon it in every moment and breaks into it in some great moments, which are the historical *kairoi* [plural of *kairos*]," *Systematic*, 3:149.

Notwithstanding his present despondency, Vincent believed "that something of the eternal which the halo used to symbolize," and which belonged to those whose "soul" he wished to convey by the "actual radiance and vibration" of his "coloring," characterized "real" man and woman, the *essential* person. It was from *within* his portraits and from *within* his paintings of still-life, seascape, and landscape that he sought to portray "spirit" intersecting with "Spirit," giving rise to the most profound meanings that art can convey. In that sense his art remains "epiphany." It offers a medium for the viewer through which the holy may manifest itself as immanently present to, and within, the viewer. The force of such epiphany is the power of love. In that sense Vincent's art is a "participation" in the holy and an "awakening" to the holy *as love*.

Paul Tillich explained the nature of this sacred participation:

> Humanity, of which each individual is a special and unique mirror, is the key to the universe. Without having the universe in ourselves we would never understand it. The center of the universe and of ourselves is divine, and with the presence of the infinite in ourselves we can *re*-cognize (I [Tillich] purposely underline the first syllable) in the universe the infinite which is within us. And what is the key to this in ourselves? . . . It is love, but not love in the sense of *agape*, the Christian concept of love, but love in the Platonic sense of *eros*. Eros is the love which unites us with the good and the true and the beautiful and which drives us beyond the finite into the infinite.[11]

From within the sphere of being-within-Being, of spirit-within-Spirit, the unified center of divine reality invests itself in the power of nature and expresses itself as love. It is the source of all loving relationships. The heart of such love is the affirmation of life itself.

Concerning the deepest purposes and meanings of a life, such as the life of Vincent van Gogh, or of anyone else, the author of the New Testament book of Acts specifically addressed both the "essentialist" and the "existentialist" dimensions[12] of human experience, without employing those

11. Tillich, *A History of Christian Thought*, 397.

12. The philosophical terms "essentialist" and "existentialist" are deliberately placed in juxtaposition to indicate that, apart from Essence, human existence is impossible since human existence is contingent upon the existence of God as Essence. God enters into both the creation and the human condition, and thereby exists historically as

philosophical terms. For, as the scripture bears witness, God dwells herein, both at the center and at the boundaries of human existence. This is why the One God alone is to be worshipped.

> Paul stood in front of the Areopagus and said: "Athenians, I see how extremely religious you are in every way. For as I went through the city and looked carefully at the objects of your worship, I found among them an altar with the inscription, "To an unknown god." What there you worship as unknown, this I proclaim to you. The God who made the world and everything in it, he who is Lord of heaven and earth, does not live in shrines made by human hands, nor is he served by human hands, as though he needed anything, since he himself gives to all mortals life and breath and all things. From one ancestor he made all nations to inhabit the whole earth, and he allotted the times of their existence and the boundaries of the places where they would live, so that they would search for God and perhaps grope for him and find him—though indeed he is not far from each one of us. For, "in him we live and move and have our being"; as even some of your own poets have said, "For we too are his offspring."[13]

Saint Paul, the theologian, speaking like a philosopher of philosophers, asserted that human existence involves a search—perhaps even a groping for—a finding of—*and a being found by*—the one God who "is not far from each one of us" precisely because this God is the One *in whom* "we live and move and have our being." In a similar though more abstract metaphor, Paul Tillich declared that all of humanity and all of nature have God as the absolute, essential, and universal "Ground of Being." Such is true whether we speak in metaphysical, ontological, or personalistic categories, though personalistic language is far more comprehensible, thus useful, than the abstractions of rarefied metaphysics and ontology. Nevertheless, through their respective metaphors both theology and psychology delve into the invisible, unconscious realms of reality in an attempt to understand and interpret them. Yet these disciplines, complex systems and languages that they are, swim in murky waters. They do so for the simple reason that the human eye and the human mind are not capable of seeing entirely below the surface of things to what lurks within the depths of the unknown.

---

constantly "becoming" that which God is, enabling humanity to become true to itself as it becomes true to the essence and existence of God.

13. Acts 17:22–28.

As Reinhold Niebuhr observed: "The self that is in dialogue with God takes the inquiry immediately beyond the limits of empirical verification."[14] Yet, that is precisely where, in faith rather than in knowledge, we venture to go. As Niebuhr reiterated, "by its memory and foresight," the self "transcends the given moment and is therefore transtemporal in one dimension of its being. The self-consciousness of the self proceeds in a particular organism. But the self is, in one dimension, non-spatial. This is a great embarrassment to any rational conception which must insist on the coherence of the various entities with which it deals."[15] In other words, science has its limits, and so do faith and reason. But faith is willing to gamble beyond the reach of rational and empirical inquiry, all the while keeping its eyes peeled on the finite temporal and spatial dimensions of reality in which clues to the infinite lurk like oysters beneath the sea, their secrets hidden between their shells.

Saint Paul was trying to be "reasonable." He was also seeking to transcend reason while taking advantage of the available but limited empirical evidence at hand. Moreover, for that moment at least, he relied not upon Jewish or Christian sources, but rather on pagan Greek authorities, one thought to be Epimenides and the other the poet Cilicia, a Stoic.[16] In so doing, it all boiled down to a simple fact. Without the necessary existence of God, all contingent beings proceeding from God, including nature itself, would cease to exist and would never have existed to begin with.

Paul Tillich put the matter in philosophical abstraction by saying that "the courage to be is possible because it is participation in the self-affirmation of being-itself."[17] But to paraphrase the British historian Herbert Butterfield, who spoke in concreteness: If God should happen to stop breathing, we would all perish.[18]

---

14. Niebuhr, *The Self and the Dramas of History*, 5.

15. Ibid., 23.

16. See footnote commentary on Acts 17:28, NRSV.

17. Tillich, *A History of Christian Thought*, 24.

18. Butterfield wrote: "Perhaps history is a thing that would stop happening if God held His breath, or could be imagined as turning away to think of something else" (*Christianity and History*, 145).

MYSTERY

The aesthetic corollary to this theological affirmation about human contingency resting upon divine necessity relates directly to what Ken Wilber advocates as the principle of "integral hermeneutics."[19] He deems this concept to be extremely useful, if not altogether indispensable, for understanding the life and art of Vincent van Gogh. For, as Wilber states, we all live in a world of "holons."

> "Holons": the word was coined by Arthur Koestler to indicate *wholes* that are simultaneously *parts* of other wholes: a whole quark is part of a whole atom; a whole atom is part of a whole molecule; a whole molecule is part of a whole cell; a whole cell is part of a whole organism. . . . In linguistics, a whole letter is part of a whole word, which is part of a whole sentence, which is part of a whole paragraph. . . . In other words, we live in a universe that consists neither of wholes nor of parts, but of whole/parts, or holons. Wholes do not exist by themselves, nor do parts exist by themselves. Every whole simultaneously exists as a part of some other whole, and as far as we can tell, this is indeed endless.[20]

Concerning then the intersection of a theory of aesthetics with the depth psychology of the self, an integral hermeneutic posits that the sphere and locus of an object of art consists of *more* than the art object in and of itself. It does so for the same reason that the self is composed of more than the determinate aspects of its being. For the self, in mind and body, in soul and spirit, is both determinate and indeterminate. It lives within, and simultaneously transcends, temporal and spatial reality.[21]

A work of art, therefore, should be considered from within the artist's multiple loci of meaning, including narrow and broad personal, familial, social, cultural, political, economic, and religious aspects of that meaning. A work of art is a creation of the artist, to be sure—but *not only* the artist—implying that its meaningful content is derived from sources and spheres both within and beyond the artist's mind as a discrete entity. Because the finite concerns of persons exist not only within their own de-

19. Wilber, *Eye of Spirit*, 97. "The aim," he says, "is to step out of the narcissistic and nihilistic endgame that has so thoroughly overtaken the world of postmodern art and literature, and to introduce instead the essentials of a genuinely integral art and literary theory—what might be called *integral theory.*"

20. Ibid., 99–100.

21. Reinhold Niebuhr elaborates upon this in a number of his writings, including *The Self and the Dramas of History.*

terminate times and spaces but also within larger, indeterminate spheres, a work of art as the product of a single artist may not be adequately understood apart from the larger commitments of the person who created it. These may embrace both ambiguous and unambiguous vistas of circumstance, purpose, and causation that illumine an artist's artistry.

Additionally, the "projected" meanings of those who view a work of art need not necessarily have anything overtly to do with the original conscious or unconscious intentions of the artist, even if such influences upon the artist are detectable within the work of art itself. Furthermore, the question may be left hanging as to just how something detectable, or potentially detectable, within a work of art will in fact become noticed, since sometimes it is not. That persons and communities have "eyes with which to see" does not mean that they will see. Some things remain enshrouded in mystery, even to those who have had a hand in creating them.

Hours upon hours, days upon days, weeks upon weeks, even years upon years of searching for buried treasures may be met with the stubborn resistance of a mysterious fact or faculty to unveil itself. Then again, an illusive phenomenon may abruptly unmask every inch of itself, and may do so without the slightest provocation. Who has not caught sight of a tarnished silver coin lying furtively within the grass, or turned up a curiously obtuse object while tilling the soil, and done so with eyes and conscious mind focused entirely elsewhere? Some people have a knack for spotting a single four-leaf clover embedded among thousands of three-leaf clovers. Others can have the four-leaf clover directly pointed out and still be unable to see it.[22] The revelation of some mysteries depends upon the kinds of questions being asked—or whether any questions are asked at all. Too often a particular point of view is held so vehemently that no other point of view can be entertained, much less curiously comprehended. Some minds cease searching altogether, satisfied with a humdrum perspective, whereas taking up a brand new perspective would be life changing. It is more than a truism to say that *one who does not search is not likely to find.* Given a world composed of both big and little surprises, no person should be mollified for complaining of excess

22. The author's maternal grandmother could spot four-leaf clovers by the dozen, simply by walking into the yard and instantly looking down, whereas her grandson could crawl on his hands and knees and search for hours through patch after patch of clover and never spot a single one.

boredom, or for protesting with disproportionate disinterest, in regard to the intricacies of how all sorts of things work. Vincent said of his father and mother: "They will never be able to understand what painting is. They cannot understand that the figure of a laborer—some furrows in a plowed field—a bit of land, sea, and sky—are serious subjects, so difficult, but at the same time so beautiful, that it is indeed worth while to devote one's life to expressing the poetry hidden in them" (CL 226).

But then, conversely, it is possible to be endlessly tilting at windmills. One can spend one's life searching with a flashlight into the wee hours of the night, in the wrong places, for the wrong reasons, and for the wrong things, or be in quest of the "poetry hidden" in "a bit of land, sea, and sky," as though the entire world were a basement wherein great mysteries are like spiders clinging to cobwebs, to be treated as common enemies until they are subdued as obliging friends. Being incessantly intent upon cracking open an ironclad mystery may be the one sure-fire way of keeping it locked up forever in solitary confinement. A mystery, like a groundhog, has its own season and timing, and should be treated with respect, even at the expense of the seeker of truth having to persist through a long and arduous winter of uncertainty before discovering whether or not the groundhog will at last reveal its shadow—and then only if the sun burns sufficiently bright to make a silhouette.

Nevertheless, despite the danger of tilting at windmills, and regardless of more pressing obligations and distractions, sometimes the mystery of a star in and of itself compels a stargazer to gaze. This is in spite of the temptation to return to pedal-pushing a bicycle along a well-trampled path. That may have its own reward, yet it prevents the eyes from tracing a steady course through the sky. Vincent recalled the physician Pascal Rougon, a character appearing in a sequel of novels written by Émile Zola. Of this "doctor . . . always in the background; a noble figure," Vincent said, "it is always possible for energy and will power to conquer fate. In his profession he found a force stronger than the temperament he had inherited from his family; instead of surrendering to his natural instincts, he followed a clear, straight path, and did not slide into the wretched muddle in which all the other Rougons perished" (CL 226). Vincent was referring not only to Pascal Rougon but also to himself, and above all to that enticing mystery that can convert a single moment into the reason for a lifetime of living. Such is what keeps archaeologists digging for "the origins of life." Like profound religion, it demands that one devote oneself tirelessly to mounds and mounds of stones and dirt where someday instead of a nugget of gold one may just turn up a trace of God. When this happens, a poetic metaphor will say more by way of description than all the prosaic language of scientific investigation.

> Those Dutchmen had hardly any imagination or fantasy, but their good taste and their scientific knowledge of composition were enormous. They have not painted Jesus Christ, the Good God and so on—although Rembrandt *did* in fact—but he is the only one (and Biblical subjects are, relatively speaking, not numerous in his work). He is the only one, the exception, who has done Christs. . . . And in his case it is hardly like anything whatever done by the other religious painters; it is a metaphysical magic.

> Thus Rembrandt has painted angels. He paints a self-portrait, old, toothless, wrinkled, wearing a cotton cap, a picture from nature, in a mirror. He is dreaming, dreaming, and his brush resumes his self-portrait, but only the head, whose expression becomes more tragically sad, more tragically saddening. He is dreaming, still dreaming, and, I don't know why or how, but just as Socrates and Mohammed had their familiar spirits, Rembrandt paints behind this old man, who resembles himself, a supernatural angel with a da Vinci smile.

> I am showing you a painter who dreams and paints from imagi-nation, and I began by contending that the character of the Dutch painters is such that they do not invent anything, that they have neither imagination nor fantasy.

> Am I illogical? No.

> Rembrandt did not invent anything, that angel, that strange Christ, the fact is that he knew them; he felt them there.

> Delacroix paints a Christ by means of the unexpected effect of a bright citron-yellow note, a colorful luminous note which pos-sesses the same unspeakable strangeness and charm in the picture as a star does in a corner of the firmament; Rembrandt works with tonal values in the same way Delacroix works with colors.

> Now there is a great distance between Delacroix's and Rembrandt's method and that of all the rest of religious painting. (CL B12)

> I very much like the last words of, I think, Silvestre, who ended a masterly article in this way: "Thus died—almost smiling—Delacroix, a painter of a noble race, who had a sun in his head

and a thunderstorm in his heart, who turned from the warriors to the saints, from the saints to the lovers, from the lovers to the tigers, and from the tigers to the flowers."

It is possible that these great geniuses are only madmen, and that one must be mad oneself to have boundless faith in them and a boundless admiration for them. If this is true, I should prefer my insanity to the sanity of the others. (CL B13)

To do good work one must eat well, be well housed, have one's fling from time to time, smoke one's pipe and drink one's coffee in peace. (CL B17)

During such off-moments (what some turn into a junket and others a binge), an artist must obtain a second wind for leaping over all impediments that cause a painter to be accused of being entirely too sane. The more mystical the art, the greater will be the need for insanity.

Just so, Vincent found himself struggling against all manner of thought that he deemed to be nothing more than a "system of resignation." He struggled against it for the simple reason that, for those who belonged to the esteemed artist guilds, membership required one to submit to the venerable rules of the "academy" and to ask no questions. Certainly, do not ask why such rules for creating art should exist to begin with. They were, after all (were they not?), divinely appointed.

He was writing to his friend and fellow art student van Rappard, who, like himself, was struggling with the "system" of "arts"— the "bête noire"—not unlike the church at its "emptiest," where "in theology there exists a system of resignation with mortification as a side branch" (CL R5). As for the arts academy—that "mistress who freezes you, who petrifies you, who sucks your blood . . . this woman of marble (or is it plaster of Paris??? how horrible!)," where they teach one to draw from dry bones and skeletons,[23] in contrast to Dame Nature who bears not only death but *life* within her—Vincent excoriated: "Listen, beautiful lady, wherever you pretend to come from, you who tell me that your fundamental intensions are 'beauty and sublimity' (which, however, can only be *results* and never *intentions*), whatever place you come from, you certainly did not issue from the body of the living God, neither did you from the body of a woman. Get you gone, sphinx, at this very instant, I tell you—you are nothing but a humbug" (CL R4).

23. "Skull with Burning Cigarette," WM, 138.

Vincent's advice to van Rappard was the same he offered himself:

> The Open Sea is your true element and even at the academy you
> do not belie your true character and nature; that is why the worthy
> gentlemen there will not recognize you in fact, and put you off
> with idle talk.

> Mr. Ten Cate[24] is not yet an able seaman, and I myself much less,
> and we cannot steer and maneuver yet as we would like to; but if
> we do not get drowned or smashed on the rocks in the seething
> breakers, we shall become good sailors. There is no help for it,
> everyone has to go through a period of worrying and fumbling
> after he has risked himself on the open sea. At first we catch little
> or no fish, but we get acquainted with our course and learn to
> steer our little vessel, and this is indispensable to begin with. And
> after a while we shall catch a lot of fish, and big ones too, to be
> sure! (CL R5)

Actually, what Vincent told his professors was this: "I said, 'Go to
hell!' And this they thought very disrespectful. Well, so be it. Whatever
may be the raison d'être of this resignation, it—the resignation, I mean—
is only for those who *can* be resigned, and religious belief is for those
who *can* believe. And what can I do if I am not cut out by nature for the
former, *i.e.*, resignation, but on the contrary for the latter, *i.e.* religious
belief, with all its consequences?" (CL R5).

Being a sly "fisherman," Vincent knew "one thing." He said: "If a
man masters one thing and understands it well, he has at the same time
insight into and understanding of many other things in the bargain" (CL
121). That is, be sure to look carefully into the mystery of one solitary
object and ask plenty of questions. Do not rely upon what others have
said. The secret to the universe may be contained within a single four-
leaf clover in which the members of the academy could see nothing but
the chlorophyll. And then trust your answer with the same religious
conviction as that "colorful luminous note which possesses the same
unspeakable strangeness and charm in the picture as a star does in a
corner of the firmament." A painting, like a star, for all we know, may
emit the very light of God.

24. An art instructor at the Antwerp Academy.

"TO AN UNKNOWN GOD"

Saint Paul declared: "Athenians, I see how extremely religious you are in every way. For as I went through the city and looked carefully at the objects of your worship, I found among them an altar with the inscription, 'To an unknown god.'"[25] Whoever happened to inscribe that altar had simultaneously mastered two arts. One was the mastery of etching a stone, the other the art of bowing down before the unknown. There is a poignant reason as to why the best artists are called "masters." As in the case of the inscription upon the Athenian altar, "masters" have situated themselves in the position of servants who have opened themselves to the "mystery within a mystery"[26]—the latter "mystery" pertaining to the one doing the inscribing, and the former to the One to whom the altar is inscribed. Vincent said:

> It is good to continue believing that everything is more miraculous than one can comprehend, for this is truth; it is good to remain sensitive and humble and tender of heart, even good to be learned in the things that are hidden from the wise and intellectual ones of the world but are revealed, as if by nature, to the poor and simple, to women and little children. For what can one learn that is better than what God has given by nature to every human soul—which is living and loving, hoping and believing, in the depth of every soul, unless it is wantonly destroyed?
>
> Nothing less than the infinite and the miraculous is necessary, and man does well not to be contented with anything less, and not to feel at home as long as he has not acquired it.
>
> Happy is [the one] who has faith in God for in the end [such a one] will overcome all the difficulties of life, albeit not without trouble and sorrow. (CL 121)

To have overcome trouble and sorrow is to have mastered the two great resistances: the resistance to God and the resistance to the true self.

Philosopher-theologian Cliff Edwards has written a superb "work of art" in its own right, which is concerned centrally with one painting. The book is entitled *Mystery of The Night Café: Hidden Key to the Spirituality*

---

25. Acts 17:22–23.

26. The title of the eleventh chapter of *Mystery of The Night Café: Hidden Key to the Spirituality of Vincent van Gogh*, by Cliff Edwards.

of Vincent van Gogh. Vincent's original painting of "The Night Café" is "housed among the towers of an old New England university and offers one of the artist's most intriguing and puzzling images."[27] Through a monumental amount of research, probing, thinking, comparing, contrasting, reflecting, and meditating upon the deepest of mysteries revealed in this painting, Edwards discovered the "mystery within a mystery" of "The Night Café."

Vincent had frequented the café, known the proprietors, and taken a number of his meals there. It was a place in Arles where the down-and-out and the destitute, the "street people," among others, gathered "after hours" in search of life in the night.

Commencing his interpretation with the prescient words of Jesus, Edwards drew the following picture of Vincent's extraordinary painting:

> "The Kingdom of God is among you." Has Vincent painted this realization in "The Night Café?" A refuge with an open invitation to the Kingdom of God resides precisely in the midst of the powers of darkness, the slaughterhouse where one is stunned. Love is the mystery within the mystery that unifies the "power of darkness" with "gaiety and good nature," locating the Kingdom of God in "the devil's furnace."
>
> In the "devil's furnace" of this painting, the meeting of the eyes of the artist with the eyes of the man in white . . . may signal a sense of sympathetic understanding passing between the caretaker of the refuge of the night café, and Vincent, future caretaker of The Yellow House—a refuge intended for homeless artists.[28]

> Vincent's work with canvas and brush brought just such broken humans into "The Night Café," placed them under the haloes of the gaslights, depicted the strangeness of such a banquet for those broken by life, and opened a passageway to a brighter, deeper, mystery.[29]

That "brighter, deeper, mystery" stands at the back of the painting as a veiled image of the risen Christ, of the "incarnation of God, a God Vincent now saw in terms of the flow of creativity itself . . . present as

27. Edwards, ibid., xiv. The painting hangs in the Yale University Art Gallery. The author of *Bone Dead, and Rising* had the experience of unexpectedly stumbling upon this painting, and sat before it, deeply moved, for several hours of meditation over the course of two days.

28. Edwards, *Mystery*, 74.

29. Ibid., 91.

an open and inviting light, leading beyond the mixed world of the café. The divine as an open space, a creative absence, beckons to us beyond the sanctuary of the café, which itself substitutes for the conventional symbol of refuge he had rejected, 'the inside of a church.'"[30]

Here, in a commonplace café, where abide the most ordinary joys and sorrows of the most ordinary kind of people—"the forgotten under-side of society, always present but seldom noticed"[31]—is a picture of the "meaning within the meaning" of *night life*. Here, within a hazy place of obscurity, where lips are thirsty for friendship and hearts are pounding to hear the word "love"—where "spirits" of laughter greet the falling tears of sorrow—Light invades Darkness and Mystery *unbolts itself*. Here, within the Night Café, is an altar to the Unknown God.

In the "Christ-shaped doorway"[32] "so draped as to resemble the image of the consoling Christ in [Ary] Scheffer's 'Christus Consolator,'"[33]—which Edwards said he could imagine as "the image so imprinted on Vincent's memory that the shape had become for him almost an archtypal symbol for consolation,"[34]—there stands the semblance of the open tomb from which Christ has been resurrected, and from which he has come to dwell in the midst of the café, offering healing, comfort, and rec-onciliation to a broken world. It brings to mind the scene in the Gospel of John in which Mary is standing outside the empty tomb, weeping, as she greets the risen Jesus, thinking him all the while to be the gardener.[35] Both scenes reveal just how subtle is the veiled presence of God in a world darkened by the clouds of unknowing.

Edwards continues:

> Vincent's act of painting in the Ginoux Café de la Gare after mid-night with those few remaining stunned laborers, the homeless, and a prostitute, was not an act of condescension. He was a part of that strange "banquet for the poor, the lame, and the blind" announced by Jesus in a parable of Luke's Gospel. Vincent dared

30. Ibid., 83.

31. Ibid., 67.

32. Ibid., 89.

33. Ibid., 82.

34. Through a sequence of events, Edwards uncovered the fact that Vincent had traced into his painting of "The Night Café" the image of the Christ figure from Ary Sheffer's painting of "Chritus Consolator," which Vincent had superimposed over the doorway at the rear of the café. See Edwards, "Christus Consolator," 79–84.

35. John 20:11–18.

paint the café in its simplicity, without the romanticizing found
in café scenes by so many of the Impressionists. He dared paint
the dispossessed as they were, worn by life and in need of refuge.
The true religion of the heart he sought was the simple act of hospitality that accepted the needy, himself included. And beyond
his own paints and easel in a corner of that café, Vincent realized that the art of life itself was of more importance than even
his art of painting. He was grateful that he had found his work
as a painter, but he experienced his work as that of a servant,
not a master. He was not so much an observer given the task of
painting the down and out, as one who struggled among them in
life's sorrows and joys. He had given up his hope for a wife and
children of his own. He had given up his plan for a studio that
would provide refuge for needy painters. He was now prepared to
accept a final renunciation, should it be asked of him, the renunciation of painting itself.[36]

Anton Kerssemakers said of his friend, Vincent: "Whenever he saw
a beautiful evening sky, he went into ecstasies, if one may use the expression. Once, when we were tramping from Nuenen to Eindhoven toward
evening, he suddenly stood stock-still before a glorious sunset, and using
his two hands as if to screen it off a little, and with his eyes half closed,
he exclaimed, 'God bless me, how does that fellow—or God, or whatever
name you give him—how does he do it? We ought to be able to do that
too. My God, my God, how beautiful that is! What a pity we haven't got
a prepared palette ready, for it will be gone in a moment" (CL 435c).

Had he been asked, it is unlikely that Vincent could have said just
when had been the very first time as a child that he had lifted his pencil to
draw a crooked line on a flat piece of paper, or under what circumstance
he had undertaken his first act of self-renunciation in a long procession
of transfiguring events. Yet, it is possible to believe that, when it finally
became perfectly clear to him what he must do, he submitted himself
to a destiny he neither fully expected nor completely understood. He
did so because he was drawn irrepressibly toward that which God had
persistently called him.

Kerssemakers once received a painting from Vincent that Vincent
had forgotten to sign. When Kerssemakers called his attention to the
oversight, Vincent said he might eventually get around to signing it, and
then added: "I suppose I shall come back someday, but actually it isn't

36. Edwards, *Mystery*, 102.

necessary; they will surely recognize my work later on, and write about me when I'm dead and gone" (CL 435c).

But what he failed to mention, as the greater reason for not having signed it, was that the painting's true signature had been inscribed by the hand of the One who, like the gardener, had appeared before the painter as a "mystery within a mystery," looking, for the life of him, to be anything other than what he was. And like most gardeners who till the soil and plant and pluck the vegetables, he would not be recognized for his true worth until after they had said of him, "He is dead and gone."

The Night Café in Arles

SIX

Art as Intimation of
the Divine

A WISH FOR THE SELF

THE MIND OF THE artist frequently embraces what the art theorist Donald Kuspit claimed to be the artist's "wish for a certain kind of audience that amounts to a wish for a certain kind of self. His art embodies both wishes."[1]

So when Vincent, being outdoors, painted a colossal yellow orb of sunlight at the edge of a purple field of autumn,[2] just as indoors he decorated the bedroom of his famous Yellow House[3] on a street corner in Arles, Vincent created for himself a wish.

That is why, when beautifying a landscape or furnishing a house, for the artist the choice of color is as crucial to the painting as lead is to the pencil for drawing the sketch. Colors are holons within which artist and viewer together "live, and move, and have their being."

Every color contains its own peculiar hue and tint of meaning. Purple is for the season of gathering darkness, yellow for the season of in-breaking light. The Sower[4] tills the soil for lying fallow in the "violet"

1. Kuspit, *The Cult of the Avant-Garde Artist*, 83.

2. "The Sower," WM, 452.

3. "Vincent's House in Arles (The Yellow House)," WM, 423; "Vincent's Bedroom in Arles," WM, 442, 548–49.

4. WM, 452.

161

hue of autumn, and sows the seed to sprout in the "yellow" tint of spring. Purple is to sorrow and sadness, as yellow is to joy and gladness. Each color, in its own way of "speaking," is the expression of "a wish for a certain kind of audience" and "a certain kind of self"—or, if not a wish, then a virtual statement of fact.

Vincent painted "Crab on Its Back"[5] within several weeks of having had his catastrophic fall-out with Paul Gauguin on the eve of Christmas 1888, which turned out to be that grim and near-fatal occasion when in emotional desperation Vincent severed his earlobe and presented it to the prostitute Rachel, who with the help of her friends called the police. "Crab on Its Back" was a scene of total dispossession. The poor, destitute crab appeared to have made it all the way up to the beach, but that was as far as it could get. Its upside-down "browned-out" shell and torso and cleaver-forked claws—the two on the right looking like collapsed paint brushes soaked in blood—were not exactly a portrait of what an artist would normally draw for the sake of fulfilling a wish, that is, not unless the wish was a not so subtle prayer for death. In this ghastly "still-life" the old "crab on its back" was *decidedly dead*. Yet, oddly enough, like the luxuriant grasses that lavish the Garden of Eden, the backdrop to this work was set forth in the plush and "wishful" color of "living green."

In the same month of January 1889, Vincent painted "Still Life: Bloaters on a Piece of Yellow Paper."[6] It was abundantly clear from the scene, which may not have been far from the site of the crime, that these two ghastly fish did not make it to the shoreline because of having swum as contestants in an aquatic triathlon. These bloaters were *dragged to shore*. And for anyone who might have stumbled upon their smoked remains—"view" them, as they say—these herrings of the sea were absolutely the most pathetic, catatonic looking creatures one could ever imagine. They were laid out on a make-do, papered-over, china "mortuary table," sideways for Sunday, head-to-tail and tail-to-head in all their naked finery, fit for the banquet of a king and ready for a ravenous "burial." Decidedly, they were the *color of death*. Yet, oddly enough, the combination of the paper, the plate, and the fish, all together, was not a "still-life" portrait whatsoever. For these dried up, swollen-to-the-gills, down-in-the-mouth creatures were now wishfully "washed *up*" in the color of resurrection yellow.

5. Ibid., 475.
6. Ibid., 474.

To the present viewer it may appear that in both of these "self-por-traits" of Vincent there was a definite "wish for a certain kind of self"—which for him would have been to be "dressed up," if not "dressed out," in the immortal color of "yellow" and the life-giving color of "green."

Psychologically, certain intrapsychic "selfobjects"—such as a pair of fish—residing as images within the self of the artist, are projected by the artist onto the canvas, then mirrored back as "artobjects" embedded within the "self" of the art. With respect to the archaic nature of such intrapsychic selfobjects, Heinz Kohut stated:

> As with all genuine experiences in human life, the adult's experi-ence of a selfobject is not segmental but sectorial. It is, in other words, an experience in depth: when the adult experiences the self-sustaining effects of a maturely chosen selfobject, the selfob-ject experiences of all the preceding states of [one's] life reverber-ate unconsciously. When we feel uplifted by our admiration for a great cultural idea, for example, the old uplifting experience of being picked up by our strong and admired mother and having been allowed to merge with her greatness, calmness, and security may be said to form the unconscious undertones of the joy we are experiencing as adults.[7]

One does well, therefore, to consider just what *colors* come to mind in association with one's mother, or father, or, for that matter, with any-one or anything serving as a selfobject of enormous power and effect.

"Still Life: Drawing Board, Pipe, Onions, and Sealing Wax"[8] was also painted in January 1889. It contains a number of valuable "selfobjects" all neatly arranged right before the artist on a brightly painted yellow wooden table. Art historians Walther and Metzger noted that "the tran-quility, the consolation and the life expressed by everyday things became a particular concern, and van Gogh steadily aimed to translate the plu-rality of things into a coherent visual texture. . . . In arranging the objects he selected as motifs, he bore in mind what was helpful and pertinent in his present condition."[9] They observed of the painting:

7. Kohut, *How Does Analysis Cure?*, 49–50.
8. WM, 473.
9. Ibid., 486.

We see Francois Raspail's *Annuaire de la Santé*, a medical self-help annual [white with pink, yellow and green]; onions (which Raspail recommended for sleeplessness) [yellow tinted bronze with green]; his beloved pipe [brackish brown] and tobacco pouch [white, tinted yellow]; a letter addressed to the artist [white, stamped blue], standing for the affection and support of his distant brother; a lighted candle [white with yellow and golden flame, in blue candleholder], defiantly stating that the flame of life has not been extinguished yet; red sealing-wax beside it, attesting confidence that he will remain in touch with his friends; and an empty [transparent green] wine bottle to suggest he has given up alcohol. . . . Van Gogh is simply recording in meticulous detail an emotional affection for the things that afforded him consolation, that gave promise of happiness and instilled new optimism and hope in him, a hope he was trying to preserve by expressing it on his canvas. The individual symbolism in his motifs becomes more significant in proportion to the diminishing reference to the objective outside world. Van Gogh's objects are no longer first and foremost the everyday, functional things they seem to be; now their magical qualities are foregrounded.[10]

In the background of the painting, directly behind and adjacent to the yellow table, stands a large, fat ceramic teakettle with looped handle and open lid, it, too, in the color of living green. Presumably it was for boiling water and steeping tea, though it could just as easily have been for displaying an extravagant, gorgeous array of Vincent's famous sunflowers, to this day one of his most enduring and endearing trademarks. Likewise, "in some of the nature studies he did that spring of 1889 he was . . . producing close-ups of the green world: *Two White Butterflies . . . Grass and Butterflies . . . Rosebush in Flower . . . Clumps of Grass . . . A Field of Yellow Flowers*."[11]

There reside in such "green" works of art, however, a more expansive universe than the particular spheres of embodied wishes that belong to either the artist creating the art or to the audience viewing it. To be sure, there are finite, embedded cultures of similar and dissimilar meaning in which the artist and the viewer alike live and work. Yet, there is also an infinite, cosmic locus of *being and meaning* that extends

10. Ibid., 486–87.
11. Ibid., 489.

beyond the margins of the mind's eye and the fields of sensory perception. Just as the artist *"lives and moves and has its being"* within finite and expressible spheres that at the same time are infinite and ineffable, so does the artist's *art* dwell in all such spheres.[12] Metaphysically and ontologically, spiritually and materially, theologically and anthropologically, nature consists of ever smaller and larger, ever narrower and broader "holons" of reality belonging to the totality of "Holon," which is God. Accordingly, as Ken Wilber has written, all material and spiritual dimensions consist of vast interlinked holons-within-holons. Yet, at the beginning and end, at the heart of all that exists, in the words of Alfred North Whitehead, "God . . . is . . . an actual entity immanent in the actual world, but transcending any finite cosmic epoch—a being at once actual, eternal, immanent, and transcendent."[13]

In other words, God is Mystery. And as "the Mystery within the mystery": "Behold, the Kingdom"—the Presence—"of God is in the midst of you."[14] And—"We declare to you what was from the beginning, what we have heard, what we have seen with our eyes, what we have looked at and touched with our hands, concerning the word of life—this life was revealed, and we have seen it and testify to it, and declare to you the eternal life that was with the Father and was revealed to us."[15]

Cliff Edwards described Vincent's revelatory encounter with the mysterious God:

> Vincent does not simply ascribe to God human attributes, as though God were a giant human being. Rather, Vincent sees God specifically in his own innermost experience of frustration, failure, and striving as an artist. Vincent experiences God in the concreteness of his own most intense and significant personal history. Because as an artist Vincent experiences life in its profundity, he not only experiences God "as if" God were an artist, he experiences God's "failed sketch" in his own failed sketches. So a mother would experience God not simply "as if" God were a mother, but would experience God's mothering in her concrete acts of child-care. A farmer would experience God not simply "as if" God were a farmer, but would experience God in the concrete

12. For a discussion of integral theory and its relation to art, see Ken Wilber's *Eye of Spirit*, 96–138, 286–301.

13. Whitehead, *Process*, 93.

14. Luke 17:21b, RSV.

15. 1 John 1:1–2.

acts of sowing and planting. Vincent's idiomorphism strains the
requirements of Buber's I-Thou description of relationship with
the Divine. Vincent, unlike Buber, seems unconcerned that the
gulf between Creator and creature disappears in intensity of personal experience viewed as Divine experience.[16]

A single person dwells within a deep blue house beneath a deep blue sky.
The deep blue house sits beside the waters of the deep blue sea. The deep
blue house and the waters of the deep blue sea dwell upon the foundation
of the deep blue Earth[17] within the firmament of the deep blue universe.
Each is integral to all, and all are integral to each. Plants within the forest
feed from sunbeams and water falling from the deep blue sky, which
arise as heat and moisture returning to the deep blue sky. For, dying is
integral to rising, and rising is integral to dying, and God is integral to
all, and all is integral to God. As Wendell Berry inscribed: "The field
must remember the forest, the town must remember the field, so that the
wheel of life will turn, and the dying be met by the newborn."[18]

So, when Vincent, as earthly pilgrim, went in search of what *intimated* the presence of God, he sought in line, perspective, curvature, and
color, to depict those mysterious aspects of the eternal that are refracted
within the concrete facets of the temporal.

> Art is something greater and higher than our own adroitness or
> accomplishments or knowledge; that art is something which, al-
> though produced by human hands, is not created by these hands
> alone, but something which wells up from a deeper source in our
> souls. . . . My sympathies in the literary as well as in the artistic
> fields are most strongly attracted to those artists in whom I see
> the working of the soul predominating. (CL R43)

By way of illustration, he explicitly mentioned the artist Jozef Israëls
and the writers Charles Dickens and George Eliot. There were others, as

16. Edwards, *Van Gogh and God*, 71. Edwards coined the term "idiomorphism" to
signify "identification between forms" (the Greek word *idios* meaning "one's own"),
thus, the divine incarnation as God's entrance into human form. The Jewish philosopher-theologian, Martin Buber, in his book *The Eclipse of God*, made a distinction between "I-Thou" and "I-It" relationships, the former representing the encounter between
human being and Divine being.

17. Consider the satellite or spaceship image of Earth as clear, deep blue.

18. Berry, *What Are People For?* 12.

well, such as Millet, Delacroix, and Rembrandt—superlative exemplars of exquisite artistry. But why did Vincent take note of any of them at all? It was simply because they possessed what he, and Kierkegaard, called "an awakening power" (CL R43). "'Let your light shine before [all]' is something that I think is the duty of every painter," he said (CL R43).

What precisely is this "light" so incumbent upon the painter to shine before others? Is it merely an artist's unique perspective—that is, *your* light that *you* alone possess, and no one else but *you* can shed in the way that *you* shed it? This would be only "partial" truth. The "whole" of truth is greater.

Vincent spoke of "spiritual ecstasy" when he wrote to his friend Émile Bernard. "Personally," he said, "*if* I am capable of spiritual ecstasy, I adore Truth, the possible, and therefore I bow down before that study—powerful enough to make a Millet tremble—of peasants carrying home to the farm a calf which has been born in the fields. Now this, my friend, all people have felt from France to America; and after that are you going to revive medieval tapestries for us? Now honestly, is this a sincere conviction? No! You can do better than that." (CL B21).

What was it about Millet's art that was such a far cry better than a medieval tapestry? It was, as Vincent knew so well for himself, that Millet *intimated* the adored "Truth, the possible." He expressed the truth *from within* the scene, *from within* the realm of the encountered experience. He did not impose a caption beneath it or place a sign above it, as though boldly declaring to the viewer: Look, you see this halo surrounding the head of Jesus. It is the golden glow of his divinity! How could you possibly fail to see his divinity so long as you can see this halo?

It is possible to do far better than that. For Vincent, as for Millet, the visual manifestation of "spiritual ecstasy," of which artist and viewer alike are capable, is encountered through the painted scene *as it is* without "signage." Truth is *experienced*, not instructed. A halo is an imposter, a surrogate, like a blinking neon light would be, set atop Mount Sinai to satisfy Moses of God's presence in the absence of personal encounter with God. Art lacking the *realization* of truth, like "cheap grace," may be compared with the Ten Commandments written on a plastic key fob hanging on the shelf next to the bubble gum machine at the Five and Ten Cents Store instead of being written upon the human heart. For art to become the medium of spiritual ecstasy, of direct encounter with Mystery, of authentic experience of God, then art must evoke, educe,

—draw out—the truth, and induce—draw in—the viewer to the truth that is "powerful enough to make a Millet tremble" or a Vincent van Gogh to "bow down."

Jesus—as the "art" of God hanging upon a wooden Roman cross, bleeding and gasping for breath, with iron nails driven into his hands and feet—had no glowing halo set about his head. There was only the crown of thorns piercing his brow. If there is any divinity to be seen in a scene such as this, then a halo simply lacks the power to convey it. One either sees such terrifying "holiness" with the eyes of faith or does not see it at all. In the same manner of speaking, "plastic" art is not religious art. If anything, it is no better than the same neon sign being posted above Jesus' tomb, blinking: "Behold, he is risen." But who in a right mind, or for that matter a wrong one, could possibly believe it to be so *without winking*?

In an evocative letter to Anthon van Rappard, Vincent sought to educe (by the subtly of a picture) rather than deduce (by an axiom) the following for his friend:

> Look Rappard, whither I am trying to drive myself, and whither I am trying to drive others too, is to be fishermen on the sea that we call the Ocean of Reality, but on the other hand I want—for myself and for the fellow creatures whom I importune now and then—that "little cottage," most decidedly I do! And in that cottage, all those things! So the open sea and that resting place, or that resting place *and* the open sea. And as regards the doctrine I preach, this doctrine of mine—"My friends, let us love what we love"—is based on an axiom. I thought it superfluous to mention this axiom, but for clarity's sake I will add it. That axiom is: "My friends, we love." (CL R6)

Saint John said it succinctly: "God is love, and those who abide in love abide in God, and God abides in them."[19] This "abiding in love" is the key to grasping the deeper meanings of Vincent's art. For if the world is meant to be anything other than what it sometimes is when it resembles anything but love, then it is meant to be the showcase of God's love. And this is true to the extent that even the apparent absence of God is the paradoxical manifestation of the presence of God.

The holon of the finite (the "little cottage") within the holon of the Infinite (the "Ocean of Reality" or "open sea") constitutes the nexus of

---

19. 1 John 4:16b. The word for "love" in this and the surrounding passage is *agape*.

broadest and deepest concentricity of *nature within Nature, of being within Divine Being*, of which "love" is the cathexis.[20] And yet "the little cottage" and the "Ocean of Reality"—the part within the Whole—are juxtaposed realities, so tightly juxtaposed that they are as likely to be divergent as they are convergent—like lovers whose love is both freeing and binding. In that sense, the entire spectrum of colors in the rainbow can dissolve in an instant into light or darkness, either one of which and both of which presume the other. It is just so with an entire universe filled with a plethora of sorrows and joys. For it is their combination that casts us upon the rocks and shoals that inhabit the calm and soothing, sometimes troubling, waters of the divine mystery.

OBSESSIONS AND EPIPHANIES

Consider what W. Paul Jones said of Annie Dillard, the Pulitzer Prize-winning author, whose love of nature is as profound as was Vincent's.

> The writings of Annie Dillard are helpful in grasping the anatomy of [the] impulsing logic, fundamental to the emergence of a theo-logical World. . . . In searching for some unifying thread in her *Pilgrim at Tinker Creek*, I find two events emerging as crucial. In fact, they keep emerging as variations on a theme. In each case, they have the power of an ache and the claim of a gestalt. The most powerful, and in that sense the most overarching, occurs as, flat on her stomach, she intently watches the surface of a pond. Her eye almost touches the water line—alert to any stirrings that might turn nature into an event. And there, no more than a foot or so from her eyes, arises out of the water the face of a frog. For a moment their eyes meet, locked together, clasped in sacred won-der. An eternal Now. But as she looks, the seeing turns into a stare, and the eyes cave in upon themselves from within. The frog's face is slowly sucked inside out, like a worn-out ball. It sinks slowly be-neath the surface. But only for a moment. Rebreaking the surface, there emerges the head of a giant water bug. Almost with an evil grin, it stares at her, as it relentlessly crunches the life out of the frog—its "mouth a gash of terror." Horror! Paralyzed . . .

---

20. From the Greek word *katechein* (to hold fast, retain), in psychoanalytic psychol-ogy denoting the idea of binding the energy between structures or substances, such as the love energy (*eros*) of attachment between a subject and an object. The most binding form of love is the unconditional love of divine *agape*.

One tries to domesticate such an invading image by enfolding it into life-as-usual. But to no avail, for by now it has become an obsession. In fact, the more it replays, the deeper it bores. Thinking about it only intensifies its grasp. Finally, the obsession sinks its teeth in all the way, when she is forced to ask, "Would I eat a frog's leg if it were offered?" The answer is as clear as it is obsessive—*Yes!* And the image, once external, becomes deeply fastened internally.

However Dillard understands such matters conceptually, viewed functionally, this image is the ground of an impulsing logic that cinches her work together as religious quest. The way this event functions as impulse is best identified as "obsessio." An obsessio is whatever functions deeply and pervasively in one's life as a defining quandary, a conundrum, a boggling of the mind, a hemorrhaging of the soul, a wound that bewilders healing, a mystification that renders one's living cryptic. Whatever inadequate words one might choose to describe it, an obsessio is that which so gets its teeth into a person that it establishes one's life as plot. It is a memory which, as resident image, becomes so congealed as Question that all else in one's experience is sifted in terms of its promise as Answer. Put another way, an obsessio is whatever threatens to deadlock the Yeses with No. It is one horn that establishes life as dilemma. It is the negative pole that functions within one's defining rhythm. The etymology of the word says it well: *obsessio* means "to be besieged" . . .

For Dillard, that obsessio means she must suffer, as the price for being, a horror that is knit into the fabric of her life. She is not to forget it—obsessio! And what is the impact of its pervasive weight? It gives the feel of exile—in her case, from nature, of which she is a part, and which is part of her. This means being a cosmic orphan, to be in and not of—or is it of but not in? Whichever, it is enough to serve as the impulsing logic of a lifetime."[21]

Consider this: For Vincent, too, the "impulsing logic of a lifetime," his obsessio, was likewise the fate of his exile. Typecast as the outcast, the derelict, the prodigal, he no longer could escape the perceived persona of a mumbling moron minus his marbles. So grievously had he tumbled from his appointed "station in life" that his father once reminded him: "Do not forget the story of Icarus, who wanted to fly to the sun, and having arrived at a certain height, then lost his wings and dropped into the sea" (CL 43). Appearing to be deranged and disordered with

21. Jones, *Theological Worlds*, 26–28.

conflict, he was afflicted with hunger and disease, and enflamed in defiance of authoritarian hypocrisies. He was the one person whom others would taunt, twice over, and think nothing of it. He was the proverbial artist, deemed to be drunk and doomed to be "mad"—"a winebibber, a friend of publicans and sinners,"[22]—who, like Jesus, was accused of being a "gluttonous man," whose gluttony, in the absence of prime rib and the priciest wine of Brittany, consisted of a scrap of canvas and a tube of paint, with a bottle of absinthe and a pipe of tobacco thrown in for effect. And when he had neither paint nor brush, he cut for himself a reed to make himself a pen, or took a knife with which to improvise his "impasto." His lot, prototypically, was that of a "cosmic orphan" dwelling in the cosmic orphanage with all the other cosmic orphans, abiding in a "little cottage" swallowed up in the "Ocean of Reality"—one could say, not exactly what makes for a painless and carefree existence. Then, on top of it all, if not because of it all, there were those doggedly persistent questions that for most of us have no quick and easy answers: In the grand scheme of things, why is it that a "frog's face is slowly sucked inside out" with its "mouth a gash of terror," but the "pilgrim at Tinker Creek" is hard-pressed to see within such a "medieval tapestry" a halo circumnavigating the frog's head?

W. Paul Jones's snapshot of Annie Dillard's "frog world" demonstrates that both Annie and the frog were "enwrapped in morose and moribund passivity within [their] obsessio." The "enwrapment," being of all conditions the most deadly, "is to experience a state of spiritual abortion. *Depression* is the clinical term for this vicious circle."[23] Kierkegaard was no prevaricator, either, when he went so far as to say that the only thing to call this beast is Despair.

"Normality, on the other hand," writes Jones, "is the term for a lively dialectic between one's obsessio and that which functions as illumination, enabling a dynamic which entertains the possibility of wholeness." Illumination is the instrument of awakening that *opens the way* to wholeness.

> The second pole we identify as *epiphania*, etymologically meaning "to show upon," that which keeps the functioning of obsessio fluid, hopeful, searching, restless, energized, intriguing, as a

---

22. Luke 7:34b, KJV.
23. Jones, *Theological Worlds*, 28.

question worth pursuing for a lifetime. It keeps one's obsessio from becoming a fatal conclusion that signals futility.

One's epiphania is as difficult to discern as one's obsessio. It too is most detectable functionally—in this case, by its evocative power. Reminiscent of the workings of an oyster, an epiphania is known by its capacity so to enfold an obsessio that the grating particle is made bearable. Indeed, quietly within its promise is the hope that the obsessio, while never lost, might become the center for a pearl of great price, flowing back to redeem the whole.[24]

This is precisely what, one might be led to believe, happened to Dillard. At least once in reality, and far more often in memory, she is so claimed. It is a very special day. Nature, from which she has been exiled by violence, lays claim to her as epiphania. It comes as a morning moment when she sees a frost-covered cedar tree suddenly ablaze with light as three hundred red-winged blackbirds fill it to overflowing. If only for that one sacramental moment, the exiled Annie belongs—the prodigal is embraced on the road! But as the Gospel according to Luke alerts us, it "vanished out of their sight."

Yet the hint is sufficiently powerful that one can wager a "Did not our hearts burn within us?" Emmaus. Resurrection. Epiphania! Thus the impulsing logic which renders each life a religious question, whether consciously or otherwise, is this rhythm, slung between obsessio and epiphania, experienced or dreamed of. It is that which marks us as fugitives, vagabonds, clowns, or sojourners. Whatever, it drives us on to seek signs that the question wrapped in foil as one's obsessio is at least worthy. It is this impulsing logic that confirms us as theologians.

For Dillard, living concretely the rhythm that flows between her obsessio and epiphania means living the intersection between oceans of horror and oceans of beauty . . . "I alternate between thinking of the planet as home—dear and familiar stone hearth and garden—and as a hard land of exile in which we are all sojourners." Here they are, set side by side.[25]

Concerning the "hard land of exile," Jones invoked the spirits of both the theologian and the psychotherapist:

This obstacle as obsessio marks the threshold of life as labyrinth, forging that driving impulse which serves both as motive and as test for meaning. While this dynamic is universal, its specificity

24. Ibid.
25. Ibid., 28–30.

in each individual illustrates functionally what theologians abstractly call the human condition. This functioning of obsessio becomes graphic in psychotherapy when the attempt is made to discern a patient's agonized life as variations on a theme. Therapy offers many techniques for uncovering such an obsessio, which in resisting identity becomes as immovable as it is insoluble. Whatever its content or intensity, we are dealing with that primal level of functioning in each of us with which one must make peace, for it will not go away.[26]

As for release from such exile, Jones invoked the spirit of the twentieth-century bard of mystery: "Poet T. S. Eliot refers to such epihanias as the 'unattended moments, in and out of time,' which serve as 'hints followed by guesses.'"[27] And this is precisely what Vincent entertained with his art. In the midst of his obsession he was looking for those "unattended moments, in and out of time"—those "epiphanias"—those "hints followed by guesses"—which he then sought to place right squarely in the middle of his canvas. Light pushing back the darkness works its way into the painting. And when at last the Light is perceived for what it *really* is, it transforms the moment. But like the red-winged blackbirds filling the Christmas tree to overflowing, usually when one is not looking, and then only for a smidgen of time, the Light flickers and quivers in the blinding darkness and then vanishes out of sight.

It is just so with resurrection. If one is—say, not just lucky enough, but sufficiently attentive enough—it is possible to catch a glimpse of something like the flash of a streaking meteorite, or the sudden twinkling of "one single star, but a beautiful, large, friendly one" bursting forth brightly in the abysmal, "unsightly" silence of the night,[28] or a glimpse of the first rose-red ray of early morning light. There it is—whether one is ready for it or not—standing forth to greet it or not—caught sleeping like a prisoner in the solitary confinement of the self, or not—as it breaks forth in a split second of splendor like the "sun" rising before disappearing behind the clouds of Mystery.[29]

Vincent once wrote in reprisal to Theo:

26. Ibid., 27.

27. Ibid., 31.

28. CL 67. See Vincent's painting of "The Café Terrace on the Place du Forum, Arles, at Night," WM, 425; "Starry Night," WM, 520–21; "Starry Night over the Rhone," WM, 431.

29. See Vincent's "Enclosed Field with Rising Sun," WM, 600–601.

> When you say in your last letter, "What a mystery nature is," I
> quite agree with you. Life in the abstract is already an enigma;
> reality makes it an enigma within an enigma. And who are we to
> solve it? However, we ourselves are an atom of that universe which
> makes us wonder: Where does it go, to the devil or to God? . . .
> Pourtant le soleil se lève [and yet the sun rises], says Victor Hugo
> . . . I feel *a power in me which I must develop, a fire that I may not
> quench, but must keep ablaze*, though I do not know to what end it
> will lead me, and shouldn't be surprised if it were a gloomy one. In
> times like these, what should one wish for? What is relatively the
> happiest fate? . . . When one is in a somber mood, how good it is to
> walk on the barren beach and look at the graying-green sea with
> the long white streaks of the waves. But if one feels the need of
> something grand, something infinite, something that makes one
> feel aware of God, one need not go far to find it. (CL 242)

In such moments, Ken Wilber proposed: "If the nature, meaning,
and value of art are not simply due to art's imitative capacity, perhaps
the essence of art lies in its power to *express* something, and not simply
to *copy* something. And indeed, in both the theory and practice of art,
emphasis often began to turn from a faithful copying and representing
and imitating—whether of religious icons or of a realistic nature—to *an
increasingly expressionist stance*."[30]

As if he were anticipating the words of Wilber, Paul Tillich wrote:
"One could say that only styles which can express the ecstatic character
of the Spiritual Presence lend themselves to religious art, and this would
mean that some expressionistic element has to be present in a style in
order to make it a tool for religious art." Such styles "are best able to
express the ecstatic quality of the Spirit."[31]

Vincent meant to say all of that when he said: "*I think I see something deeper, more infinite, more eternal than the ocean in the expression
of the eyes of a little baby when it wakes in the morning, and coos or laughs
because it sees the sun shining on its cradle. If there is a 'rayon d'en haut
[ray from on high],' perhaps one can find it there*"[32] (CL 242).

---

30. Wilber, *Eye of Spirit*, 105.
31. Tillich, *Systematic Theology*, 3: 213.
32. Italics added.

Mother Roulin with Her Baby

SEVEN

The Art of Being the Self before God

FAITH AND DESPAIR

R ECALL THE CONUNDRUM: As the sun rises from darkness, then
returns to it, the artist's true vision requires of the artist that self-
assertion be relinquished to self-abnegation—an impossible assignment,
at best.[1] With this in mind, we attend further to Kierkegaard:

> Now something happens that impinges . . . upon this immediate
> self and makes it despair . . . and the despair is nothing more than
> a submitting. By a "stroke of fate" that which to the man[2] of im-
> mediacy is his whole life, or, insofar as he has a minuscule of re-
> flection, the portion thereof to which he especially clings, is taken
> from him; in short, he becomes, as he calls it, unhappy, that is, his
> immediacy is dealt such a crushing blow that it cannot reproduce
> itself: he despairs. . . . But to despair is to lose the eternal—and of
> this loss he does not speak at all, he has no inkling of it. In itself,
> to lose the things of this world is not to despair; yet this is what
> he talks about, and this is what he calls despairing. In a certain

---

1. See chapter 2, section 2: "The Plight of Darkness." The metaphor should not be
taken literally since the sun emits light constantly. The metaphor works only from the
perspective of being earth-bound, from which the sun has the "appearance" of light
arising from and receding into darkness.

2. The masculine noun ("man") and masculine personal pronouns, due to their fre-
quency of usage, have been retained in the interest of the grammatical flow and literary
integrity of this passage, and are meant to be inclusive of both female and male genders.

sense, what he says is true, but not in the way he understands it; he is conversely situated, and what he says must be interpreted conversely: he stands and points to what he calls despair but is not despair, and in the meantime, sure enough, despair is right there behind him without his realizing it. It is as if someone facing away from the town hall and courthouse pointed straight ahead and said: There is the town hall and courthouse. He is correct, it is there—if he turns around. He is not in despair—this is not true—and yet he is correct in saying it. He claims he is in despair, he regards himself as dead, as a shadow of himself. But dead he is not; there is still, one might say, life in the person. If everything, all the externals, were to change suddenly, and if his desire were fulfilled, then there would be life in him again, then spontaneity and immediacy would escalate again, and he would begin to live all over again. This is the only way immediacy knows how to strive, the only thing it knows: to despair and faint—and yet, that about which he knows the least is despair . . .

Meanwhile, time passes. If help arrives from the outside, the person in despair comes alive again, he begins where he left off; a self he was not, and a self he did not become, but he goes on living, qualified only by immediacy. If there is no external help, something else frequently happens in actual life. In spite of everything, there is still life in the person, but he says that "he will never be himself again." He now acquires a little understanding of life, he learns how to copy others, how they manage their lives—and he now proceeds to live the same way. In Christendom he is also a Christian, goes to church every Sunday, listens to and understands the pastor, indeed, they have a mutual understanding; he dies, the pastor ushers him into eternity for ten rix-dollars—but a self he was not, and a self he did not become . . .

Immediacy actually has no self, it does not know itself; thus it cannot recognize itself and therefore generally ends in fantasy. When immediacy despairs, it does not even have enough self to wish or dream that it had become that which it has not become. . . . So when the externals have completely changed for the person of immediacy and he has despaired, he goes one step further; he thinks something like this, it becomes his wish: What if I became someone else, got myself a new self.[3]

This, however, works no better than the former. It is a superficial analgesic precisely because it is not possible. But then comes the day perhaps when the bottom falls out of everything and the self experiences the effects of a sudden self-emptying. And

3. Kierkegaard, *Sickness*, 51–53.

then what? The youth despairs over the future as the present *in futuro* [in the future]; there is something in the future that he is not willing to take upon himself, and therefore he does not will to be himself. The adult despairs over the past as a present *in praeterito* [in the past] that refuses to recede further into the past, for his despair is not such that he has succeeded in forgetting it completely. This past may even be something repentance really should have in custody. But if repentance is to arise, there must first be effective despair, radical despair, so that the life of the spirit can break through from the ground upward. But in despair as he is, he does not dare to let it come to such a decision. There he stands still, time passes—unless, even more in despair, he succeeds in healing it by forgetting it, and thus instead of becoming a penitent, he becomes his own receiver of stolen goods . . .

But essentially the despair of a youth and of an adult remains the same; there is never a metamorphosis in which consciousness of the eternal in the self breaks through so that the battle can begin that either intensifies the despair in a still higher form or leads to faith. . . . When the self in imagination despairs with infinite passion over something of this world [such as loss of limb, loved one, position, power, ambition, kingdom, or empire], its infinite passion changes this particular thing, this something, into the world *in toto*; that is, the category of totality inheres in and belongs to the despairing person. . . . Consequently, the self infinitely magnifies the actual loss and then despairs over the earthly *in toto*.[4]

Kierkegaard insists upon what must happen: "You must go through despair of the self to the self."[5] But this is precisely what the false self resists, lest it lose its immediate, more superficial, illusory self, which it mistakes for its actual self. For, there is a constitutional order to the self in despair of itself.

First comes despair over the earthly or over something earthly, then despair of the eternal, over oneself. . . . The despair that is the thoroughfare to faith comes also through the aid of the eternal; through the aid of the eternal the self has the courage to lose itself in order to win itself. Here, however, it is unwilling to begin with losing itself but wills [instead] to be itself.[6]

4. Ibid., 59-60, italics added except for already italicized Latin phrases.

5. Ibid., 65.

6. Ibid., 67.

The conflict between self-assertion and self-abnegation presents a choice: become a false self by disclaiming the true self (self-assertion) or become a true self by disclaiming the false self (self-abnegation). In either case a disclaimer must be made and a renunciation must take place. Something must be forfeited. "No one can serve two masters." For, as Jesus said, to do so is to "either hate the one and love the other, or be devoted to the one and despise the other."[7] One of the selves must fall away. Kierkegaard once again addressed this issue by going straight to the heart of the matter.

> The self is its own master, absolutely its own master, so-called; and precisely this is the despair, but also what it regards as its pleasure and delight. On closer examination, however, it is easy to see that this absolute ruler is a king without a country, actually ruling over nothing. . . . Consequently, the self in despair is always building only castles in the air, is only shadowboxing. . . . In despair the self wants to enjoy the total satisfaction of making itself into itself, of developing itself, of being itself . . . the way it has understood itself. And yet, in the final analysis, what it understands by itself is a riddle; in the very moment when it seems that the self is closest to having the building completed, it can arbitrarily dissolve the whole thing into nothing.[8]

On the other hand, when the self goes through the despair of the self—to the Self—it becomes its true self. "This self is no longer the merely human self but is what I, hoping not to be misinterpreted, would call the theological self, the self directly before God. . . . In fact, the greater the conception of God, the more self there is; the more self, the greater the conception of God. Not until a self as this specific single individual is conscious of existing before God, not until then is it the infinite self."[9] Finally, Kierkegaard arrives at a crucial definition of faith. "Faith is: that the self in being itself and in willing to be itself rests transparently in God." Sin, therefore, is "'whatever does not proceed from faith.'"[10] Indispensible for understanding Vincent's life and his art is his implicit trust that "in God we live and move and have our being." In that sense the artist who stands before his canvas creating his art is the theological self standing directly before God, resting transparently in God.

7. Matthew 6:24.

8. Kierkegaard, *Sickness*, 69–70.

9. Ibid., 79–80.

10. Ibid., 82; Romans 14:23.

This means that art and life are fully art and life to the extent that the distance separating subject and object is overcome within the transcendent unity that exists between the self and God. The dynamic harmony between the human and the divine comprises the experience of "spiritual ecstasy." The vertical dimension of life is encountered within the horizontal. This is what turned Vincent's art into vocation and his vocation into art as an "expression" of the eternal, in so far as "a conceptual identification of infinity with finitude"[11] is artistically possible. Here lies the profound depth and meaning of his portraiture and paintings, in that he pursues his own development in semblance to the consciousness of Jesus. "One will succeed," he said, "in developing one's conscience to such a point that it becomes the voice of a better and higher self, of which the ordinary self is the servant. . . . One sees the same thing in Jesus too; first he was an ordinary carpenter, but raised himself to something else, whatever it may have been—a personality so full of pity, love, goodness, seriousness that one is still attracted by it" (CL 306).

As Vincent said two years before his death to his friend Bernard: "Christ alone—of all the philosophers, Magi, etc.—has affirmed, as a principal certainty, eternal life, the infinity of time, the nothingness of death, the necessity and the raison d'être [reason for being] of serenity and devotion. He lived serenely, as a greater artist than all other artists, despising marble and clay as well as color, working in living flesh. That is to say, this matchless artist, hardly to be conceived of by the obtuse instrument of our modern, nervous, stupefied brains, made neither statues nor pictures nor books; he loudly proclaimed that he made . . . living [people], immortals." (CL B8)

Such mysteries expressed within the forms and content of visual art are parallel to what Rudolf Otto said of musical art when describing Johann Sebastian Bach's B-Minor Mass: "Its mystical portion is the 'Incarnatus' in the Credo, and there the effect is due to the faint, whispering, lingering sequence in the fugue structure, dying away pianissimo. The held breath and hushed sound of the passage, its weird cadences, sinking away in lessened thirds, its pauses and syncopations, and its rise and fall in astonishing semitones, which render so well in the sense of awe-struck wonder—all this serves to express the mysterium by way of intimation, rather than in forthright utterance."[12]

11. A phrase employed by Thomas Altizer, *Van Gogh's Eyes*, 397.

12. Otto, *The Idea of the Holy*, 72.

And so it was when Vincent painted a certain pair of shoes.

"A Pair of Shoes"

"LIFE" AND "ART": WHAT IS CONTAINED WITHIN A PAIR OF SHOES?[13]

Shoes are worn for walking. They transport a person from place to place, as in a pilgrim making a pilgrimage. Along the way the pilgrim lies down for rest, leaning back against a tall haystack. He kicks his shoes off of his feet. He covers his face with his straw hat, raises his arms, and folds his hands behind his head. As he falls asleep, his anxious thoughts and weary sack of troubles are carried away into a "still life"[14] dream. When he awakens, he stares down at the wrinkles, the tears, and the abrasions in his "shoes." His "leathers," like his life, are frayed, "worn," and profligate. His "strings are loose."

13. "A Pair of Shoes," WM, 183.
14. "Noon: Rest from Work," ibid., 610–11.

Many considered Vincent to be a "madman." His demeanor, his strange behaviors, and his acts of self-flagellation were taken as *prima facie* evidence of his "madness." By inference, a madman is supposed to produce mad art. His works of art are an expression of the strange and dislocated world he inhabits inside and outside himself: broad strokes across the canvas—dark, swirling clouds upon the horizon—bright, "oddish" colors juxtaposed in "loud," vivid contrast—and a self-portrait in which, from the look of the bandage over his ear, he appears to flaunt the fact that he is painfully missing a part of himself.

According to an account of someone connected with the Antwerp art academy, Vincent painted "feverishly, furiously, with a rapidity that stupefied his fellow students. 'He laid on his paint so thickly,' Mr. Hageman told us, that his colors literally dripped from his canvas onto the floor" (CL 458a). Vincent, "the young Dutchman, rustic *(sic!)* of the Danube *(sic!)* (or of the Lower Meuse) whose rudeness had terrified the fair clients of Goupil's at Paris, flew into a violent passion, and roared at his professor, who was scared out of his wits: 'So,' [says Vincent to Mr. Sieber], 'you don't know what a young woman is like, God damn you! A woman must have hips and buttocks and a pelvis in which she can hold a child!" (CL 458a).

What child? —one might ask.

Another witness offered the following footnote: "The drawing master [at the academy] sent Van Gogh down to a lower class, and there Vincent, who scorned nothing, did drawings of 'noses and ears'" (CL 458a). On top of that, in spite of his overall intellectual lucidity mixed with an enormous capacity for aesthetic sensitivity and personal empathy, he once described himself as that awful "shaggy dog." "So if remarks are made about my habits—meaning dress, face, manner of speech—what answer shall I make . . . that such talk annoys me?" (CL 190).

A photograph taken of Vincent at age eighteen lent credence to his frenzy. When years later the neighbors in Arles took up a petition against this bizarre character living in their neighborhood (a man who mortifies his own flesh must be considered dangerous), to them it appeared perfectly clear that there was ample cause to declare this man "mad."

Finally, there was Vincent's suicide. What else would be needed for sufficient proof of the fact that this man decidedly had gone off his rocker? —Mad, mad, mad!

But, back now to the shoes.[15] The philosopher Martin Heidegger once set about to interpret the meaning of Vincent's painting of a pair of shoes. Ken Wilber explained that Heidegger, whose essay was entitled "The Origin of the Work of Art"[16] (as it turns out, an ironic title), wanted to convey the fact that a work of art "can disclose truth." Yet, what truth?

Heidegger assumed that here was a pair of peasant shoes, and he said, "with reference to the painting alone," that he, Heidegger, could "penetrate to the essence of its message." So, Heidegger concluded: "There is nothing surrounding this pair of peasant shoes in or to which they might belong, only undefined space. There are not even clods from the soil of the field or the path through it sticking to them, which might at least hint at their employment. A pair of peasant shoes and nothing more. And yet."[17]

"And yet," as Wilber said, "Heidegger will reach deeply into the form of the artwork, all by itself, and render the essence of its meaning."[18]

Again, Heidegger is speaking:

> From the dark opening of the worn insides of the shoes the toilsome tread of the worker stands forth. In the stiffly solid heaviness of the shoes there is the accumulated tenacity of her slow trudge through the far-spreading and ever-uniform furrows of the field, swept by a raw wind. On the leather there lies the dampness and saturation of the soil. Under the soles there slides the loneliness of the field-path as the evening declines. In the shoes there vibrates the silent call of the earth, its quiet gift of the ripening corn and its enigmatic self-refusal in the fallow desolation of the wintry field. This equipment is pervaded by an uncomplaining anxiety about the certainty of bread, the wordless joy of having once more withstood want, the trembling before the advent of birth and the shivering at the surrounding menace of death. This equipment belongs to the earth and it is protected in the world of the peasant woman. From out of this protected belonging the equipment itself rises to its resting-in-self.[19]

Wilber continued: "That is a beautiful interpretation, beautifully expressed, lodging itself carefully in the details of the painting, which

15. Vincent's painting of "A Pair of Shoes," WM, 183.

16. Wilber, *Eye of Spirit*, 121.

17. Ibid., 122.

18. Ibid.

19. Ibid.

makes it all the sadder that virtually every statement in it is wildly inaccurate."[20] How so? It turns out, as Wilber determined:

> To begin with, these shoes are Van Gogh's shoes, not some peasant woman's. He was by then a town and city dweller, not a toiler in the fields; under its soles there are no corn fields, no slow trudging through uniform furrows, no dampness of the soil and no loneliness of the field-path. Not an ounce, nary a trace, of enigmatic self-refusal in the fallow of the desolation of the wintry field can be found. "Van Gogh's painting is the disclosure of what the equipment, the pair of peasant shoes, is in truth," exclaims Heidegger.
>
> Perhaps, but Heidegger has not come near that truth at all. Instead—and while not in any way ignoring the relevant features of the artwork holon itself—we must go outside the artwork, into larger contexts, to determine more of its meaning.[21]

Actually, Vincent was living in his "Yellow House" in Arles at the time he painted the shoes. He was sharing a room with his fellow artist Paul Gauguin. Gauguin had noticed this "pair of badly worn shoes," which "seemed to have a very important meaning" for Vincent. Gauguin told the story as he heard it from Vincent.[22] Gauguin is speaking:

"In the studio was a pair of big hob-nailed shoes, all worn and spotted with mud; he made of it a remarkable still life painting. I do not know why I sensed that there was a story behind this old relic, and I ventured one day to ask him if he had some reasons for preserving with respect what one ordinarily throws out for the rag-picker's basket."[23]

Vincent proceeded then to give Gauguin an explanation: "My father," he said, "was a pastor, and at his urging I pursued theological studies in order to prepare for my future vocation. As a young pastor I left for Belgium one fine morning, without telling my family, to preach the gospel in the factories, not as I had been taught but as I understood it myself. These shoes, as you see, have bravely endured the fatigue of that trip."[24]

Wilber asked: "Why exactly were these shoes so important to Vincent? Why had he carried them with him for so long, beaten and

20. Ibid.

21. Ibid., 122–23.

22. Ibid. See also Gauguin's account as reproduced in Stein, *Van Gogh*, 121–22.

23. Wilber, *Eye of Spirit*, 123. See Wilber's footnote documenting his combining of two of Gauguin's accounts from Meyer Shapiro's *Theory and Philosophy of Art*.

24. Wilber, *Eye of Spirit*, 123.

worn as they were?"[25] For, they were of little or no practical use to anyone, including the owner. The shoes were important, however, precisely because they had meaning. They had meaning beyond the shoes themselves. The shoes were figurative "selfobjects," which in and of themselves alone were mostly meaningless apart from their function of protecting the feet and transporting the wearer to his intended destination once upon a time. That is to say: this was so unless their true meaning—their Meaning within the meaning—the Self within the self, the Time within the once upon a time—came from beyond the shoes themselves.

Wilber said: "And then a vision came upon Vincent, a vision that he disclosed to his friend Gauguin, a vision that explains why this incident was so important to him."[26]

The fourth holon consisted of the vision—"infinitely" larger than the first three holons.

The third holon consisted of the shoes, "frayed, worn, and profligate" from the great "firestorm"—which explained why their "strings were loose."

The second holon consisted of the shoes worn by the preacher on his preaching mission.

The first holon consisted of the shoes themselves.

Back to the fourth holon, where, again, Gauguin is speaking:

> When we were together in Arles, both of us mad, and in constant war over the beauty of color—me, I loved the color red; where to find a perfect vermillion? He traced with his most yellow brush on the wall, suddenly turned violet:[27]

> I am whole in Spirit
> I am the Holy Spirit

Gauguin is still speaking:

> In my yellow room—a small still life: violet that one. Two enormous worn-out misshapen shoes. They were Vincent's shoes. Those that he took one fine morning, when they were new, for his journey on foot from Holland to Belgium. The young preacher had just finished his theological studies in order to be a minister like his father. He had gone off to the mines to those whom

25. Ibid.
26. Ibid., 124.
27. Stein, *Van Gogh*, 121. This is almost identical to the translation in Wilber's account.

he called his brothers,[28] like the simple workers, such as he had read of in the Bible, oppressed for the luxury of the great.[29]

Contrary to the teachings of his instructors, the wise Dutchmen, Vincent believed in Jesus who loved the poor; his soul, entirely suffused with charity, desired by means of consoling words and self-sacrifice to help the weak, to combat the great. Decidedly, decidedly, Vincent was already mad.[30]

Wilber commented: "'Vincent was already mad'—Gauguin repeats this several times, thick with irony; that we all should be graced enough to touch such madness!"[31]

Gauguin is speaking again:

His teaching of the Bible in the mines was, I believe, profitable to the miners below, but disagreeable to the authorities on high, above ground. He was quickly recalled, dismissed, and a family council convened that judged him mad, and advised rest at a sanatorium. He was not, however, confined, thanks to his brother Theo.

One day the somber black mine was flooded by chrome yellow, the fierce flash of firedamp fire, a mighty dynamite that never misfires. The beings who were crawling and teeming about in filthy carbon when this occurred bid, on that day, farewell to life, farewell to men, without blasphemy.

One of them, terribly mutilated, his face burnt, was taken in by Vincent. "And yet," the company doctor had said, "he is a finished man, barring a miracle or very costly nursing. No, it would be folly to attend to him."

Vincent believed in miracles, in maternity.

The mad man (decidedly he was mad) kept watch for forty days at the bedside of the dying man; he prevented the air from ruthlessly penetrating into his wounds and paid for the medications. He spoke as a consoling priest (decidedly he was mad). The works of a madman had revived a Christian from the dead.[32]

Wilber added: "The scars on the man's face—this man resurrected by a miracle of care—looked to Vincent exactly like the scars from a

28. Wilber, *Eye of Spirit*, 124.

29. Stein, *Van Gogh*, 121. Stein includes the last clause of the sentence, which was omitted by ellipsis in Wilber's account.

30. Ibid., italics added.

31. Wilber, *Eye of Spirit*, 124.

32. Stein, *Van Gogh*, 121–22.

crown of thorns. 'I had,' Vincent says, 'in the presence of this man who bore on his brow a series of scars, a vision of the crown of thorns, a vision of the resurrected Christ.'" Vincent then "picks up his brush and says, referring to the 'resurrected Christ': 'And I, Vincent, I painted him.'"[33]

Gauguin repeated: "Tracing with his yellow brush, suddenly turned violet, Vincent cried:

> I am Holy Spirit
> I am whole in Spirit

"Decidedly, this man was mad."[34]

Ken Wilber offered a "midrash":

> Psychoanalysis, no doubt, would have some therapeutic inter-pretations for all of this. But psychoanalytic interpretations, relatively true as they might be, do not in themselves touch deeper "realms of the human unconscious," such as the existential or the spiritual and transpersonal. . . . And at the upper reaches of the spectrum of consciousness—in the higher states of consciousness—individuals consistently report an awareness of being one with the all, or identical with spirit, or whole in spirit. . . . The attempt of shallower psychologies, such as psychoanaly-sis, to merely pathologize *all* of these higher states has simply not held up to further scrutiny and evidence. Rather, the total web of crosscultural evidence strongly suggests that these deeper or higher states are potentials available to all of us, so that, as it were, "Christ consciousness"—spiritual awareness and union—is available to each and every one of us. . . . Thus, Vincent's central vision itself most likely was not pathological, not psychotic, not madness at all—which is why Gauguin keeps poking fun at those who would think that way: decidedly, he was mad. Which means, decidedly, he was plugged into a reality that we should all be so fortunate to see. Thus, when Vincent said he saw the resurrected Christ, that is exactly what he meant, and that is very likely ex-actly what he saw. And thus he carried with him, as a dusty but dear reminder, the shoes in which this vision occurred. And so, you see, an important part of the primal meaning of the painting of these shoes—not the only meaning, but a primal meaning—is

33. Wilber, *Eye of Spirit*, 125.
34. Ibid.

very simple: these are the shoes in which Vincent nursed Jesus, the Jesus in all of us.[35]

The last thing that Gauguin said of "these shoes" was this: "Vincent took up his palette again; silently he worked. Beside him was a white canvas. I began his portrait. I too had the vision of a Jesus preaching kindness and humility."[36]

This is the "life" and the "light" that are Christ's shoes. This is the "life" and the "light" that are the "art" of Christ's shoes. If a person—any person—has a pair of shoes belonging to Christ, what does she or he do with them?

It is simply not possible to understand Vincent van Gogh, or his art, without considering what happened *in* these shoes and *in* a thousand other *epiphanies of God* just like them. Hans-Georg Gadamer called this a "'fusion of horizons.'" In Wilber's symbolization, "a *new holon emerges*, which itself is a new context and thus carries new meaning."[37] It is just as Vincent said, and just as he painted for all to see: "Art is something greater and higher than our own adroitness or accomplishments or knowledge; that art is something which, although produced by human hands, is not created by these hands alone, but something which wells up from a deeper source in our souls" (CL R43).

The consequence is enormous once it becomes apparent exactly what has happened here, by way of the "art" that has been painted here. Whoever we might be—no matter what psychological, or theological, or ideological "pennant" beneath which we happen to sail our ships upon the "Ocean of Reality," as persons who are "treated as impostors, and yet are true"[38]—"as unknown, and yet are well known,"[39] this much remains true as well: as much as we may in fact be unprepared for it, or opposed to it, we are always subject to being opened to *Epiphany*.

35. Ibid., 125–26.

36. Ibid., 126.

37. For elaboration see Wilber, *Eye of Spirit*, 127ff.

38. 2 Corinthians 6:8b. There is a sense in which pastoral and spiritual counselors may invariably be viewed as "imposters" by those whose first allegiance is to the secular "legions of priests and priestesses from the pantheon of classical and popular psychology" who "have bowed the knee to an unknown God as though there were no God, and turned Psyche herself into a fragmented oracle" (Davidson, "Change," 425).

39. 2 Corinthians 6:9a. "Well known" in the sense that God knows us better than we know ourselves, for it is God who ultimately judges both the worker and the work, as the One who is present in the midst of it.

As Kierkegaard declared: "There is no disciple at second hand."[40] For the one at "second hand" is in the same place of encounter and decision as the one at "first hand," where one must decide what one believes about what one *sees* and *hears*:

Jesus of Nazareth, a Jew—royal descendant of Abraham and Sarah (too old to bear children)—of Isaac and Rebekah (hardly the ideal of a happily married couple)—of Jacob (who colluded with his mother to deceive his father and rip off his brother)—of Judah (who "went into" his daughter-in-law, Tamar, the Canaanite disguised as a prostitute)— of Rahab (the "woman" of Jericho, the harlot, the mother of Boaz and protector of spies)—of David (who killed the husband, Uriah, and with lustful eyes took the wife, Bathsheba, who bore them Solomon, the despot)—of Mary (the beautiful, innocent young woman of Nazareth) and Joseph (the strong and handsome out-of-town carpenter)—who by the wind of the Spirit gave birth to a mamzer[41] who befriended publicans and sinners—crossed the demarcation line between Jew and Samaritan—cast out demons, for which he was called Beelzebub, prince of demons—thrown out of his own congregation for claiming that the "Kingdom of God is present to you *here* and *now*"—who lived the life of a renegade prodigal and caused enough commotion to threaten the entire establishment of Jerusalem as well as the Pax Romana—who was mocked and crowned "king" of Israel with a brow full of thorns—and who, being secretly given over to the Roman authorities, was booked and beaten and taunted and spat upon him—a political prisoner whom

40. Kierkegaard, *Philosophical Fragments*, 131.

41. A "mamzer" was a "silenced one." Bruce Chilton writes: "The term *mamzer* refers specifically to a child born of a prohibited sexual union, such as incest (see Mishnah Yebamot 4:13). The fundamental issue was not sex before marriage (which was broadly tolerated) but sex with the wrong person. An unmarried woman impregnated by a man outside her own community was in an invidious position, suspected of illicit intercourse. // Unless she could bring witnesses to show she had been in the company of a licit father, it was assumed she had been made pregnant by a *mamzer* or another prohibited person, so that her child was a *mamzer* (Mishnah Ketubot 1:8–9). Mary's sexual relations with Joseph had not been prohibited, but given that Joseph had lived in Bethlehem and she in Nazareth when she became pregnant, it was virtually impossible for her to prove that he was the father. In the absence of proof, Jesus was considered a *mamzer*, what the Mishnah at a slightly later period calls a *shetuqi*, or "silenced one" (Qiddushin 4:1–2; see also Qiddushin 70a in the Talmud), without a voice in the public congregations that regulated the social, political, and religious life of Israel (Deuteronomy 23:2)" (Chilton, *Rabbi Jesus*, 12–13).

they made to carry his own cross, by means of which they summarily and *brutally executed him*.

The trouble is that most of us, living within a host of holons but confining ourselves at best to *one or two*, do not recognize such things as epiphanies. Nor do we permit ourselves the power of such things to transform us.

- We do not "re-cognize" them for the same reason that we consider despair to be nothing more than what in the immediacy of the moment it appears to be, as merely the dark "obsession" of a "depression" in which the self is deathly afraid of losing itself.

- For we have considered the self to be a true self when in fact it has not yet sufficiently emptied itself of its immediate, false self to become its infinite, true self before God.

- "*I will speak to my Lord, I who am but dust and ashes. If I repute myself greater than this, behold, You stand against me, and my sins bear witness to the truth which I cannot contradict. But if I abase myself and humble myself to nothingness, if I divest myself of all self-esteem (as I really am) and account myself as the dust which I am, Your grace will favor me, Your light will enshroud my heart, and all self-estimation, no matter how little, will sink in the depths of my nothingness and there lose itself for ever.*" —Thomas à Kempis, *The Imitation of Christ* [42]

---

42. Composite translation, Bruce (100) and Burns (163).

"The Pieta (after Delacroix)"

Van Gogh painted his own face into the face of the deceased Jesus,
completing the painting ten months before his own death

EIGHT

This Holy "Madness"

GETTING INSIDE THE TEXT AS THE TEXT GETS INSIDE OF US

A SCROLL OF SCRIPTURE SUCH as the Gospel of Luke, or a painting by van Gogh such as "The Potato Eaters,"[1] was, and still is, an *ars facta*—"something made of a profession" or "made to be professed"—which is what an "art-i-fact" is.

The Gospel book, like the field lark on its maiden flight, spread its wings within a local, historical, social, cultural, and religious con-"text." The "artist" who created the book, was in mind, manner, speech, appearance, and dress, also contextualized—embedded in time, place, and circumstance, and, despite great doubts and difficulties, was capable of transcending them.

From the outset, prior to and contemporaneous with the Gospel "artist," there were formed audiences of one, two, or three, and soon a few more, then a few more still, until there were hundreds gathered here and there within community—the like-minded and not-so like-minded with whom, about whom, for whom, these "evangels" were "arranged" and "composed" from "materials" discovered and received in bits and pieces from this place and that: things "handed down" from long and short synopses, collected sayings, oral traditions, stories, proverbs, sermons, speeches, apocalypses, and first-hand eye-witness reports wrapped in second-hand "this is what he said and did" packaging.

1. WM, 96–97.

There was—to open a scene—the oft repeated "in the days of" and "now the time came," the "once, when" and "then they said," with the introjections "blessed are you!" and "woe to you!" thrown into the middle, for good measure, or bad, followed by "soon afterwards he went on" and "when a great crowd gathered," "as they were going along the road," then "he said to them," and "someone in the crowd said to him," until, at the end, the narrator said to all: "then he opened their minds to understand."

Looping back to the beginning, the Gospel "artist" announced: "Since many have undertaken to set down an orderly account of the events that have been fulfilled among us, just as they were handed on to us by those who from the beginning were eyewitnesses and servants of the word, I too decided, after investigating everything carefully from the very first, to write an orderly account for you, most excellent Theophilus, so that you may know the truth concerning the things about which you have been instructed."[2]

In the course of time—overnight, years, decades, centuries later—there was received into the presence of this "art-i-fact" a multiplicity of visitors from newly emerging contexts. Some were curiosity seekers and others "potato eaters" hungry for a meal—"beholders" together of this "art-i-fact," wanting not only to see but also to touch it. Some of them, a diverse bunch, were Roman Christian or Christian Roman (some neither)—some Johnny-come-lately—Protestant, Holy Roller, Quaker, Shaker, Old Light, New Light, liberal-evangelical. They took this evangel into hand, minimally or maximally became attached to it, blew the dust off, unfurled it, sniffed it for mold, scanned the scroll—with God looking on, not exactly like a stand-by museum docent but looking on nonetheless. And in some cases they "sank their teeth" into this "art-i-fact."

Its "con-textuality" à "storied" reality, once told, twice told, many times over retold from within a formerly three-storied universe, now one story—post-Copernican, round, flat (technologically), subject to being "checked-out" through the telescope, microscope, "horror-scope" of higher, lower criticism—it is a document having been studied, carbon-dated, and, amid the most rigorous of debate, its most recent red-letter edition presented to a committee of scholars for a majority vote.

From Jerome to Jeremias—having first been preached, this Gospel book subsequently has been copied, analyzed, passed beneath lenses of

2. Luke 1:1–5.

scrutiny (there's always more than one)—every jot and tittle examined, interpretations formed and re-formed within neo-contexts, fluid and shifting, alternately frigid and fracturing (the generations come and go), as the "text" moves mouth-to-mouth, hand-to-hand, translation-to-translation, community-to-community, through the ages.

This "art-i-fact" has been re-discovered time and time again, but this time it has been set down, shelved between Tom Clancy's *The Hunt for Red October* and Maya Angelou's *I Know Why the Caged Bird Sings*. For this "art-i-fact"—otherwise to the faint of heart little more than an historic "artifice," a slight of hand, a ruse, a lie, a deception, or a cultural accretion—at some point, many points, unexpected points, suddenly, out of nowhere, becomes epiphany for the not so faint of heart. For "then," as it says: "he opened their minds to understand."

Some "greater artist than all other artists" had put his hand to this art-i-fact himself, and declared: This scroll shall not dwell among the treasures hidden in the rubble of dark, damp, and musty old basements of marble museums. Bring it out, and set it forth before the people—before the rabble!

St. Luke's Gospel and Vincent's painting of "The Potato Eaters"—not to be confused with one another—are nevertheless intimately and contiguously connected. Each is a holon-within-a-holon, that "projects a 'world' that shapes the judgments of the . . . interpreter who enters it."[3] For not only does the interpreter interpret the text, but also the text interprets the interpreter—just as the art interprets the viewer who interprets the art. The one becomes the one transfigured, the other the one transfiguring. In that sense scripture possesses the potency of art, and art the potency of scripture.

So now we ask: Of what effect and to what end is great art? What has the "scroll" to say, this "painting" to speak—to do with—all these sundry throngs of rabble, of curiosity seekers, sports spectators, stock brokers, tea-party sippers, Fortune 500 CEOs, casino crap-shooters, pimps, and prostitutes passing along the boulevard, some in their block-long limousines, others peddling bicycles, and a few pumping wheel chairs? Most are just perambulating between appointments in

3. Thiselton, *New Horizons in Hermeneutics: The Theory and Practice of Transforming Biblical Reading*, 10.

their more or less beleaguered, conflicted, and at times tragic "holons" of "contextuality"—when to look in the mirror is to see the full-blown demeanor of "madness."

Anthony Thiselton wrote: "Every tradition in the New Testament about the cross challenges any context-relative or ethnocentric understanding of its status: the cross impinges equally on 'Jew and Greek, slave and free, male and female,'"[4]—even though all may not receive it equally, and many may refuse it altogether for seeming to be preoccupied with nothing less than their own versions of sheer "madness."

Jesus said: "Truly I tell you, unless you change and become like children, you will never enter the kingdom of heaven."[5] This, too, within any context, sounds much like madness. In ancient Semitic cultures, children and women had no autonomous rights and privileges equivalent to those of men. Children and women were owned and possessed as chattel property. They belonged to the patriarchy and were bound to conditions of subservience and lived within states of dependency.

The disciples had asked Jesus (an argument having arisen among them[6]): "Who is the greatest in the Kingdom of heaven?" Jesus answered: "Whoever becomes humble like this child is the greatest in the kingdom of heaven."[7] A picture—a "painting"—is worth a thousand words. So, "he called a child, whom he put among them."[8] He disrupted the disciples' "universe" of "self"-construction, commanding them instead to look squarely upon the face of this child!

To become one with the reality of a painting is to become one with the reality of the one who paints the painting: "Whoever welcomes one such child in my name welcomes me, and whoever welcomes me welcomes the one who sent me; for the least among all of you is the greatest."[9] This "child" is not the "property" of itself. This "child" is the property of "Another." This "child"—this disciple—belongs to none other than God,

---

4. Ibid., 613; Galatians 3:28.

5. Matthew 18:3.

6. Luke 9:46

7. Matthew 18:4.

8. Matthew 18:2.

9. Composite of Luke 9:48 and Matthew 18:5.

as Jesus belongs to none other than "Abba."[10] This disciple, this child—by virtue of the one to whom it belongs—is now transformed into a portrait of Jesus himself.

This "Artist" had invited "certain women" into the intimate inner circle of his friends and followers. This, too, at the time, within the context, looked and sounded like madness. He deliberately unbound these women from self-constructions imposed by patriarchal dictates and cultural imperatives. He gave them a new status in relationship to the divine power already at work in them. To repeat: "Every tradition in the New Testament about the cross challenges any context-relative or ethnocentric understanding of its status." As Saint Paul declared: "As many of you as were baptized into Christ have clothed yourselves with Christ. There is no longer Jew or Greek, there is no longer slave or free, there is no longer male and female; for all of you are one in Christ Jesus."[11] For this is so, according to the book that pronounces the revelation: "Behold, I make all things new."[12]

On December 9, 1877, while Vincent was engaged in preparatory theological studies in Amsterdam, memorizing Latin and Greek nouns and verbs under the tutelage of Dr. Mendes da Costa, he wrote the following to his brother Theo:

> Mendes gave me the works of Claudius. . . . I had sent him *Thomae Kempensis, De Imitatione Christi*, and on the flyleaf I wrote: "In him there is neither Jew nor Greek, nor servant nor master, nor man nor woman, but Christ is all and in all."
>
> This week I had a conversation with Mendes about "the man who hates not his own life, cannot be my disciple." Mendes asserted that that expression was too strong, but I held that it was the simple truth; and doesn't Thomas a Kempis say the same thing when he speaks about knowing and hating oneself? When we look at

10. W. Paul Jones quotes from Joachim Jeremias's *The Prayers of Jesus*, 57, 63: "'There is *no analogy at all* in the whole of Jewish literature or practice' for Jesus' use of Abba in addressing God. For Jesus, the Sovereign Creator of the Universe is 'daddy.' In teaching the Lord's Prayer to his disciples, Jesus invited them into that familial relationship with God which encapsulated Jesus' own uniqueness. Thus for this World, the clue both to Christology and to epiphania resides in the nature of this relationship" (Jones, *Theological Worlds*, 157).

11. Galatians 3:27–28.

12. Revelation 21:5a.

others who have done more than we and are better than we, we
very soon begin to hate our own life because it is not as good
as others'. Look at a man like Thomas a Kempis, who wrote his
little book with a simplicity and sincerity unequaled by any other
writer, either before or since; or, in another sphere, look at Millet's
work or Jules Dupre's "The Large Oaks"—that is it. (CL 116)

The fact was that in Jesus' day children and women, collectively and in-
dividually, were already in the position of the self-renunciated—those
who possessed no self-determined "self." No Jew—no Greek—no slave—
no free—no male—no female—no "self"—falsely constructed of lesser
selves than the true self—shall stand between the self that is void of itself
and the self that has received its fullness from the divine Self—and this
interpreted, according to Jesus Christ. No substitute "self"—enshrined
as ethnic "self" (Jew/Greek), class "self" (slave/free), or gender "self"
(male/female)—shall preside over the self belonging to Christ. To be
"clothed with Christ" is to stand naked before God, stripped of all other
selves—Brooks Brothers and Yves Saint Laurent being no exceptions.
"So if anyone is in Christ, there is a new creation"[13]—a new self.

"The Potato Eaters"[14] went through several renditions before the final
one was completed within a month or so after Vincent's father's death. It
is a dark painting full of shadows, with but one "lamp," clearly in view,
dimly but sufficiently casting light upon all gathered around the table
for the "breaking of bread." Potatoes are a peasant's substitute for bread
when there is no grain to grind.

Walther and Metzger wrote of this painting: "In order to understand
what it is that gives The Potato Eaters manifesto status it is sufficient to
grasp van Gogh's deliberate rejection of virtuoso technique. . . . Everyday
drudgery had left its mark on the faces of these people. Their backs were
bent."[15] Drudgery bends not only the back but also, along with it, the
self. "The Potato Eaters" is a dark painting enshrouded by existential
shadows. Those very shadows frame a light shining in the faces of the
potato eaters, illuminating the "communion" of which they partake.

13. II Corinthians, 5:17a.
14. WM, 96–97.
15. Ibid., 176.

Meyer Schapiro commented: "The table is their altar and the food a sacrament for each one who has laboured. Under the single light at

"The Potato Eaters"

this common table, the solitude of the individual is overcome and the harshness of nature, too. . . . In the homely faces and hands of these peasants—in color and modeling they are like the potatoes that nourish them—there is a touching purity. It is the purity of familial souls in whom care for one another and the hard struggle with the earth and weather leave little space for self-striving."[16]

Schapiro notices that a transfiguration has taken place: "The eyes of the two figures at the left shine with an inner light and the shadows on their features are more a modeling of character than a phenomenon of darkness."[17] They belong to Christ. They are new selves, a new creation.

Ludwig "Willem" Reijmert Wenkebach, a Dutch painter and illustrator, once had the good fortune, mixed with a few tense moments ("it was the most remarkable experience I ever had"), to visit Vincent while he was

16. Schapiro, *Van Gogh*, 40.
17. Ibid.

living in Nuenen and painting from a room that "was in a farmhouse of the sexton of the Catholic church."[18]

> It was crowded with all sorts of articles, spread around in the greatest disorder. The first things my eyes caught were the characteristic, violently painted canvases as well as the expressive drawings which covered the walls. They were most striking. Then I discovered a great many birds' nests and eggs on several tables. Then there were wooden shoes, old caps and bonnets such as the womenfolk wear, some very dirty; old chairs without seats, rickety and broken, and in a corner all sorts of working tools. In a little room at the back sat Vincent before an easel; the room seemed much too small for a studio.
>
> After shaking hands, it seemed to me as if Vincent was very pleased to see me. He showed me everything and he talked volubly and interestingly about his aim and his work, his difficulties in working with the peasants, and so forth.
>
> It seemed so strange to me that, although he lived amongst them, he flew into a rage and was so provoked at them. Yet even more he railed against the "decent" people and the bourgeois, kicking now and then against his easel. During the conversation some of his drawings fell to the floor and, as I picked them up, my shirt cuff, which was fastened with a gold cufflink, showed. Vincent's eye fell on it, and looking at me in a contemptuous manner, he said furiously: "I can't stand people who wear such luxuries!" This unusual, unkind, and rude remark made me feel most uncomfortable, but I pretended not to notice it and paid no attention to it. Vincent himself forgot it immediately, for in the pleasantest way he proposed that we take a walk through the country.
>
> It was during this walk that he gave me a glimpse of his sublime soul, his sensitive artistic feeling; he noticed all the colors, the delicate atmosphere, the bright sun and mighty clouds, the crops, the shady trees; he was full of enthusiasm about all the beauty of the country, every detail of light and shade on cottage and field. . . . I felt that I had met a mighty artist!"[19]

Here was a first-hand, eyewitness account (second hand to the reader) of an encounter with the artist. What did Mr. Wenkebach mean when he said, "it was the most remarkable experience I ever had"? What made it remarkable? And what did he mean when he said, "I felt that I had met a mighty artist"? What made Vincent such a "mighty" artist?

18. Stein, *Van Gogh*, 67.
19. Ibid., 67.

Hugo von Hofmannsthal was an Austrian poet and playwright, "perhaps best known for his librettos for Der Rosenkavalier and other Strauss operas." He reminisced of his experience one particular day when, with an hour to waste during a visit to the 1901 Bernheim Jeune exhibition, and due to pure happenstance, he "turned into a quiet side street" and "there, in a building was a very decent-looking shop without show windows, and next to the entrance a sign saying: 'Comprehensive exhibition; Paintings and Drawings."[20] He wrote about what he had stumbled upon.

> My dear friend, this was no coincidence; I was meant to see these pictures. . . . First they seemed to me coarse and shrill in color tones, agitated and quite strange; I had to first find a way to see them as pictures, as a unity, but then, then I saw them all that way, each one individually, and all of them together, and Nature in them, and the strength of the human soul that had been at work here, shaping Nature, and tree and bush and field and slope, and in addition, something else, that which was "behind" the painted surface, the true reality, the indescribably fateful—all this I perceived in such a way as to lose my self-awareness while looking at these pictures, and then I regained it, only to lose it again! My dear friend, for the sake of that which I want to say here and yet will never divulge, I have written you this whole letter! But how could I ever put into words something so incomprehensible, so sudden, so strong, so indivisible! I could obtain photographs of the paintings and send them to you, but what could they give you—what could these pictures by themselves give you of the impression they made on me, which is most likely something altogether personal: a secret between my fate, the pictures, and myself. A peasant plowing his field, a row of powerful trees seen against the evening sky, a dirt road between crooked scotch pines, a garden corner near the back wall of a house, peasant carts with skinny horses in a pasture, a copper basin and a clay pitcher, peasants around a table eating potatoes—but what good is this to you? So, should I tell you about the colors? There is an incredible, most powerful blue that keeps recurring, a green like molten emeralds, a yellow-orange. But what are colors if the innermost life of objects does not burst out of them? And this innermost life was there, tree and stone and wall and road revealed their innermost personality, as though they were casting it at me, but not the delight and harmony of their beautiful, inanimate lives, like the magic currents that at times seemed to emanate toward

20. Ibid., 313.

me from old master paintings: No, only the enormous power of their existence, the raging, incredible miracle of their presence attacked my soul. How can I explain to you that here, every being—the being of every tree, every strip of yellow or greenish field, every fence, every ravine that cuts across the rocky hillside; the being of the pewter pitcher, the earthenware bowl, the table, the clumsy armchair—lifted itself as though newly born out of the terrible chaos of nonexistence, out of the abyss of Non-Being, toward me, so that I felt—no, knew—that these beings were born out of horrible doubt about the world and were now covering up by their existence a horrible abyss, a gaping nothingness, for all time. How can I even begin to tell you how this language reached my soul, revealed to me an enormous justification for the strang- est, seemingly most unresolvable conflicts of my inner depths, al- lowed me to understand all at once what, in my dull gloominess, I could hardly bear to feel, and yet felt so strongly, but was yet unable to tear out of myself—and here an unknown soul of unbe- lievable strength answered me with a world of revelations! I felt like one who, after having whirled in boundless frenzy, feels the solid ground under his feet while the storm rages all around. In a storm these trees were born before my eyes, and on my account, their gnarled roots in the soil, their twisted branches reaching for the clouds; in a storm these rifts in the crust of the earth, these valleys between the hills, surrendered themselves; even within the weighty boulders was a frozen storm. Now, going from one painting to another, I could feel something, feel the accumulation and the reciprocity of the beings, how their inner life burst out in colors, how the colors seemed to exist for one another, and how one, mysteriously, powerfully, seemed to carry all others; and in all this one could sense a heart, the soul of the man who created it, who, with this vision, did himself answer his own most terrible doubt; I could see, could know, could delight in viewing peaks and valleys, inside and outside, one and all, in a ten-thousandth of a particle of the time that has taken me to write this down, and I rejoiced in a sensation of having two-fold powers, over my life, over my strength, my reason.[21]

Here was a first-hand account of an encounter one step removed from the artist (two steps removed from the reader), through the me- dium, the "art-i-fact," the painting, of the "gospel" of the artist. What did Mr. von Hofmannsthal mean when he said that "this was no coinci- dence; I was meant to see these pictures"?

21. Ibid., 313–14.

Here was a man who said that he had not looked at any paintings in twenty years, but who stumbled upon these paintings of Vincent's, including one of "peasants around a table eating potatoes." Of what was he speaking when he said: "something else, that which was 'behind' the painted surface, the true reality, the indescribably fateful—all this I perceived in such a way as to lose my self-awareness while looking at these pictures, and then I regained it, only to lose it again!"? "But how could I ever put into words something so incomprehensible, so sudden, so strong, so indivisible!" "A secret between my fate, the pictures, and myself." "An incredible, most powerful blue that keeps recurring, a green like molten emeralds, a yellow-orange." "But what are colors if the innermost life of objects does not burst out of them?" "This innermost life was there, tree and stone and wall and road revealed their innermost personality, as though they were casting it at me."

"The colors seemed to exist for one another, and how one, mysteriously, powerfully, seemed to carry all others."

"How can I explain to you that here, every being . . . lifted itself as though newly born out of the terrible chaos of nonexistence, out of the abyss of Non-Being, toward me, so that I felt—no, knew—that these beings were born out of horrible doubt about the world and were now covering up by their existence a horrible abyss, a gaping nothingness, for all time." "An unknown soul of unbelievable strength answered me with a world of revelations!"

"In all this one could sense a heart, the soul of the man who created it, who, with this vision, did himself answer his own most terrible doubt." "I could see, could know, could delight." "I rejoiced in a sensation of having two-fold powers, over my life, over my strength, my reason."

"Peasants around a table eating potatoes—but what good is this to you?"

What good is the gospel to anyone?

Epiphany is a thing of madness. According to Saint Luke, it is mystifying. Cleopas and friend were perambulating between "appointments." They were walking along the road from Jerusalem to Emmaus, somewhere between "bitter disappointment" and "ultimate despair." He was dead. He had been brutally executed. What was there left to say?

But they were going to tell this perfect stranger about it anyway—couldn't help it. And they said to him that some—of the women—

reported having seen "a vision of angels who said that he was alive." The stranger walked ahead of them as they approached the village. "But they urged him strongly, saying, 'Stay with us, because it is almost evening and the day is now nearly over.'" They took their seats at the supper table—these peasant folk.

"When he was at the table with them, he took bread, blessed and broke it, and gave it to them. Then their eyes were opened, and they recognized him; and he vanished from their sight."[22]

It is perfectly conceivable that, just after his father died—somewhere along the road to Nuenen or Emmaus—on the day when Vincent finally completed "The Potato Eaters"—he was "saying," in effect, that every single last one of us—father, mother, sister, brother, himself included— all of them—all of us—truth be known—are seated as "peasants around a table eating potatoes."

And the one who seems most absent is the Very One who is most present as he vanishes from the sight of those who recognize him.

THE EYE OF THE OBSERVER AND THE EYE OF THE OBSERVED: THE SOUL AS A MIRROR BEFORE IT BECOMES A HOME

Here is Vincent again. He is existentially no different from the rest of us. Like the rest of us, he is in pain.

I have had in all four great crises, during which I didn't in the least know what I said, what I wanted and what I did. Not taking into account that I had previously had three fainting fits without any plausible reasons, and without retaining the slightest remembrance of what I felt.

I am unable to describe exactly what is the matter with me; now and then there are horrible fits of anxiety, apparently without cause, or otherwise a feeling of emptiness and fatigue in the head. I look upon the whole thing as a simple accident. There can be no doubt that much of this is my own fault, and at times I have attacks of melancholy and of atrocious remorse; but you know, the fact is, that when all this discourages me and gives me spleen, I am not exactly ashamed to tell myself that the remorse

22. From the Emmaus story, Luke 24:13–35.

and all the other things that are wrong might possibly be caused
by microbes too, like love. Every day I take the remedy which the
incomparable Dickens prescribes against suicide. It consists of a
glass of wine, a piece of bread with cheese and a pipe of tobacco.
This is not complicated, you will tell me, and you will hardly be
able to believe that this is the limit to which melancholy will take
me; all the same, at some moments—oh dear me . . . (CL W11)

The "Oh dear me" is the voice of the "true self" seeking itself, in
order to speak itself. It is the voice of the "false self" sighing as the "not-
me," for in order to become the "real me" it must lose itself in its en-
tirety. "When the world is taken away from the self and one despairs, the
despair seems to come from the outside, even though it always comes
from the self; but when the self despairs over its despair, this new despair
comes from the self, as the counter-pressure (reaction), and it thereby
differs from defiance, which comes directly from the self."[23]

Vincent had not only lost his "father" on that fateful Christmas
of 1881 when he was ordered out of the house. He had also lost a significant part of himself, the part that could no longer pretend to be his
true self. This constituted "the break" with the idealized selfobject that
his father had been for him since early childhood, though less so as the
years passed by. Besides his own father, the church "fathers" as idealized
selfobjects had deeply wounded him by failing to mirror him and by
rebuking him (from their perspective, understandably so). Vincent left
the church, in effect, because he had been cast out like a demon, and
ever since that exodus his "soul" had not found its "home" in any land of
promise except for the one that was within himself.

His "nuclear self," his "cohesive self," had not sufficiently consoli-
dated, but it was on its way toward becoming so. He continued to suffer
from battering self-defeat. As a portrait of Heinz Kohut's "Tragic Man,"[24]
Vincent's nuclear ambitions and highest ideals had not yet materialized.
Thus, he continued on, limping out of "Egypt" as an "ex-slave" having
departed from the household of "Pharaoh," whose exile brought him
straight into the middle of a "desert" wilderness. A painter and a monk

23. Kierkegaard, *Sickness*, 62.

24. "The psychology of the self is needed to explain the pathology of the fragmented self (from schizophrenia to narcissistic personality disorder) and of the depleted
self (empty depression, i.e., the world of unmirrored ambitions, the world devoid of
ideals)—in short, the psychic disturbances and struggles of Tragic Man" (Kohut,
Restoration, 243).

he was becoming. Insofar as his defiant self was capable of exercising counter-rejection of those who had rejected him, he had still fallen short of "the mark of the prize of the high calling of God in Christ Jesus"[25]—like all who wander in the wilderness, short of their prized destination.

There remained those "certain barriers, certain gates, certain walls" from which the "caged bird . . . looks through the bars at the overcast sky where a thunderstorm is gathering, and inwardly he rebels against his fate. 'I am caged, I am caged, and you tell me I do not want anything, fools! You think I have everything I need! Oh! I beseech you liberty, that I may be a bird like other birds!' . . . A justly or unjustly ruined reputation, poverty, unavoidable circumstances, adversity. . . . And one asks, "My God! is it for long, is it forever, is it for all eternity?" (CL 133). This is the cry of an existentialist who turns to his brother Theo and asks what to do. And Theo says: Take up your "palette" and paint. Your art will reveal your salvation.

Every lost, abandoned, or deficient selfobject requires its replacement, for the self cannot exist apart from its objects of attachment. A future attachment must emerge. Otherwise the self disintegrates, fragments, bends back upon itself, and spirals downward. Some, who cannot help themselves, bid against the future by turning to alcohol, the brothel, the high stakes wager, flights of illusion, overt aggression, the lonely corner of the "night café," or fantasies of love in the gaping absence of love. These gambled-upon substitutes for the true self are in some manner of speaking like thin sheets of paper that tear easily but do no make for a solid canvas upon which to paint a genuine portrait. Painting the true self, on the other hand, entails an act of faith and positive envisioning. It sustains the hope of being re-created.

For Vincent, Dame Nature had become the great surrogate selfobject—a replacement for a whole host of other intermediaries, a few of great value, most of little value and not worth keeping, while still others remained painfully missing. And so it was that Vincent again, at the last, turned to Dame Nature as he had done time after time before, as the one visible and tangible constant, the one lover still within reach of the eye and the hand. Like Moses, Vincent could strike it as a rock, in the faith that it would pour forth water. When like a snake it bit back, the sting would last only for a while until the storm had passed and the sun had burst out. Vincent experienced Dame Nature as God's playground,

25. Philippians 3:14, KJV.

despite the fact that humans knew only too well how to turn it into the Devil's battleground. Theo was right. Vincent was called to take up his "palette" and paint.

Thomas Altizer wrote:

> It must never be forgotten that Van Gogh alone among our great painters was a preacher of the Gospel, but this does not cease when he fully becomes a painter, it becomes profoundly deeper, and while Van Gogh ever more fully distanced himself from all ecclesiastical Christianity, and could even believe in the advent of a new religion, one altogether new and which will have no name . . . he surely created an iconography for this new religion, and above all so in his final painting. Wheat Field with Crows,[26] painted shortly before his suicide, is perhaps his greatest painting, and surely his most purely sacred work, it certainly embodies a new iconography, one in which the traditional icon is truly reversed, as the ecstatic light of this field is inseparable from the dark abyss of these heavens . . .
>
> If only because of this ecstasy we can respond to these crows as eyes, eyes which see in our own when we are caught up in this ecstatic moment, then the very blackness of the crows captures the darkness of death, but now death is the very opposite of all possible passivity, and is ecstatically present, a presence releasing truly new eyes, eyes which now see the fullness and the finality of death itself. Here, that finality is an ecstatic finality, and one which we actually see, but we do so only with new eyes, and if these are the eyes of Van Gogh, they are eyes that are given us in this painting, eyes which may be understood as a consummation of Van Gogh's work, but eyes which perhaps impelled that suicide which almost immediately followed the completion of this painting, a suicide seemingly occurring even here, and one which we enact in fully responding to this painting.
>
> Certainly this is a sanctification of darkness, and of the deepest darkness and the deepest abyss, and precisely thereby darkness finally becomes indistinguishable from light, and while these crows are darkness and darkness alone, now such darkness becomes light itself, and does so in that ultimate turbulence which is here released, a turbulence which is chaos itself, but now a truly sanctioned or holy chaos. . . . Now our eyes not only truly see darkness, but become transfigured in that very seeing, and if this is an ecstatic transfiguration, releasing a truly new joy, this is a joy inseparable from the depths of darkness and abyss, but now abyss

26. WM, 690–91.

is a transfigured abyss, they are eyes not only in which we actually see the depths of abyss, but see these depths with the very eye of abyss itself. That is an eye which our traditional iconography could know as the very eye of God, but that is an eye of absolute light, whereas this eye is an eye of absolute darkness, but an absolute darkness that here is transfigured into an absolute light. . . . Thus we can see this wheat field as the very Body of God, but its glory is inseparable from the dark and abysmal sky which is its ground, and the crows are not simply intermediaries between the sky and the field, not simply messengers whether heavenly or demonic, but enactors of this glory, enactors who can be understood as the Eye of God, but now an eye that is not only an omniscient eye, but an ubiquitous eye, and hence an eye seeing in our own.[27]

So, when the beholder looks into the eyes of the one beheld, and the beheld looks into the eyes of the beholder, whose Eye is upon whose? And when the stars come out upon a dark night, whose Eye is upon the heavens, and whose Eye is upon the earth?

Vincent said: "I am unable to describe exactly what is the matter with me." "I am not exactly ashamed to tell myself that the remorse and all the other things that are wrong might possibly be caused by microbes too, like love" (CL W11).

- "If you ever fall in love and get the answer, 'No, never never,' do not resign yourself to it" (CL 153).
- "'When all sounds cease, God's voice is heard under the stars'"[28] (CL 100).
- "His eye is also upon us; and I am sure that He plans our life and that we do not quite belong to ourselves" (CL 98).

Some, no doubt, would say this is "sheer madness"—and then proceed to believe it.

27. Altizer, "Van Gogh's Eyes," 394–95. Altizer says: "Van Gogh could even be said to have anticipated quantum physics, at least insofar as that revolutionary new physics dissolves the boundary between the observer and the observed, and yet while quantum physics destroys all possibility of visualization, Van Gogh's mature painting fully envisions a new totality in which subject and object are indistinguishable" (394).

28. Line from the poem "Under the Stars," by Dinah Maria Mulock Craik. See footnote 15, The Museum Letters Project, http://vangoghletters.org/vg/letters/let119/letter.html. Original: "When earth-sounds cease, God's voice is heard / Under the stars."

A week after Vincent's funeral, Theo wrote a letter to his sister Wil. In it he expressed something about which many a person wonders. At the end of one's days, no matter how the end may come, thus when all is said and done, shall we have sufficiently died to ourselves so that we shall be able at last, perhaps for the very first time, to live fully before God?

In the voice of lamentation, Theo spoke not only for himself but also for Vincent and for all who grieve:

> To say we must be grateful that he rests—I still hesitate to do so. Maybe I should call it one of the greatest cruelties of life on this earth and maybe we should count him among the martyrs who die with a smile on their face.
>
> He did not wish to stay alive and his mind was so calm because he had always fought for his convictions, convictions that he had measured against the best and noblest of his predecessors. His love for his father, for the gospel, for the poor and the unhappy, for the great [ones] of literature and painting, is enough proof for that. In the last letter which he wrote me and which dates from some four days before his death, it says, "I try to do as well as certain painters whom I have greatly loved and admired." People should realize that he was a great artist, something which often coincides with being a great human being. In the course of time this will surely be acknowledged, and many will regret his early death. He himself wanted to die; when I sat at his bedside and said that we would try to get him better and that we hoped that he would then be spared this kind of despair, he said, "La tristesse durera toujours" (The sadness will last forever). I understood what he wanted to say with those words.
>
> A few moments later he felt suffocated and within one minute he closed his eyes. A great rest came over him from which he did not come to life again.[29]

Anyone long steeped in the life and art of Vincent van Gogh, who may wish to add a few words to what Theo said of his dear brother, might simply rephrase Theo's last sentence to read like this: A great rest came over him from which he did come to life again—face to face with God and here upon the earth.

The "painter" who sanctified Vincent's painting, and whom Vincent admired above all other painters, was the one of whom he said: "Christ alone—of all the philosophers, Magi . . . has affirmed, as a principal certainty, eternal life, the infinity of time, the nothingness of death, the

29. Hulsker, *Vincent and Theo Van Gogh*, 450.

necessity . . . of serenity and devotion. He lived serenely, as a greater artist than all other artists, despising marble and clay as well as color, working in living flesh"—whose life, death, and resurrection were "the very highest summit—reached by art" (CL B8).

"Wheatfield with Crows"

Epilogue

L IKE "LAZARUS" ARISING FROM his tomb, Vincent stumbled forth
many a day, lame, broken, and exhausted, and yet eagerly clinging
to life.[1] From the wide "expanse of the heavens"[2] and the "narrow confines of the earth"[3] he portrayed with riveting attention, transcending
imagination, exceeding empathy, and waning energy amid intensified
self-depletion and excruciating psychic pain, what he believed to be true
above all about people and in all about God. He did so until the last
splatter of agony and the final smear of defeat, his and that of others,[4]
drew out of him the closing "shades of his life."[5]

"Be a painter,"[6] he said, "and as a human being . . . you will in the
course of these years gradually become something better and deeper in
the end" (CL 339a).

Drawing close to his own end, depleted from the effects of disease
and psychic torment, and fearful that Theo in his weakened condition
could not afford to support his own wife and child, much less his brother, Vincent painted the holy "Pietà" after Delacroix, the *Imitatio Christi*,
placing the ashen visage of himself into the gaunt face of the crucified
Jesus—"the perfect symbol of suffering."[7]

From the standpoint of divine paradox—which is the reversal
of customary human expectation and protocol—Vincent deliberately

1. "The Raising of Lazarus," WM, 626.

2. "La Crau with Peach Trees in Blossom," WM, 496–97.

3. "Backyards of Old Houses in Antwerp in the Snow," WM, 142.

4. "Sien's Daughter Wearing a Shawl," WM, 707.

5. "Vincent van Gogh on his deathbed, drawing by Dr. Paul Gachet," Hulsker,
Vincent and Theo, 441.

6. "The Painter on His Way to Work," WM, 386.

7. "Pietà" (after Delacroix), WM, 542.

embraced the way of genuine self-denial and authentic self-abasement, what he called "the resignation, the real kind, not that of the clergymen." To be self-abased, he said, is to "suffer without complaining." It is "the great science, the lesson to learn, the solution of the problem of this life" (CL 181).

Of immense importance to Vincent, and to understanding the entire scope of his life, was the fact that, despite any and all second thoughts he had about being a Christian, he immersed himself, early on, in the theology of Thomas à Kempis' *The Imitation of Christ*. He submerged himself so deeply in it that he once copied the entire book by hand. The longstanding effect was like an indelible blot of ink, marking not only how he perceived the world but also how he lived in it, despite those moments when clearly he was not his best self.

The art historians Ingo Walther and Rainer Metzger concluded: "To van Gogh, Jesus Christ was the personification par excellence of his own view of the world. That view was based on the paradox of suffering that is welcome, sorrow that pleases."[8] That paradox persisted until Vincent's dying day, and remains visible in his art and letters as a living testimony to how he and others have been called by Christ to live.

He once remarked to Theo: "I take things seriously and will not let myself be forced to produce work that does not show my own character" (CL 180). Deeply imbedded in that character was the very image of Christ—who, more than anything, and more than anyone else, comprised Vincent's truest self.

VINCENT, IN HIS OWN WORDS

"The Sorrowing for God"

> It may be that there is a time in life when one is tired of everything and feels, perhaps correctly, as if all one does is wrong—do you think this is a feeling one must try to avoid and to banish, or is it "the sorrowing for God," which one must not fear, but cherish to see if it may bring some good? Is it "the sorrowing for God" which leads us to make a choice which we never regret? And at such a time, when one is weary of oneself, one should think with devotion, hope and love of the words: "Come unto me, all ye that

8. WM, 46.

labour and are heavy laden, and I will give you rest. Take my yoke
upon you, and learn of me; for I am meek and lowly in heart: and
ye shall find rest upon your souls." "If any man will come after
me, let him deny himself, and take up my cross, and follow me."
At such a time one may well think: "Except a man be born again,
he cannot see the kingdom of God." If we let ourselves be taught
by the experience of life, and led by the sorrowing for God, vital
strength may spring from the weary heart. If only we are truly
weary, we shall believe in God all the more firmly, and shall find
in Christ, through His word, a friend and a Comforter. (CL 85)

"Because I Must Speak"

I want to be silent—and yet, because I must speak—well then—as
it seems to me: to love and to be lovable—to live—to give life, to
renew it, to restore it, to preserve it—and to work, giving a spark
for a spark, and above all to be good, to be useful, to be helpful in
something, for instance lighting a fire, giving a slice of bread and
butter to a child, a glass of water to a sufferer. (CL R4)

"The Other Half of Our Existence"

The patron saint of painters—St. Luke, physician, painter,
evangelist—whose symbol is, alas, nothing but an ox, is there
to give us hope.

Our real and true lives are rather humble, these lives of us
painters, who drag out our existence under the stupefying yoke
of the difficulties of a profession which can hardly be practiced
on this thankless planet on whose surface "the love of art makes
us lose the true love."

But seeing that nothing opposes it—supposing that there are
also lines and forms as well as colors on the other innumerable
planets and suns—it would remain praiseworthy of us to maintain a certain serenity with regard to the possibilities of painting
under superior and changed conditions of existence, an existence
changed by a phenomenon no queerer and no more surprising
than the transformation of the caterpillar into a butterfly, or of
the white grub into a cockchafer.

The existence of painter-butterfly would have for its field of
action one of the innumerable heavenly bodies, which would
perhaps be no more inaccessible to us, after death, than the black
dots which symbolize towns and villages on geographical maps
are in our terrestrial existence.

Science—scientific reasoning—seems to me an instrument that will lag far, far behind. For look here: the earth has been thought to be flat. It was true, so it still is today, for instance between Paris and Asnières. Which, however, does not prevent science from proving that the earth is principally round. Which no one contradicts nowadays.

But notwithstanding this they persist nowadays in believing that life is flat and runs from birth to death. However, life too is probably round, and very superior in expanse and capacity to the hemisphere we know at present.

Future generations will probably enlighten us on this so very interesting subject; and then maybe Science itself will arrive—willy-nilly—at conclusions more or less parallel to the sayings of Christ with reference to the other half of our existence.

However this may be, the fact is that we are painters in real life, and that the important thing is to breathe as hard as ever we can breathe. (CL B8)

"The Need of Religion"

It does me good to do difficult things. That does not prevent me from having a terrible need of—shall I say the word?—of religion. Then I go out at night to paint the stars, and I am always dreaming of a picture like this with a group of living figures of our comrades. (CL 543)

"The Bible"

Is the Bible enough for us? In these days, I believe, Jesus himself would say to those who sit down in a state of melancholy, it is not here, get up and go forth. Why do you seek the living among the dead? If the spoken or written word is to remain the light of the world, then it is our right and our duty to acknowledge that we are living in a period when it should be spoken and written in such a way that—in order to find something equally great, and equally good, and equally original, and equally powerful to revolutionize the whole of society—we may compare it with a clear conscience to the old revolution of the Kristians.[9] (CL W1)

---

9. "Vincent uses the unusual spelling '*Kristenen*' here instead of '*Christenen*,' thereby expressing his aversion to all religious conventionalism" (CL W1, footnote by Johanna van Gogh-Bonger, III, 426).

It is a very good thing that you read the Bible. I start with this because I have always refrained from recommending it to you. Whenever I read the numerous sayings of Moses, St. Luke, etc., I couldn't help thinking to myself, Look, that's the only thing he lacks, and now there it is in full force . . . the artistic neurosis. For the study of Christ inevitably calls it forth, especially in my case where it is complicated by the staining black of unnumerable pipes.[10] The Bible is Christ, for the Old Testament leads up to this culminating point. St. Paul and the evangelists dwell on the other slope of the sacred mountain . . . But the consolation of that saddening Bible which arouses our despair and our indignation—which distresses us once and for all because we are outraged by its pettiness and contagious folly—the consolation which is contained in it, like a kernel in a hard shell, a bitter pulp, is Christ. The figure of Christ, as I feel it, has been painted only by Delacroix and Rembrandt . . . and later Millet painted . . . the doctrine of Christ . . . (CL B8)

"A Thoroughly Good Laugh"

In every [person] who is healthy and natural there is a germinating force as in a grain of wheat. And so natural life is germination. What the germinating force is in the grain of wheat, love is in us. Now I think we are apt to stand staring with a long face, and at a loss for words, as soon as we are frustrated in our natural development and see this germination made impossible, and find ourselves placed in a situation as hopeless as that of the wheat between the millstones must be. If things go like that with us, and we are absolutely bewildered by the loss of our natural life, there are some among us who, though wanting to submit to the course of things as they are, yet do not want to relinquish their self-consciousness and self-respect, and insist upon knowing what is the matter with them, and what is really happening. And if with good intentions we search the books which it is said shed light in the darkness—though inspired by the best will in the world, we find extremely little that is certain, and not always the satisfaction of being comforted personally. And the diseases which we civilized people labor under most are melancholy and pessimism. So I, for instance, who can count so many years in my life during which a desire to laugh was grievously wanting—wholly leaving out of consideration whether this was my own fault or not—I, for instance, feel first of all the need of a thoroughly good laugh. (CL W1)

10. Vincent is referring to his love for smoking tobacco in a pipe.

"My Study of Old Whores"

> At the end you produce morality. You tell Society that it is in-
> famous, because the whore reminds us of meat in the market
> place. That's all right, the whore is like meat in a butcher's shop.
> I, though, having become a mere brute; I understand, I feel it, I
> rediscover a sensation in my own life; I say, That is well spoken—
> for sonorous rhythm of the colorful words evoke for me with real
> intensity the brutal reality of the slums, but on me, the brute, the
> reproaches directed against society, such hollow words as "le bon
> Dieu"—the good God—no longer make any impression. I say,
> that isn't the real thing—and I sink back into my brutish state;
> I forget poetry, which was powerful enough at first to dispel my
> stupefaction. Is this true or not? Establishing fact, as you do in
> the beginning, is cutting with the scalpel as the surgeon does
> when he explains anatomy. I listen attentively and full of interest,
> but when the dissecting surgeon later starts moralizing at me like
> that, then I don't think his final tirade is the same value as his
> demonstrations. Studying, analyzing society means more than
> moralizing any time. Nothing would seem queerer to me than
> saying, for instance, Here is that meat from the market place;
> now observe how, in spite of everything, it may be electrified
> for a moment by the stimulus of a more refined and unexpected
> love. Just like the sated caterpillar that doesn't eat any more, that
> crawls on a wall instead of crawling on a cabbage leaf, so this
> sated female can no longer love, even if she does her best. She
> is seeking, seeking, seeking—does she herself know what? She
> is conscious, alive, sensitive, galvanized, rejuvenated for a mo-
> ment—but impotent. Yet she can still love, so she is alive—here
> no prevarication is possible—although she may be finished and
> dying the death of a terrestrial beast. Where will this butterfly
> emerge from the chrysalis? This butterfly that was a sated cater-
> pillar, this cockchafer that was a white grub? Well, this is where I
> have got to in my study of old whores. I too should like to know
> approximately what I am the larva of myself, perhaps. (CL B9)

"Our Own Metamorphoses"

> I cannot very well write about Mauve;[11] I think of him every
> day, but that's all. It was a great shock to me; but personally, as a

---

11. Mauve is recently deceased as of the writing of this letter to Vincent's sister,
Wil. Vincent once had said of Mauve: "Mauve takes offense at my having said, 'I am
an artist'—which I won't take back, because, of course, these words connote, 'always

human being, he may have been quite different from what people said of him once in a while—that is, more deeply engrossed in life itself than in art perhaps; and I loved him as a human being. Now it is so hard for me to imagine that those who penetrate to the core of life, who for the rest judge themselves as if they were dealing with somebody else, and who treat others as unceremoniously as though they were taking themselves to task—I find it so hard to imagine that such can cease to exist. Now I know that it is hardly to be supposed that the white potato and salad grubs which later change into cockchafers should be able to form tenable ideas about their supernatural existence in the hereafter. And that it would be premature of them to enter upon supernatural researches for enlightenment about this problem, seeing that the gardener or other persons interested in salad and vegetables would crush them underfoot, considering them harmful insects. But for parallel reasons I have little confidence in the correctness of our human concepts of a future life. We are as little able to judge of our own metamorphoses without bias and prematureness as the white salad grubs can of theirs, for the very cogent reason that the salad worms ought to eat salad roots in the very interest of their higher development. In the same way I think that a painter ought to paint pictures; possibly something else may come after that." (CL W)

"A Choice"

Many people, arriving at the moment in life when they must make a choice, have chosen for their part "the love of Christ and poverty," or rather, "give me neither poverty nor riches; feed me with food convenient for me." (CL 109)

"Sheep" and "Wolves"

Suppose that it's not just in our imagination, but that you and I are really like sheep among our fellow creatures.[12] All right—granting the existence of rather hungry and false wolves, it would not be impossible that we should be devoured someday. Well, this may not be so very pleasant, but I tell myself: It is, after all, better to be ruined than to do the ruining. I mean, there is no reason to lose

seeking without absolutely finding.' It is just the opposite of saying, 'I know, I have found it'" (CL 192).

12. See Vincent's painting of "Shepherd with Flock of Sheep," WM, 46.

one's serenity if one should realize that one might have to lead a life of poverty, even if one possess all the qualities, the knowledge, the capacities, which make other people rich. I am not indifferent to money, but I do not understand the wolves. (CL 344)

"The New Art"

In the fullness of artistic life there is, and remains, and will always come back at times, that homesick longing for the truly ideal life that can never come true.

And sometimes you lack all desire to throw yourself heart and soul into art, and to get well for that. You know you are a cab horse and that it's the same old cab you'll be hitched up to again: that you'd rather live in a meadow with the sun, a river and other horses for company, likewise free, and the act of procreation.

And perhaps, to get to the bottom of it, the disease of the heart is caused by this; it would not surprise me. One does not rebel against things, nor is one resigned to them; one's ill because of them, and one does not get better, and it's hard to be precise about the cure.

I do not know who it was who called this condition—being struck by death and immortality. The cab you drag along must be of some use to people you do not know. And so, if we believe in the new art and in the artists of the future, our faith does not cheat us. When good old Carot said a few days before his death—"Last night in a dream I saw landscapes with skies all pink," well, haven't they come, those skies all pink, and yellow and green into the bargain in the impressionist landscapes? All of which means that there are things one feels coming, and they are coming in very truth.

As for those of us who are not, I am inclined to believe, nearly so close to death, we nevertheless feel that this thing is greater than we are, and that its life is of longer duration than ours.

We do not feel we are dying, but we do feel the truth that we are of small account, and that we are paying a hard price to be a link in the chain of artists, in health, in youth, in liberty, none of which we enjoy, any more than the cab horse that hauls a coachful of people out to enjoy the spring.

So what I wish for you, as for myself, is to succeed in getting back your health, because you must have that. That "Espérance" [hope, trust, expectation] by Puvis de Chavannes is so true. There is an art of the future, and it is going to be so lovely and so young that if we give up our youth for it, we must gain in serenity by it.

Perhaps it is very silly to write all this, but I feel it so strongly; it seems to me that, like me, you have been suffering to see your youth pass away like a puff of smoke; but if it grows again, and comes to life in what you make, nothing has been lost, and the power to work is another youth. (CL 489)

"This Good Old God"

Did you ever hear Mauve preach? I heard him imitate several clergymen . . . and then he imitated Father Bernhard: God—God is Almighty—He has made the sea, He has made the earth, and the sky, and the stars, and the sun, and the moon; He can do everything—everything—everything—no, He is not almighty, there is one thing He cannot do. What is the thing the Almighty cannot do? God Almighty cannot cast out a sinner. (CL 164)

I feel more and more that we must not judge of God from this world, it's just a study that didn't come off. What can you do with a study that has gone wrong?—if you are fond of the artist, you do not find much to criticize—you hold your tongue. But you have a right to ask for something better. We should have to see other works by the same hand though; this world was evidently slapped together in a hurry on one of his bad days, when the artist didn't know what he was doing or didn't have his wits about him. All the same, according to what the legend says, this good old God took a terrible lot of trouble over this world-study of his.

I am inclined to think that the legend is right, but then the study is ruined in so many ways. It is only a master who can make such a blunder, and perhaps that is the best consolation we can have out of it, since in that case we have a right to hope that we'll see the same creative hand get even with itself. And this life of ours, so much criticized, and for such good and even exalted reasons, we must not take it for anything but what it is, and go on hoping that in some other life we'll see something better than this. (CL 490)

Appendix

A Chronology of the Life of Vincent van Gogh[1]

March 30, 1853—July 29, 1890

MARCH 30, 1853. Vincent was born in Groot Zundert, Holland, one year to the day after the still birth of his parents' first child, whose name was also Vincent van Gogh. Vincent's father was a Dutch Reformed pastor, Theodorus van Gogh (1822–1885), and his mother, Ann van Gogh-Carbentus (1819–1907), formerly of The Hague. Their second child was Anna Cornelia (Anna) (1855–1930), their third, Theodore (Theo) (1857–1891), four years younger than Vincent. The others in descending order were Elizabeth Huberta (Lies) (1859–1936), Willemein (Wil) (1862–1941), and Cornelius Vincent (Cor) (1867–1900).

Age 8. "Little Vincent" with "a great love for animals and flowers," attended the village school for a short while and was thereafter home-schooled by a governess. During his early childhood he drew and sketched, taking lessons from his mother, a capable artist.

Age 12. Vincent was sent to Mr. Provily's boarding school at Zevenbergen.

Age 16. Vincent entered the House of Goupil & Co. at The Hague, thanks to an arrangement by his Uncle Vincent van Gogh, and worked there as an apprentice art dealer under the direction of Mr. Tersteeg, boarding with the Roos family on Beestenmarkt.

---

1. Based upon the "Memoir of Vincent van Gogh" by Johanna van Gogh-Bonger, Vincent's sister-in-law, who was married to Vincent's brother, Theo (CL, "Memoir," xv–liii).

1872. In August, Vincent began a lifelong correspondence with his closest brother, Theo, lasting until the end of July 1890.

1873. In January, Vincent, age 20, apprenticed with Goupil in Brussels. In May he was transferred to Goupil in London, and boarded at the home of the Loyers, falling in love with their daughter, Ursula, who rejected his overtures since she was engaged to someone else. He had his first serious inklings of wanting to become a painter.

1874. Vincent visited his family at their home in Holland, "thin, silent, dejected" and then returned to London, his depression continuing. In August, his Uncle Vincent moved him to the Paris branch of the firm, which angered Vincent, who thereupon returned to Goupil in London in December as an "eccentric," ceasing to draw and taking up a life of solitude.

1875. In May, he was transferred to Goupil of Paris, where he roomed with Harry Gladwell, spending much of his time reading the Bible. For Christmas he went to Holland for a visit with his family.

1876. In April, he was dismissed from Goupil, his Uncle Vincent saying he "washed his hands of him." Theo suggested Vincent become an artist. Vincent obtained a position teaching languages and math at Mr. Stokes' school in Ramsgate, England. In July, the school was moved to Isleworth where Vincent received board and lodging but no salary. He moved to the school of Mr. Jones, a Methodist minister. In October, he delivers his first sermon at the Wesleyan Methodist Church in Richmond. In December, he came home for Christmas and did not return to England but stayed in touch with Mr. Jones.

1877–1878. In January 1877, Vincent moved to Dordrecht where, again with the help of his Uncle Vincent, he worked as a clerk at the Blussé and Van Braam Bookshop. With his heart set on becoming an evangelist in the coal-mining district of Belgium, he began theological studies in Amsterdam to prepare for university entrance exams, learning Latin and Greek under the tutelage of Dr. Mendes da Costa, and reading theology with his mother's brother-in-law, The Rev. Johannes Stricker, a Dutch Reformed pastor and biblical scholar. Vincent later described this as "the worst time of my life." In July, after giving up on theological studies, he traveled to the School of Evangelization at Brussels, accompanied by his father and Mr. Jones, there meeting with the Committee of Evangelization, which accepted him into the school. Beginning in August, he studied for three months but did not receive his nomination as an evangelist. He then went on his own, without official endorsement, to the coal-mining district of the Borinage and taught children in the evenings, visited the poor, and held adult Bible classes.

1879–1881. Vincent was given a six-month temporary nomination as an evangelist at Wasmes. Taking Jesus' call to discipleship seriously, he gave away all of his possessions to the poor and lived in "a miserable hut where every comfort was wanting." In February 1879, when the Rev. Mr. Rochelieu came for an inspection, Vincent was found to be "a person who neglected himself so [that he] could not be an example to others." During a mine explosion and a subsequent miners' strike, Vincent attended lovingly and directly to the physical and spiritual needs of the miners. In July, after six months of probation, he was not reappointed by the committee and was given three months to find another position.

He left Wasmes and traveled to Brussels, seeking the advice of the Rev. Mr. Pietersen, an artist. Vincent resolved to stay in the Borinage and boarded with Evangelist Frank in Cuesmes, where he becomes focused on his drawing. In August, he visited his parents at Etten, to which they had moved. His mother said: "He reads Dickens all day and speaks only when he is spoken to; about his future, not a single word." In the fall of 1879, he returned to the Borinage where he "wandered about without work, without friends and very often without bread." With a permanent appointment of his own to Goupil in Paris, Theo visited Vincent and advised him to devise a plan for his life. Struggling through "the awful winter of 1879–1880," without any further contact with Theo, Vincent eventually made his way to Courrières in the hope of meeting Jules Breton, an artist and poet. He then returned to the Borinage penniless and "slept either in the open air or in a hayloft. Sometimes he exchanged a drawing for a piece of bread."

In the spring of 1880, he returned to the vicarage at Etten, where his father was pastor, but then went again to the Borinage in the summer, living with the miner Charles Decrucq at Cuesmes. He made drawings of miners going to work, copied large drawings after the artist Millet, and took his work into the garden. In October, he moved to Brussels where he met the Dutch painter Anthon van Rappard at the Art Academy, studying anatomy, drawing from living models, and taking lessons in perspective. In spring 1881, he moved back to Etten and stayed with his parents for eight months, all the while drawing and painting. Theo reconnected with Vincent during a visit home at Easter. After falling in love that summer with his recently widowed first cousin, Kee Vos, who summarily rebuffed him, leaving him utterly embittered and dejected, at Christmastide Vincent had "a violent altercation with his father," and was ejected from his own home.

1882–1883. Vincent moved immediately to The Hague and sought the help and instruction of his cousin Anton Mauve, an accomplished artist. For two years he remained there, during which time he met "a poor neglected woman approaching her confinement," a former prostitute named Clasina Maria Hoornik, called "Sien," whom "he took . . . under his protection." While Vincent continued his work as an artist, the two lived together with her two children for a year until September 1883, when Vincent started out "alone for Drenthe" where he remained depressed and in debt. By December, he "hastened back to the parental vicarage, now located at Nuenen, the only place where he could find safe shelter." With his studio behind the manse, he painted scenes from the Brabant landscape and figures of the local peasants.

1884–1885. In January 1884, Vincent's mother Anna fractured her thighbone. Vincent and his sister Wil nursed their mother to recovery. In May, Vincent moved to a larger studio consisting of two rooms in the house of the sexton of the Catholic Church. In July, he and a next-door neighbor, an older woman by the name of Margot Begemann, fell in love. Her family protested their plans to marry, after which Vincent found Margot suffering from a failed suicide attempt. While continuing to draw and paint "in the gloomy cottages of peasants and weavers," on New Year's Day, 1885, he wrote to Theo, "I've hardly ever begun a year with a gloomier aspect, in a gloomier mood." His father wrote of Vincent, "He seems to become more and more estranged from us."

On March 25, his father wrote his last words about Vincent: "May he meet with success anyhow." Suddenly and unexpectedly, on the 26th, Theodorus dropped dead at the front doorstep of the manse. He was buried on Vincent's birthday, March 30. In the autumn of that year, Vincent made a brief trip to Amsterdam to see the "Rijksmuseum, including paintings by Rembrandt." After disagreement within the family,

Vincent left the manse and took up residence in a rented studio from May through November. He concentrated on painting peasant life and sent Theo "his first great picture," "The Potato Eaters," composed "from the heart of the peasant's life." He conducted many studies and wrote about the artist Delacroix's laws of color, as well as first mentioned his awareness of a school of art called Impressionism. Due to his association with certain models whose portraits he painted, the Catholic priest "forbade his parishioners from posing for Vincent." At the end of November, Vincent packed up and headed for Antwerp, "leaving all his Brabant work behind." Unfortunately, for the most part, it was sold for junk when his mother later moved from the manse.

1886–1887. Vincent became a pupil at the Academy of Art in Antwerp, until in February, physically exhausted after "many disagreements with his teachers," he left all his work behind and moved to Paris to live with Theo. There he met many of the Impressionists, became enthralled with Japanese art, and took up work in Cormon's studio. By June, he and Theo had moved to the Montmartre section of Paris where Theo was working, and where Vincent had his own studio and came under the influence of the French "plein air" painters, Monet, Sisley, and Pissarro.

Late in 1886, Vincent had fallen "back into his old irritability . . . his temper that winter worse than ever." On the Boulevard Montmartre, Theo made "the gallery . . . a center of the impressionists." In the spring of 1887, Vincent befriended the artist Émile Bernard, fifteen years younger. They painted together in Émile's studio in Asnières until Vincent had a "violent quarrel" with Émile's father, which the friendship managed to survive. During the winter, Vincent painted numerous self-portraits, among his many other works.

1888–1889. In February 1888, Vincent left Paris for southern France, taking up residence in Arles, where in September he moved into the "Yellow House" he intended to make the hub of an artists' colony. He reached the peak of his abilities as an artist in a period of "immense productivity." As Vincent said in his own words, "Life is almost enchanted after all." Then in October, his friend and fellow artist, Paul Gauguin, arrived at the Yellow House so the two could paint, share expenses, and render one another mutual support. The relationship proved tumultuous and conflict arose between them. On Christmas

Eve, "Vincent had in a state of violent excitement . . . an attack of high fever, cut off a piece of his ear and brought it as a gift to a woman in a brothel." Upon Theo's arrival, Gauguin left town, and Vincent slowly recovered during hospitalization, thanks to being befriended by the Protestant clergyman, the Rev. Mr. Salles, as well as by the kindly Postman Roulin and his family. Due to subsequent complaints in the form of a petition by neighbors, Vincent was involuntarily hospitalized in February 1889. In April, Theo married his fiancée, Johanna Bonger. In May, Vincent voluntarily entered the Asylum of Saint-Paul-de-Mausole at Saint-Rémy, where for a year he lived and painted between debilitating "attacks" of what was diagnosed at the time as epilepsy.

In August, in hope of a cure, Vincent suffered from a breakdown and declared, "I no longer see any possibility of having courage or hope . . ." His painting, the "Reaper," he said, was of "an image of death as the great book of nature speaks of it." By winter he completed his famous "Pieta" after Delacroix, the "Resurrection of Lazarus" and the "Good Samaritan" after Delacroix, as well as the "Four Hours of the Day" after Millet.

1890. In the middle of May, Vincent was discharged from the asylum, feeling better and hopeful of continued improvement. He planned to spend several days in Paris with Theo, Jo, and their newborn son Vincent, his namesake. On May 21, he set out for Auvers, where he was to lodge at an inn and be cared for by Dr. Paul Gachet. On June 10, Theo, Jo, and little Vincent spent a day with Vincent in Auvers, where he gave his nephew "a bird's nest as a plaything." Early in July, Vincent visited them in Paris, then returned to Auvers. Distraught over the thought that Theo may lose his job with Goupil, and that he, Vincent, would lose the financial support he had been receiving from his brother all these years, he plummeted again into despondency. Jo said that "his last letters and pictures show . . . the threatening catastrophe . . . approaching like the ominous black birds that dart through the storm over the wheat fields" appearing in one of Vincent's very last paintings. On the evening of July 27, in a field where he had been painting, Vincent shot himself in the chest with a revolver and died two days later on July 29 in the arms of his beloved brother Theo. He was buried on July 30 in the presence of Theo and many of his fellow artists during a brief ceremony in a cemetery at the edge of a field in the village of Auvers.

On January 25, 1891, having been hospitalized for several months in a state of complete mental insanity, Theo died.

The physical remains of the two of them now lie in death as they had for so long resided in life, side by side, impartibly as brothers.

The graves of Vincent and Theo

Bibliography

Altizer, Thomas J. J. "Van Gogh's Eyes." In *Hermeneutic Philosophy of Science, Van Gogh's Eyes, and God*, edited by Babette E. Babich, 393–402. Dordrecht: Kluwer Academic, 2002.

Arnold, Wilfred Niels. *Vincent van Gogh: Chemicals, Crises, and Creativity.* Boston: Birkäuser, 1992.

Baker, Howard. "Vincent van Gogh: Selfobject Factors in Motivating, Facilitating, and Inhibiting Creativity." In *Progress in Self Psychology*, vol. 6: *The Realities of Transference*, edited by Arnold Goldberg, 189–215. Hillsdale, NJ: Analytic, 1990.

Bangs, Carl. *Arminius: A Study in the Dutch Reformation.* Nashville: Abingdon, 1971.

Benedict, Saint. *The Holy Rule of St. Benedict* (1949 edition). Translated by Boniface Verheyen. No pages. Online: http://www.ccel.org/ccel/benedict/rule2/files/rule2 .html#ch42.

Berry, Wendell. *What Are People For?: Essays.* San Francisco: North Point, 1990.

Bonafoux, Pascal. *Van Gogh Self Portraits: with Accompanying Letters from Vincent to His Brother Theo.* New York: Tabard, 1989.

Brooks, David. *Vincent van Gogh: The Complete Works.* CD-ROM Database. Sharon, MA: Barewalls, 2002.

Bruins, Elton, and Robert P. Swierenga. *Family Quarrels in the Dutch Reformed Churches in the Nineteenth Century.* Grand Rapids: Eerdmans, 1999.

Brusse, M. J. "Among People." In *The Complete Letters of Vincent van Gogh*, edited by Johanna van Gogh-Bonger, 1:107–14. Boston: Little, Brown, 1978.

Buechner, Frederick. *Telling Secrets.* San Francisco: Harper, 1991.

Butterfield, Herbert. *Christianity and History.* London: Fontana, 1957.

Chilton, Bruce. *Rabbi Jesus: An Intimate Biography.* New York: Doubleday, 2000.

Conn, Walter E. *The Desiring Self: Rooting Pastoral Counseling and Spiritual Direction in Self-Transcendence.* New York: Paulist, 1998.

Davidson, Charles N. "A Theory of Natural Change Revisited: Theology, Psychology, and Pastoral Counseling." *Pastoral Psychology* 47 (1999) 425–37.

———. "Vincent van Gogh, Son of the Manse: A portrait in Self-Psychology." *Pastoral Psychology* 45 (1997) 237–57.

Denvir, Bernard. *Vincent: The Complete Self-Portraits.* Philadelphia: Running Press, 1994.

Denzin, Norman. "The Art and Politics of Interpretation." In *Collecting and Interpreting Qualitative Materials*, edited by Norman K. Denzin and Yvonna S. Lincoln, 313–34. Thousand Oaks, CA: SAGE, 1998.

Dillard, Annie. *Pilgrim at Tinker Creek.* New York: Harper's Magazine Press, 1974.

Edwards, Cliff. *Mystery of the Night Café: Hidden Key to the Spirituality of Vincent van Gogh*. Albany: State University of New York/Excelsior, 2009

———. *The Shoes of Van Gogh: A Spiritual and Artistic Journey to the Ordinary*. New York: Crossroad, 2004.

———. *Van Gogh and God: A Creative Spiritual Quest*. Chicago: Loyola University Press, 1989.

Erickson, Kathleen Powers. *At Eternity's Gate: The Spiritual Vision of Vincent van Gogh*. Grand Rapids: Eerdmans, 1998.

Erikson, Erik H. *Young Man Luther: A Study in Psychoanalysis and History*. Austen Riggs Center Monograph 4. New York: Norton, 1958.

Friedman, Edwin H. *Generation to Generation: Family Process in Church and Synagogue*. The Guilford Family Therapy Series. New York: Guilford, 1985.

Gay, Volney. "Augustine: The Reader as Selfobject." In *The Hunger of the Heart: Reflections on the Confessions of Augustine*, edited by Donald Capps and James E. Dittes, 185–201. Society for the Scientific Study of Religion Monograph Series 8. West Lafayette, IN: Society for the Scientific Study of Religion, 1990.

Gedo, John E. *Portraits of the Artist: Psychoanalysis of Creativity and Its Vicissitudes*. Hillsdale, NJ: Analytic, 1989.

Grotstein, James S. "Winnicott's Importance in Psychoanalysis. In *The Facilitating Environment: Clinical Applications of Winnicott's Theory*, edited by M. Gerard Fromm and Bruce Lazar Smith, 130–55. Madison, CT: International Universities Press, 1989.

Harrison, Robert. *Van Gogh's Letters*. Unabridged and annotated. No pages. Online: http://www.webexhibits.org/vangogh/.

Heiman, Marcel. "Psychoanalytic Observations on the Last Painting and Suicide of Vincent van Gogh. *The International Journal of Psycho-Analysis* 57 (1976) 71–79.

Heppner, P. Paul et al. *Research Design in Counseling*. 2nd ed. New York: Brooks/Cole-Wadsworth, 1999.

Hessert, Paul. *Christ and the End of Meaning: The Theology of Passion*. Rockport, MA: Element, 1993.

Hulsker, Jan. *Vincent and Theo Van Gogh: A Dual Biography*. Edited by James M. Miller. Ann Arbor, MI: Fuller Publications, 1990.

Jansen, Leo, et al. *Vincent van Gogh: The Letters* ("The Museum Letters Project"). Amsterdam: Van Gogh Museum and Huygens Institute (2009). Online: http://www.vangoghletters.org/vg/.

Jones, W. Paul. *Theological Worlds: Understanding the Alternative Rhythms of Christian Belief*. Nashville: Abingdon, 1989.

Kegan, Robert. *The Evolving Self*. Cambridge, MA: Harvard University Press, 1982.

Kempis, Thomas à. *The Imitation of Christ*. Milwaukee, WI: Bruce, 1940.

———. *The Imitation of Christ*. London: Burns & Oats, n.d.

Kierkegaard, Søren. *The Concept of Anxiety: A Simple Psychologically Orienting Deliberation on the Dogmatic Issue of Hereditary Sin*. Edited and translated by Reidar Thomte and Albert B. Anderson. Princeton, NJ: Princeton University Press, 1980.

———. *Philosophical Fragments or A Fragment of Philosophy by Johannes Climacus*. Edited and translated by David Swenson and Niels Thulstrup. Princeton, NJ: Princeton University Press, 1962.

———. *The Sickness unto Death: A Christian Psychological Exposition for Upbuilding and Awakening*. Edited by Howard V. Hong and Edna H. Hong. Princeton, NJ: Princeton University Press, 1980.

Kohut, Heinz. *The Analysis of the Self.* New York: International Universities Press, 1971.
———. *How Does Analysis Cure?* Chicago: University of Chicago Press, 1984.
———. *The Kohut Seminars.* Edited by Miriam Elson. New York: Norton, 1987.
———. *The Restoration of the Self.* New York: International Universities Press, 1977.
———. *Self Psychology and the Humanities.* New York: Norton, 1985.
Kuspit, Donald. *The Cult of the Avant-Garde Artist.* Cambridge: Cambridge University Press, 1993.
Lee, Ronald R., and J. Colby Martin. *Psychotherapy after Kohut: A Textbook of Self Psychology.* Hillsdale, NJ: Analytic, 1991.
Levy, Terry M., and Michael Orlans. *Attachment, Trauma, and Healing: Understanding and Treating Attachment Disorder in Children and Families.* Washington, DC: CWLA, 1998.
Longfellow, Henry Wadsworth. *The Seaside and the Fireside.* Boston: Ticknor, Reed, and Fields, 1849.
Lubin, Albert J. *Stranger on the Earth.* New York: Da Capo, 1972.
Masheck, Joseph D. *Van Gogh 100.* Westport, CN: Greenwood, 1996.
Meissner, W. W. *The Psychology of a Saint: Ignatius of Loyola.* New Haven, CT: Yale University Press, 1992.
———. *Vincent's Religion: The Search for Meaning.* New York: Peter Lang, 1997.
Meyer, Donald B. "A Review of Young Man Luther: A Study in Psychoanalysis and History." In *Psychoanalysis and History,* edited by Bruce Mazlish, 174–80. The Universal Library. New York: Grosset and Dunlap, 1971.
Moore, Thomas. *Original Self.* New York: HarperCollins, 2000.
Muslin, Hyman L. "Heinz Kohut: Beyond the Pleasure Principle, Contributions to Psychoanalysis." In *Beyond Freud: A Study of Modern Psychoanalytic Theorists,* edited by Joseph Reppen, 203–29. Hillsdale, NJ: Analytic Press, 1985.
Nagera, Humberto. *Vincent van Gogh.* Madison, CT: International Universities Press, 1990.
Niebuhr, Reinhold. *The Self and the Dramas of History.* New York: Charles Scribner's Sons, 1955.
Otto, Rudolf. *The Idea of the Holy.* London: Oxford University Press, 1924.
Rizzuto, Ana-Maria. *The Birth of the Living God.* Chicago: University of Chicago Press, 1979.
Schwartz, Richard C. *Internal Family Systems Therapy.* New York: Guilford, 1995.
Shapiro, Meyer. *Vincent Van Gogh.* New York: Abrams, 1994.
Siegel, Allen M. *Heinz Kohut and the Psychology of the Self.* London: Routledge, 1996.
Smith, Bruce L. "The Community as Object." In *The Facilitating Environment: Clinical Applications of Winnicott's Theory,* edited by M. Gerard Fromm and Bruce Lazar Smith, 516–34. Madison, CT: International Universities Press, 1989.
Stein, Susan A. *Van Gogh: A Retrospective.* Beaux Arts Editions, 1986.
Stolwijk, Chris, and Richard Thomson. *Theo van Gogh.* Amsterdam: Van Gogh Museum, n.d.
Stricker, Johannes P. *Jezus van Nazareth Volgens de Historie Geschetst.* Amsterdam: Gebroeders Kraay, 1868.
Sund, Judy. *True to Temperament: van Gogh and French Naturalist Literature.* New York: Cambridge University Press, 1992.
Sweetman, David. *Van Gogh: His Life and His Art.* New York: Simon & Schuster, 1990.

Taylor, Charles. *Sources of the Self: The Making of the Modern Identity*. Cambridge: Harvard University Press, 1989.

Taylor, Steven J., and Robert Bogdan. *Introduction to Qualitative Research Methods*. 3rd ed. New York: John Wiley, 1998.

Templeton Read LLC. *The Van Gogh Gallery* (January 2008). No pages. Online: http://www.vangoghgallery.com/.

Thiselton, Anthony C. *New Horizons in Hermeneutics: The Theory and Practice of Transforming Biblical Reading*. Grand Rapids: Zondervan, 1992.

Tillich, Paul. *The Courage to Be*. New Haven, CT: Yale University Press, 1952.

———. *A History of Christian Thought*. New York, NY: Simon & Schuster, 1967.

———. *Systematic Theology*. Vols. 1–3. Digswell Place, UK: James Nisbet, 1964.

Van Gogh, Theo, and Jo Bonger. *Brief Happiness: The Correspondence of Theo van Gogh and Jo Bonger*. Edited by Leo Jansen and Jan Robert. Amsterdam: Van Gogh Museum, 1999.

Van Gogh, Vincent. *The Complete Letters of Vincent van Gogh*. Edited by Johanna van Gogh-Bonger. 3 Vol. Boston: Little, Brown, 1978.

Walther, Ingo F., and Rainer Metzger. *Vincent van Gogh: The Complete Paintings*. 2 vols. Cologne, Germany: Benedikt Taschen, 1993.

Weldon, Keith. *Van Gogh*. Greenwich, CT: Brompton, 1989.

Whitehead, Alfred N. *Process and Reality*. Corrected Edition. New York: Macmillan, The Free Press, 1978.

Wilber, Ken. *The Eye of Spirit*. Boston: Shambhala, 1998.

———. *Integral Spirituality*. Boston: Integral, 2007.

———. *No Boundary*. Boston: Shambhala, 1979.

Wilkie, Ken. *In Search of van Gogh*. Rocklin, CA: Prima, 1991.

Woodman, Marion. *The Pregnant Virgin*. Toronto, Canada: Inner City, 1985.

Zemel, Carol. *Van Gogh's Progress: Utopia, Modernity, and Late-Nineteenth-Century Art*. Berkeley, CA: University of California Press, 1997.

Subject Index

self-portraits, 79, 115

servant girls and fellows, "a power
and vitality," 81

sketches of rural life, 75

student, of anatomy, 2; human
figures, 72; perspective, 24;
water colors, 40, 72

studio in Catholic church, 199

"*studio with a cradle*, a baby's
crapper," 59

symbolism, 55–56, 161–64; colors,
55, 161–64; divine presence, 55;
rebirth, healing,

resurrection, 55; rising yellow sun,
55; stars, points through which
eternity enters time, 55–56;
"we take death to reach a star,"
55; yellow, signifying love and
light, 55

Gogh, Vincent Willem van (as person),
passim

alcohol and tobacco usage, 41, 83

bone dead to himself, and his art, 70

"books and reality and art are alike
to me," 94

"break" within himself,
psychologically and
vocationally, 36, 120

cat, drawing of, 114, 117, 118, 121;
mirror for mother's affection,
self, 118

"caged bird," 13, 22, 205

chameleon and circus clown, 22

"Christ of the Coalmine," 28

church attendance, 34

clergyman, desire to become, 9–10,
24

conflict with teachers, 155

contrary worldview, 94

"cosmic orphan," 171

death of (described by Theo), 208,
226–27

diet, 41

dog, 117–21; "big rough" 117,
121; "desecrated," 121; lonely,
abandoned, 118

double nature, monk and painter, 123

earlobe, xvii, 87, 116, 162; "guard
this object carefully," 116

eccentric, 5

ecclesiastical birthright, 90

elephant, Vincent's childhood clay
model, 113–19, 121

evangelist (in Belgium), 16–18

faith, 28

French naturalist literature, 94

genius, "roams along such
mysterious paths," 85

health, mental, 20, 21, 22, 34, 35,
40, 41–42, 72, 87, 101, 116,
133, 137n, 145; calmness and
serenity, 82; "heavy depression,"
42; "I should prefer my insanity
to the sanity of others," 154;
mania and depression, 62;
melancholy" and remorse,
133; mental illness, diagnoses,
xii; partial suicide, 116;
psychological splitting (split),
101; psychotic episodes, 87;
rage, 35; suicide, 137n

health, physical, 38, 40, 65;
gonorrhea, 65

"I am in for it now. And the die is
cast," 36, 138

"I cannot live without love, without a
woman," 122

"idle bird," 22, 43; idleness, 19, 22

illusions and reality, 37–38; and the
sublime, 39

inner exile, 103

"lark" as thematic metaphor, 3, 12,
24, 26, 27, 32, 36, 38, 48, 62, 65,
67, 69, 70, 125, 138

letters to Theo and others, 42, 72,
passim; last letter, 42, 138; great
literature, 72

"little culprit," 111

logic, "that damned wall is too cold
for me," 30

madman, 182–88

"madness," 192–209

mirroring, by parents, 36; through
art, 66n

"molting time," 20

monk, 86, 123, 204; "I would rather
shut myself up in a cloister like
the monks," 86

Jesus Christ, *passim* (*continued*)
  in all of us, 188
  incognito, in human guise, 52
  "mamzer," 189
  "neither Jew nor Greek, slave nor
    free, male nor female, in Christ,"
    196–97
  parents' prohibited sexual union,
    189n
  personification of Vincent's
    worldview, 212
  resurrection appearance to Mary, 158
  scribes and Pharisees, 119
  self-emptying (kenosis), 49
  suffering of, 55
  "very highest summit reached by
    art," 209
  Vincent's identification with, 143
  "unless you change and become like
    children," 195
  vision of Kingdom of God, 49
  vision of resurrected Christ, 187
  "who is greatest in the kingdom of
    heaven?" 195
  wilderness test, 49
  winebibber, friend of publicans and
    sinners, 171
*Jezus van Nazareth volgens de Historie
  Geschetst* (Stricker), 9
John (the beloved disciple), 121
Joie de vivre, La (Zola), 95–96
Jones, W. Paul, 169–73, 196n
Joseph (father of Jesus), 189, 189n
Judah (son of Jacob), 189

kairos, 146n
Keats, John, 5
Kegan, Robert, 132n
Kempis, Thomas à. *See* Thomas à
  Kempis
Kerssemakers, Anton, 124, 159–60
  recollections of Vincent, 124
Kierkegaard, Søren, xii, xiv, 144, 145,
  167, 176–79, 189, 204
  disciple at first and second hand, 189
  faith and despair, 176–79, 204;
    despair, thoroughfare to faith,
    178; despair, loss of the eternal,
    176; faith, consciousness of

    the eternal, 178; faith, resting
    transparently in God, 179
  man of immediacy, 176–77
  self, losing itself through aid of the
    eternal, 178; its own master, in
    despair, 179
  sin, what does not proceed from
    faith, 179
  town hall and courthouse, 177
King Willem I, 99
Koestler, Arthur, 150
Kohut, Heinz, xiv, xv, xvii, 36, 41, 42n,
  46n, 54n, 58n, 62, 62n, 65–66,
  67, 67n, 75, 96–97, 105n, 163;
  see Self-Psychology
Kuspit, Donald, art as "a wish for a
  certain kind of self," 161

Labor and Bourgeois classes, 38, 3
  labor strikes, 39
Lamartine, Alphonse de, epigraph, 117
Lazarus, 52, 53, 121, 211
Lesbianism, 86
Les Miserables (Hugo), 70
Leyden [Leiden] University, 9
light and darkness, 52, 67
Longfellow, Henry Wadsworth, 5, 80
  "Gaspar Becarra," 80
love, *eros* and *agape*, 147
Loyer, Eugenie, 5, 58, 78
Loyola, Ignatius of, xv
Luijten, Hans, xxii, xxiii
Luke, Gospel of, 192–94,
  ars facta, 192
  banquet for the poor, the lame, and
    the blind, 158–59
  Emmaus, 172, 202–3
  patron saint of painters, 213
  prodigal son, 172
  sayings of Jesus, 215
  resurrection, 172
Luther, Martin, xvi
Luxembourg, museum, 5

Maes, Nicholas, 46
Marcasse (coal mine), 17, 53
Marriage, "one doesn't marry only the
  woman herself, but the whole
  family in the bargain," 61

Scripture Index

Van Gogh Drawings, Sketches, and Paintings Index